Parents and Teachers as Partners

Issues and Challenges

Parents and Teachers as Partners

Issues and Challenges

Robert E. Rockwell
Southern Illinois University at Edwardsville

Lynda C. Andre
Edwardsville Community Schools

Mary K. Hawley
St. Clair County Regional Office of Education
Illinois STARNET Region IV

Harcourt Brace College Publishers

Fort Worth   Philadelphia   San Diego   New York   Orlando   Austin   San Antonio
Toronto   Montreal   London   Sydney   Tokyo

Vice President, Publisher	Ted Buchholz
Editor in Chief	Christopher P. Klein
Senior Acquisitions Editor	Jo-Anne Weaver
Developmental Editor	Tracy Napper
Project Editor	Elizabeth Cruce Alvarez
Production Manager	Jane Tyndall Ponceti
Senior Art Director	David A. Day
Art Director	Scott Baker

Cover Photo: © 1995 Robin Sachs

Art Program: Candice Swanson/on call

To Donna, who has been a wife, parent, and grandmother extraordinaire. To Susan and Janet, my daughters, who are living the joys of parenthood. To my grandchildren, Teri, Robert, Amanda, Kathryn, and Michael, who continue to give me endless happiness. And to my mother, Erma Lee, for bringing me into this world. I love you all.

Robert E. Rockwell

To Michael, Chris, Lindsay, and Betsy for the inspiration they provide. To my husband for his support and encouragement. To my mother and father, who taught me the importance of it all!

Lynda C. Andre

With love and gratitude to all who have taught me family involvement: my mother and father; my children, Erin and Joel, who have been my first and best teachers; and to the special families who have shared their children and their lives with me over the years.

Mary K. Hawley

Preface

Parents and Teachers as Partners is directed at everyone in education, both public and private, concerned with building partnerships with parents. Such involvement bridges prenatal, neonatal, infant stimulation, preschool, kindergarten, primary, and elementary levels. And, it has an impact on students of parent involvement in junior and senior colleges, professionals involved in the development, administration, and evaluation of programs, and educators of all kinds in home, classroom, or child-care settings.

As a child's first caregiver and teacher, a parent has both the right and the responsibility to be involved in the child's formal education. Early childhood programs need to begin to involve parents in this education. It has never been possible to help children grow and develop without mutual respect and cooperation between home and school. Today, this cooperation is more important than ever to children's achievement.

Research has clearly shown that parental involvement is a critical variable in a child's education. Studies conducted in a variety of educational and care settings over the past years suggest that parents who established a strong learning environment in the home, who stimulated interest in learning, and who supported their children's natural curiosity fostered attitudes that were important to success in school. Parents who were involved with the school also developed more positive attitudes toward the school and its goals.

Early childhood programs must not only welcome parents, but actively encourage and seek their participation in the education of their children. Teachers and administrators must have the skill and desire to involve all families in meaningful roles within the school community. Parents of cultural, ethnic, and familial differences must perceive the school as "their" school.

There are many approaches to parent involvement, and a teacher or an administrator can easily become overwhelmed and confused. The main strength of this book is that it organizes and presents strategies and techniques in an easily accessible way that enables the reader to understand them and to know when to implement each one.

Parents and Teachers as Partners is divided into three parts followed by an appendix:

- Part One focuses on some of the specific issues and challenges in implementing parent involvement: why parent involvement is necessary (Chapter 1), how parents and teachers can learn to become partners in children's education (Chapter 2), special information on working with families from diverse backgrounds (Chapter 3), and families with children who have special needs (Chapter 4).

- Part Two describes several categories of strategies for communicating successfully with parents: written correspondence (Chapter 5), verbal communications (Chapter 6), home visits and how to make them effective (Chapter 7), strategies for successful parent group meetings (Chapter 8), and parent–teacher conferences (Chapter 9).
- Part Three discusses support systems for parent involvement: volunteers (Chapter 10), parent empowerment as decision makers (Chapter 11), and community networks (Chapter 12).
- The Appendix provides a comprehensive listing of resources for all types of families.

Some important features of this book include individual chapter objectives, bold-face key terms, practical examples, questions for discussion, expansion, and application, chapter bibliographies, and a large listing of resources.

Throughout this book, we have utilized several key vocabulary words that deal with parental involvement interchangeably. Please keep this in mind as you read, and assign the context that best fits your individual frame of reference. Some important definitions are:

Early Childhood: Period of a child's life from birth through age 8.

Parent: Biological parent(s), family member, or designated primary caregiver of the child, including a stepparent or foster parent.

Early Childhood Professional: Any adult who interacts with children and families and who is identified with an early childhood program. This could be an early interventionist, therapist, social worker, child-care provider, classroom assistant, or other staff member. Used interchangeably with teacher/educator.

Program: Any attendance center for children in a private, public, not-for-profit preschool, child-care, community, or agency program. Used interchangeably with elementary school.

Administrator: Individual involved in a leadership role for management, direction, and supervision of personnel or programs. Includes principals, directors, and coordinators.

Acknowledgments

We wish to thank Kathy L. Long for her devoted attention to the typing of the manuscript. We also are grateful to our reviewers Gayle Mindes, DePaul University; Elizabeth Dodd, Valdosta State College; Jean Krasnow, Wheelock College; Carolyn Rybicki, St. Louis Community College–Florissant Valley; Bob Foster, University of Northern Alabama; and Tommie Lawhon, University of North Texas.

At Harcourt Brace, we thank senior acquisitions editor Jo-Anne Weaver for her never-ending patience, development editor Tracy Napper, photo researcher Lili Weiner, project editor Beth Alvarez, art directors David Day and Scott Baker, and production manager Jane Ponceti.

Thanks also to our families and friends for their unfailing patience, encouragement, and support.

Lastly, Lynda and Mary K. offer a special thanks to Bob Rockwell, our teacher, mentor, and friend.

About the Authors

Dr. Robert E. Rockwell received his PhD from St. Louis University and is now Professor and Program Director of Early Childhood Education in the Department of Curriculum and Instruction at Southern Illinois University, Edwardsville. He is the author of various books addressing topics that include fitness and nutrition, parent involvement, and science education. He has had many years of personal experience as a teacher, administrator, and consultant developing parent–teacher partnerships that work. He also conducts workshops across the United States. Bob is the father of two daughters and has five grandchildren.

Lynda C. Andre received her MS in early childhood education from Southern Illinois University, Edwardsville, and her BS in child development from Western Illinois University. She is completing the doctoral program at Southern Illinois University at Edwardsville with an emphasis in early childhood administration. Lynda has worked extensively with young children and parents for the past 20 years. An early childhood teacher with experience in preschool through third grade, she currently teaches kindergarten in the Edwardsville Community Schools and is the coordinator of a Model Early Childhood Parental Training program that serves parents whose children are newborn to age 6. Lynda has taught parent involvement classes at Southern Illinois University. She also is the mother of four children.

Mary K. Hawley is a birth-to-age-5 resource specialist and consultant with Illinois STARNET Region IV in Belleville, Illinois. She received a bachelor's degree in elementary education from Illinois State University and a master's degree in special education from Southern Illinois University, Edwardsville. Her educational background includes credentials in teaching elementary, early childhood, early intervention, and special education, as well as nearly 20 years of working with children in middle school and private and public preschool programs in both rural and urban settings. Mary K. has developed strategies for parent involvement in her own school programs and now works closely with teachers in southern Illinois. A parent of two teenagers, she lives in Staunton, Illinois.

Contents

Part Two Communication   98

Chapter 5 Written Correspondence   101

Chapter 6 Verbal Communications   150

Parents and Teachers as Partners

Issues and Challenges

PART ONE

Issues and Challenges

Chapter 1

WHY PARENT INVOLVEMENT?

READERS WILL BE ABLE TO:

- Define parent involvement in early education programs.
- Outline Epstein's model of involvement.
- Support a rationale for involvement, with justification from research.
- Explain how involvement benefits children, parents, families, and programs.
- Identify challenges to family involvement.
- Describe federal, state, and local initiatives that support involvement.

Early childhood educators have long recognized the need for communication and collaboration with the parents and families of the children they teach. The home-school connections developed during the preschool years are valuable in enhancing a program's positive impact on a child's development. Family members gain an understanding of their important role during these formative years and can assist programs by sharing their expertise and resources. Yet, despite the best of intentions, parent involvement in early childhood programs can be elusive, causing confusion and frustration for staff members. Why should we try to involve parents and families? This chapter will examine the definition, rationale, benefits, and challenges of involving parents and families in the child's educational program.

CHANGING TIMES, CHANGING EXPECTATIONS

Parenthood is historically accepted as a natural occurrence, one that carries with it a responsibility to nurture each child's growth and development. Yet in today's complex society, we recognize that parenting abilities, skills, and insights don't necessarily come with the birth of a baby, nor are they necessarily imbedded within a parent's experience. Raising physically and emotionally healthy children, equipped with the necessary skills to meet the challenges of the world they will inherit, has become a formidable challenge for today's parents.

Home-school connections developed during the early years are valuable.

An explosion of research and knowledge surrounding children's development and educational success has flooded the media over the past 30 years. The public has been showered with books, magazines, and media broadcasts that reveal "new" aspects of child development or parenting. "Experts" have shared their knowledge and opinions on how parents should raise their children and what impact particular family, educational, or societal situations have upon the young. Although parents have accepted this public approach to parent education and counseling that once was directed exclusively to families in therapy or crisis situations, the profusion of information on child rearing and learning is often perplexing.

In the process of deciphering this often-conflicting information on early development and education, parents may become overanxious about doing the "right thing" for their children. With so many early education options available, it has become increasingly difficult for families to identify what is best for their children. The desire to have children maximize their learning potential early sometimes results in expectations for children to demonstrate academic abilities and skills at younger ages. This has created a consumer market for early education programs in all aspects of learning, including computers, languages, art, music, and movement. Parents often seek information and guidance from early education program brochures, and from teachers, professionals, and other parents.

On the other hand, many parents are unaware of the value that early exposure to a stimulating learning environment has upon their child's later development and academic success. Parents may be uninformed of the early education options available, or may encounter difficulties in accessing early childhood services. The existence of this disparity is cause for concern among professionals in education, social science, and government, and has been the impetus for many parent involvement programs.

FAMILIES FACE CHANGE

Over the past 30 years, there have been dramatic changes in individual lifestyles and in society at large. As a result, the family, one of the oldest human institutions, has been challenged and changed. The 1950s family stereotype, consisting of a working father, a mother who stays home, and two or more children, has become increasingly rare in today's economic climate. In an age where one in two marriages ends in divorce, children commonly spend part of their childhood living with a single parent; the relationship with the other parent may fade or become restricted by visitation rights. Over time, adults frequently find their parenting roles extending to nonbiological children as well. The newer dynamics of blended families—stepchildren and stepsiblings—impact the family system dramatically. Consequently, today's child may see the family portrait change several times during his or her childhood.

Teen pregnancy rates continue to rise, creating a generation of children parenting children. The stresses of being a young parent, the dilemmas of balancing personal growth and parental responsibilities within a new social framework, and the harsh economic realities of family needs place many young families at risk.

Grandparents (and extended family), once nearby for parenting assistance and advice, may become physically distanced in an age of employment mobility. Consequently, family members may visit infrequently, and the family system may lack a traditional source of support, increasing the family's sense of isolation. As the fabric of support in the community unravels, family stress escalates and optimism for parenting success diminishes. When parents are unable to fulfill their responsibilities to their children, then grandparents, extended family, or other individuals in the community may assume a dominant parenting role.

Economic and financial realities have dramatically changed the dynamics of family life. Today, many women are employed outside of the home. Consequently, preschool children are commonly cared for by family members or are in child-care settings, play groups, or a variety of early education programs, both private and public. Families across all income levels are experiencing greater stress from the dual responsibilities of work and family life. Child poverty has risen to record levels, and inadequate nutrition, health care, and housing undermine the early development of a growing number of children. As the result of these and other factors, the family, overwhelmed by the demands of daily living, may perceive the young child's development to have a lower priority amidst other family concerns.

These variations in families have broadened the definition of parent and have increased the complexity of involving them in early childhood programs.

Today, "parent" may refer to a single adult, to a couple, or to other family members (such as grandparents, aunts, or older siblings) who serve in a parenting role. Teachers may then need to build partnerships with several parent/family configurations that foster a child's development. Programming for parents must extend to meet the concerns of a broader family group. Effective parent involvement can provide and secure valuable additional support for families facing new situations, whether it is the birth of a baby, the diagnosis of a disability, or the guardianship of a grandchild.

PARENT INVOLVEMENT: A DEFINITION

What actually is parent involvement? Many programs have defined parent involvement through a selected "model" that uses a specified format for parent-educator interactions, such as home visitation, conferences, or parent education classes. Yet, parent involvement exists in a broad continuum of activities and strategies. **Parent involvement,** therefore, is the practice of any activity that empowers parents and families to participate in the educational process either at home or in a program setting. Each parent involvement program is based upon a philosophy of child-adult and adult-adult interaction that assigns roles to both the parent and the educator. Because educating our children has become a shared responsibility between families and early childhood professionals, the authors of this text support a philosophy of home-center or home-school partnership.

PARTNERSHIPS WITH PARENTS: DEVELOPMENTAL COLLABORATIONS

This partnership philosophy is the critical foundation of parent involvement activities. Parents are recognized as a child's first and most important teachers. Teachers are viewed as sensitive and caring partners in the early education process. This relationship is guided by a common concern for the well-being and developmental progress of the children.

This collaboration goes beyond "parent education." It builds, often slowly, upon mutual respect and trust. Through active communication and support, adults are empowered to fulfill their roles as parents. Teachers share with parents their knowledge of child development, as well as practical information and strategies to assist young learners in developing their potential, all the while recognizing the special needs of the child, the family, and the educational program. Parents educate teachers about their child's strengths and needs, as well as family interests and concerns.

This bridge from home to center allows families to have a valued and meaningful presence in the program. Parental time, skills, and experience are shared at the center, at home, and through connections with other families, parent-to-parent. Parents are partners in joint decision making that affects their child's program and in the selection and design of family support activities. They often are active as program advisers, evaluators, developers, and, sometimes, team administrators. This home-center bridge also allows staff to bring pertinent, individualized information into children's homes through special communication strategies and activities.

It becomes evident that the concept of parent involvement encompasses a wide variety of options. Commitment is the key to them all. Without the dedication and perseverance of early childhood administrators, educators, and the families they serve, early education would lose one of the most valuable factors in effective programming—parent involvement.

PROGRAM ACTIVITIES DEFINE PARENT INVOLVEMENT

The activities of the early childhood program define the organization's broad or narrow interpretation of parent involvement. Some share information through a prescriptive program of parenting education, which may utilize a parent textbook, speaker, or video presentation during a group meeting. On the other hand, some early childhood programs define parent involvement by more informal strategies for communicating with parents. This may be through newsletters, notes, telephone calls, or short conversations as parents come to the center to pick up their children. Parents may become involved in the activities of the curriculum at home via an activity calendar or a lending library kit, or at the center as volunteers. Programs are continually experimenting with strategies for involving parents that meet program goals and the needs of the families they serve.

EPSTEIN'S FIVE TYPES OF PARENT INVOLVEMENT

Joyce Epstein, a researcher at Johns Hopkins University, has conducted studies for over 10 years on teachers' practices of parent involvement and the effects of family-school connections on students, parents, and teachers. She designed a model of parent involvement made up of five types with corresponding goals. Each component serves a distinct role in the process of developing parents who are actively in charge of and committed to their child's education (Brandt, 1989; Epstein, 1989). (Strategies and techniques described in this text are included as examples of practices that promote parent involvement. Further information on these particular strategies can be found in later chapters.)

The five aspects of Epstein's model of parent involvement are Parenting, Communication, Volunteering, Learning at Home, and Representing Other Parents.

1. PARENTING

Goal: To Help All Families Establish Home Environments to Support Learning and Positive Parenting.   Schools have the obligation to recognize that the family exerts the greatest influence over the child in terms of determining the success or failure that the child experiences in school. Attitudes toward literacy, the ability to provide a healthy, safe environment, and the development of language all begin at home. Schools that acknowledge the family's importance can utilize opportunities to work cooperatively with parents by providing information to them. This can be accomplished via the sharing and support offered through:

- parent education programs
- parent support groups
- parent rooms and spaces
- social service directories
- parent resource libraries

2. COMMUNICATION

Goal: To Design Effective Forms of Communication to Reach Parents.
Communication between parents and schools is generally found in two forms: written and face-to-face contact. A strong parent involvement program will address both of these in varying proportions to fit the needs of the individual family. The attitudes a parent develops about the program and its teachers will often stem from his or her contacts with program staff members. A parent involvement program in the early childhood and primary classroom carries the increased responsibility to initiate a positive rapport with parents, since this experience may shape attitudes toward schools that last throughout the child's educational career. Because parents have widely differing expectations, attitudes, and prejudices toward schools and teachers based upon their own experiences, a variety of approaches is needed to reach and involve each family. These methods of communication have been used successfully:

- parent handbook
- newsletter
- audio/video tapes
- parent resource library
- yearbooks
- parent meetings
- parent conferences

- activity calendar
- surveys/questionnaires
- screenings
- passport journals
- orientation meetings
- home visits
- notes/letters

3. VOLUNTEERING

Goal: To Recruit and Organize Parent Help and Support.   The third level of parent involvement refers to parents as volunteers, both in and out of the center. Traditionally, volunteering has included everything from assisting during field trips and making cookies for a bake sale to helping with clerical chores in the office. While these opportunities still exist, volunteering has expanded in an effort to involve working parents and those busy at home with small children. Alternative activities for at-home volunteers allow family members to participate when it is convenient for them. These alternative activities include:

- telephoning other parents when needed
- coordinating volunteers
- fundraising
- constructing instructional games
- volunteering in the classroom and the library
- supervising on the playground
- maintaining and constructing playground equipment
- sharing talents, skills, hobbies, and resources

4. LEARNING AT HOME

Goal: To Provide Ideas and Materials to Parents on How to Help Their Child at Home.   The fourth component in this model concerns parent involvement in learning activities in the home. One important aspect of promoting the "parents as teacher" philosophy involves giving parents the proper tools with which to teach. Often a parent feels inadequate and ill prepared for the role of "teacher." The assumption that educators have the sole knowledge of appropriate methods for instruction is erroneous. Parents need to be guided to see that they have important advantages critical to their child's learning: they know their child on many levels (emotionally, socially, behaviorally); they have a history with that child; they are aware of the child's likes and dislikes, interests, strengths, and weaknesses; and they have the opportunity to build an ongoing relationship with the child. Activities that support this are:

- parent meetings
- book and activity bags to use at home
- workshops/seminars
- parenting books to loan

5. REPRESENTING OTHER PARENTS

Goal: To Recruit and Train Parent Leaders.   The formation of a parent advisory council represents advocacy and governance on the part of parents, indicating a bond between schools and families. Parents in decision-making roles have a powerful effect on the curriculum and policies that a program chooses to adopt; and, by getting involved, they show both commitment and responsibility. Researchers call this upper level "empowerment" and suggest that it is at this point that parents and teachers reach a level of trust and respect, working together as members of an educational community (Fredericks & Rasinski, 1989). At this level, parents can participate as an advisory board member or as a member of a curriculum committee.

THE VALUE OF PARENT INVOLVEMENT: SUPPORT FROM RESEARCH

One of the goals of early childhood education is to support and encourage children to develop their potential for learning. Another is to support parents and families in this joint responsibility. Parent involvement is a multifaceted component of early childhood programs, and the rationale supporting it is multidimensional as well. Why value parent involvement and what benefit does it have in early childhood programs?

Education is the business of transmitting information and developing abilities in the learner. Successful strategies for parenting education have been identified and accepted over time. These "truisms" or beliefs are linked to logical and practical concepts concerning parent interaction. From these selected ideas, recommended practices have evolved. The following statements are samples of experience-based successes:

- Programming for parent involvement can help families by providing sound information on child development and the importance of appropriate early educational experiences.
- Parents learn to better focus their parenting energies on activities that are developmentally suitable and accomplishable within the daily routine. This increases support for the child's learning and actively engages parents in the process, which enhances their enjoyment and appreciation of the unique individual their child is becoming.
- With a greater number of families under stress, parent involvement programming can encourage the development of positive parenting skills, which promote desirable adult-child interactions as well as realistic expectations for learning and social-emotional behaviors during the early years.
- Professionals involved with families can assist them in locating needed human services within the community and foster a supportive, caring network for children.

Families are unique systems that face intricate challenges to survival. Families struggle to understand complex situations, deal with frustrations, and develop coping strategies that protect vulnerable members—typically, the children.

Parenting is one role in life that few adults are fully prepared to undertake. In the 1970s, Keniston and the Carnegie Council on Children recognized that all families would benefit from support in raising their children, not just "needy" families, then the beneficiary of many federal initiatives (Keniston, 1977). In 1994, the Carnegie Corporation Task Force issued *Starting Points: Meeting the Needs of Our Youngest Children*. It documents the effectiveness of positive parenting practices, parental social supports, and early childhood development stimulation in enabling children to achieve a good start in life. The report also warns that the country's future work force and citizenry are being compromised by inadequate social policies and a devaluing of children and the family. It upholds that all young people should be prepared for parenthood and receive information on child development, models of child rearing, parenting skills, and the significance of environment upon children (Carnegie Corporation Task Force, 1994). Ann Henderson, the author of *The Evidence Continues to Grow: Parent Involvement Improves Student Achievement* (1987), concluded that school and home cannot be viewed in isolation from one another—educators must recognize how they interconnect. Educators and other human service personnel have acknowledged the increased need to provide parents with information and support in today's complex world.

IMPACT OF PARENT INVOLVEMENT ON CHILDREN AND FAMILIES

Regardless of changing family circumstances, the home remains the major source of a child's developmental experiences, including language, social, emotional, moral, and intellectual. Children under 5 are developing language, motor, and cognitive abilities more rapidly than at any other stage in their life. During this critical period, adults play a major role in early learning. Most desire to help their children grow into healthy, productive adults and are capable of providing the necessary support. The best strategies for involvement offer avenues of information and access to a network of supports that can adapt to particular family needs and interests. These opportunities encourage parents to see themselves as the child's most important teachers and empowers them to support their young child's efforts to learn.

Having recognized the many benefits of parent involvement for the child, the family, and the program, early childhood programs have a long history of nurturing children's development in partnerships with parents. Federal education programs during the 1960s, many of which studied the effects of parent involvement, opened doors for parents to become active participants in the education of their children. Research on the effects of programs that aim to enhance parental competence in child-rearing practice indicates that the quality of care that parents give their children does make a difference, and that children do change as a result of their parents' involvement. Evaluations of intensive parent/family-oriented early childhood programs serving low-income populations have found positive effects on child competence and maternal behaviors. Research findings have been substantiated many times over (Epstein, 1986; Levenstein, 1988; Lyons, Robbins, & Smith, 1983; Powell, 1989).

Parent involvement in a child's program and educational activities is critical to sustaining program accomplishments after a young child's participation in an early education program ends. In 1983, The Consortium for Longitudinal Studies released its report, *As the Twig Is Bent*. This data and that of The Perry Preschool Program (Berrueta-Clement, Schweinhart, Barnett, Epstein, & Weikart, 1984, Schweinhart, Barnes, & Weikart, 1993) reports substantiated long-term benefits to early intervention well beyond the school years. When parents are interested and involved with their child's program, they support the child's need for attention and provide motivation for future learning. This was substantiated in the early years of Head Start and Follow Through programs. After researching parental involvement in the Follow Through program, Ira Gordon concluded in 1977 that all forms of parent involvement help a child, but the more roles parents can play in the program and the longer the involvement lasts, the more positive the effects will be. Honig (1975) concluded that the young child enrolled in the program isn't the only one who benefits—younger siblings also gain as the result of parent involvement. Parents do not have to be well educated to help their children; parental involvement benefits all children, but especially those from low-income and minority families (Henderson, 1987). Children whose parents are involved in their educational program recognize that their parents are an integral part of learning and see them in different roles. Children begin to value education when they experience the connection between home and school. Most important, children who share learning experiences with parents feel special and cared about (Horowitz & Faggella, 1986).

Research indicates that a planned program of parent involvement has a positive impact on parents as well (Hester, 1989). When parents are involved, they:

- Believe they should help.
- Understand more about the educational program.
- Change their behavior at home to be more supportive of their child.
- Appreciate teacher efforts more.

Involved parents also are better able to define appropriate levels of expectations for their child's development and begin to perceive their child's developing abilities and skills. Parents have greater access to teachers and other parents and develop an appreciation of their own abilities as parents (Horowitz & Faggella, 1986). The noted social scientist Urie Bronfenbrenner stated:

> Not only do parents become more effective as parents, but they become more effective as people. It's a matter of higher self-esteem. Once they saw they could do something about their child's education, they saw they could do something about housing, their community, and their jobs. (Liontos, 1992)

Bronfenbrenner strongly concluded in 1974 that ". . . the family is the most effective and economical system for fostering and sustaining the development of the child. The evidence indicates further that the involvement of the child's family as an active participant is critical to the success of any intervention program." Preschool programs are especially valuable because they have the potential of providing early intervention for the family as well as the child. "Reaching parents early is the key," writes Jones (1989), "because the process that contributes to school success begins at birth. Many children drop out before they drop in. The seeds of failure are sown early, and early intervention is critical." Research with older children builds evidence that parent involvement is critical to later student and school improvement as well (Epstein, 1987; Greenberg, 1989; Hester, 1989). Parent involvement:

- Raises the academic achievement of students.
- Improves the attitudes and performance of children in school.
- Increases self-esteem and motivation.
- Reduces behavior problems and lowers student dropout rates.
- Helps parents understand the work of the school.
- Builds school-community relationships in an ongoing, problem-preventing way.

Parental involvement has not gone unnoticed by leadership organizations in education. In *Perspectives on Early Childhood Education, Growing with Young Children Toward the 21st Century* (1991), editor David Elkind collected monographs from organizations that offer support for family involvement, including the Association for Childhood Education International, American School Counselor Association, Council of Chief State School Officers, Education Commission of the States, National Alliance of Black School Educators, National Association of Elementary School Principals, National Association for the Education of Young Children, National Association of State Boards of Education, National Association of School Psychologists, the National Education Association, and the Parent Teacher Association.

Another advantage to parental involvement is that parents who are known in their children's programs are treated with greater respect by teachers and administrators. Administrators also learn about parents' concerns and can better respond to their needs. Schools that provide family support and involvement show their commitment to families and their communities, thus enhancing the educational system's esteem in the eyes of the community. In times of fiscal uncertainty, community support has proven critical for the continuing survival of school programs (Lyons, Robbins, & Smith, 1983).

IMPACT OF PARENT INVOLVEMENT ON PROGRAMS

Concern has spread across the United States for increasing the effectiveness of our nation's schools. We confront growing evidence that the educational preparation of our youth is not adequate. Although many components factor into effective school programs, parental involvement consistently ranks high among the characteristics of effective schools, according to researchers, practitioners, and policymakers. Yet not all programs actively encourage parent involvement, and not all families realize how to become involved (Epstein, 1987). A 1990 survey on parent involvement, commissioned by the National PTA and Dodge, found that relatively few parents are actively involved in their children's school, although most parents do help their children with homework and talk about school (Lynch, 1991). Preschool and kindergarten teachers generally utilize multiple strategies to maintain contact with families—contact that often

All families are unique and special.

withers in elementary school (Lynch, 1991). Horowitz and Faggella (1986) assert that teachers gain valuable resources when they involve parents in the school program. Aside from the practical assistance that parents offer, teachers who involve parents in their programs gain new insights about the children they teach and enrich their curriculum with fresh, new resources in the parents themselves.

Early education programs have increasingly become a recognized factor in the U.S. economic and educational agenda. As more mothers enter the work force, early education concerns for preschoolers become more of a public responsibility. In 1990, President George Bush and the nation's governors developed the National Education Goals, which reflected the concern that all U.S. children should begin school with a readiness to learn. The first of these goals states that by the year 2000, all children in America, especially low-income and disabled children, will reach school age with a minimum level of developmental preparedness. The president and state governors concurred that all levels of government need to contribute to the accomplishment of this goal (Miller & McDowelle, 1993). The variable political climate of the succeeding years, the nature of politics, and the difficult fiscal and moral issues faced by all levels of government make the realization of these educational goals a challenge for citizens and lawmakers alike.

Epstein has researched teachers' practices of parent involvement and the effects of family-school connections on children, parents, and teachers. She upholds that the most basic obligations of parents to perform from infancy onward are providing food, clothing, and shelter; assuring health and safety; providing child rearing and home training; and positive home conditions for learning. These are basic parenting responsibilities that help make children "ready" for school. Furthermore, practices that empowered parents to take an active role in the education of their children led to higher levels of school achievement, irrespective of the economic, racial, or cultural background of the family.

The National Association of State School Boards of Education, in its 1988 research-based policy statement, *Right From the Start*, states that parental involvement is essential (Galen, 1991). Strategies the organization recommends include:

- Promoting an environment in which parents are valued as primary influences in their children's lives and are essential partners in the education of their children.
- Recognizing that the self-esteem of parents is integral to the development of the child and should be enhanced by the parents' positive interactions with the school.
- Promoting an exchange of ideas and information between teachers and parents that will benefit the children.
- Ensuring opportunities and access for parents to observe and volunteer in classrooms.
- Including parents in decision making about their own children and in the early childhood program overall.

CHALLENGES TO PARENT INVOLVEMENT

Eliciting parental participation in the multidimensional process of parent involvement can be made more challenging by a variety of conditions that limit the extent of home-program communication and parent cooperation. Many researchers have investigated the factors that impede parent involvement from family, professional, and programmatic perspectives (Brown, 1989; Galinsky, 1988; Honig, 1975; Miller & McDowelle, 1993; Rich, 1987a, 1987b).

FAMILY FACTORS

Educators must realize that it is not easy for all families to become involved in program activities. For many families, a major barrier to involvement is a lack of time. Working parents are often unable to attend program events during the day because of inflexible work schedules. Evening events may be jeopardized by the competing demands of home and family. Parents may choose to spend this time catching up on home responsibilities, rather than attending meetings.

Finding time to be involved is an issue for both families and teachers.

Colds, the flu, or other medical problems sometimes prevent participation. Parents today may be afflicted by stress-related problems, constant fatigue, or depression. Evening meetings may cause concerns for personal safety in some areas. Families also may have difficulty securing adequate child care, especially if the family includes a child with special needs. For some families, there may be an overwhelming number of personal problems involving basic needs, like transportation, a problem with the landlord, or difficulties with family relationships which impede involvement within the program.

Parents may choose to be uninvolved due to intrapersonal or interpersonal difficulties. Some parents may have difficulty seeing themselves as the "first teacher" and feel overwhelmed by a professional's expectations, whether real or imagined. Some parents lack self-confidence and do not value themselves as participants in the parent program. They may lack the skills to adequately (in their eyes) participate. These feelings may be compounded by different linguistic, cultural, or socioeconomic backgrounds. Some parents also may think that the teachers do not really respect or listen to them. Likewise, professionals may project a "teacherish" attitude and treat parents more like children than adults. Parents whose own school experiences were not positive may feel uncomfortable interacting with teachers again. Just returning to a school building may bring back unpleasant memories of educational failure or social discrimination. Consequently, parents may feel mistrust when dealing with educators and staff members. Teachers are viewed by many parents as authority figures, and some parents may feel they are being helpful by keeping a respectful distance from the schools.

PROFESSIONAL FACTORS

Professionals can also have difficulties with parent involvement. They may object to expanding their program responsibilities to include parents. Frequently, a lack of time is cited by busy teachers who may feel that planning program activities for children is enough of a responsibility. Many educators are working parents who share the same constraints of fatigue, stress, and home–work conflicts, especially when it comes to evening events that follow a full day on the job. Sometimes professionals take on parent involvement activities without compensation, and some educators may not desire to make the commitment to involve parents. Other roadblocks include feeling insufficiently trained to work with families and overwhelmed by the problems they face; difficulties in relating to culturally different families; and discouragement because of past problems with parent involvement. Teachers can become frustrated by their inability to reach parents who might benefit the most. Some parents, by rejecting active participation in their child's program, may appear to want the teacher to take over parental responsibilities. Other parents want educators to "fix" what they perceive as the problem, insisting that the solution be simple, failproof, and immediate. Frustrations over these demands may prompt teachers to abandon efforts toward parent involvement.

PROGRAMMATIC FACTORS

Not all programs actively encourage and support parent involvement. Programmatic barriers to parent involvement may occur at either the philosophical or the practical level. Insufficient parent involvement may be due to a lack of administrative support. There may be an absence of policy guidelines regarding parent involvement, or a lack of coordinated planning to execute activities in an organized manner. Inadequate staff time or money for family programs can be barriers to parent activities. Occasionally, parent involvement programming is concentrated at particular centers and is not available systemwide; this occurs when a few centers receive special grant or program funds. Previous difficulties in reaching or sustaining participation from a particular segment of the parent population may discourage a program from attempting to reestablish parent programming. This is particularly common when there is a large number of working or single parents in the program.

Despite the obstacles, parents want to know more. Curran (1989) has analyzed professionals' responses to parent involvement and discovered that parents are motivated and receptive to new ideas. Since the majority of adults raise their children in the same way their parents raised them, they may find their knowledge inadequate to the challenges their children offer. Parents are eager to learn skills that will lessen parenting frustrations. They realize they don't have all the answers and are willing to listen and to try new techniques. Despite sometimes overwhelming conditions, they never give up hope. That optimism is a definite motivation for professionals. By working with parents, individuals who entered teaching to make a positive difference can find the affirmation and reassurance they need to keep going.

▓ FEDERAL, STATE, AND LOCAL INCENTIVES FOR PARENT INVOLVEMENT

In the past 30 years, the issues and benefits of involving parents have captured the interest of federal, state, and local policymakers. Fueled by a history of successful efforts that have brought widely documented positive outcomes in intellectual development for participating children and increased awareness of child development as a result of family involvement, commitment to the parent-school partnership continues to grow.

FEDERAL INITIATIVES

At the federal level, several major initiatives have mandated parent involvement components in programs serving economically disadvantaged or educationally at-risk preschoolers. Head Start has been this country's most extensive investment in preschool education. Since its inception in 1965, Head Start has piloted innovative strategies for involving low-income families with children ages 3 to 5. Parent and Child Centers, which are supported by the national Head Start program, are comprehensive child-development and family support programs that serve children younger than 3 and their families. These programs, which ask parents to make a commitment to them, aim to prevent deficits in the child and strengthen parenting skills and confidence. Another program, Title I of the Elementary and Secondary Education Act, targets parents along with their educationally deprived children. The law provides guidelines to schools for parent involvement in the planning, design, and implementation of programs, as well as for parent training in centers and homes. Several federally funded programs offer services to children and families with particular needs, such as migrant or bilingual families, or those headed by teen mothers. The Even Start initiative integrates early childhood education and adult education by cooperating with federal programs that offer adult education and literacy skills, employment training, and preschool education.

Federal legislation also has provided the impetus for parents to become involved in the educational planning and evaluation of children with disabilities through the Individuals With Disabilities Education Act. Public Law 94-142 (1975) authorized public education to serve 3- to 5-year-olds with disabilities, and PL 99-457 (1986) expanded these services to children from birth through age 2. Under the law, parents give input into the child's program as part of a multidisciplinary team. Services are to be directed to the family, as well as to the child, under an Individualized Family Service Plan. Services could include referrals to community resource providers, training, counseling, and home visits. Public Law 102-119 (1991) strengthened the statutory provisions and regulations for family-centered programming in these programs, as well as at the state and local coordination level. (See Chapter 4 for more information.)

STATE AND LOCAL INITIATIVES

Early childhood programs that focus on parent involvement have also been spearheaded by state governments. In 1990, public schools in 35 states were implementing prekindergarten programs. While some were federally supported, a growing number of states, such as Connecticut, Illinois, Maryland, Minnesota, Missouri, New Jersey, Oklahoma, Vermont, and Wisconsin, had begun their own initiatives to provide family support and education. In Minnesota, all children from birth to kindergarten age and their parents are eligible for the state's Early Childhood and Family Education Program, which was begun in 1975. One of the oldest state efforts, it operates through local school districts to provide parent discussion groups, classes, home visits, newsletters, access to toys and books, and other strategies to support parental efforts in raising children.

In many states, parent involvement is a component of the state school improvement plan. Federal and state program initiatives are interpreted at the local level, and one program alone may not be sufficient to accomplish the goals or meet the community needs. Collaboration, therefore, is a key strategy in the development of local community parenting programs, which meet needs by merging government and community support.

Many programs have discovered the importance of building a stronger educational and political base. The Family Resource Coalition is a national organization begun in 1981 as a consortium of diverse community-based programs involving parents. The coalition has communicated the importance of parent involvement and has promoted the development of research and programs nationwide. Locally, many community groups, businesses, and organizations offer parenting resources, parent training, and group meetings on parent involvement. The National PTA has produced strong leadership in promoting collaborative interactions between parents and local PTA programs that go beyond fundraising and token parent involvement. Communication, cooperation, and collaboration provide the grassroots advocacy to bring about acceptance and appreciation for the value of parent involvement.

SUMMARY

Parent involvement can be defined in many ways and is supported by varied rationales that target the partnership between individual parents and teachers, and the relationship between educational programs and the parent community. While difficulties can challenge the success of communication and collaboration, parent involvement provides enomous benefits for the children, their families, the programs, and the community.

Educators are the catalysts who can make parent involvement work for the benefit of all. To reap the rewards of positive parent collaborations, educators must demonstrate interpersonal skills, develop effective strategies, and maintain a commitment to the process. This involves an ongoing dedication to personal growth as a professional, supported by comprehensive preservice and inservice programs. Teachers may need to collaborate with others to muster philosophical and financial support. Working together, early childhood personnel and policymakers can successfully meet the challenges of parent involvement and make partnerships a reality for our children, families, and communities.

ACTIVITIES FOR DISCUSSION, EXPANSION, AND APPLICATION

1. Select three early childhood settings in your community. Contact members of the program staff and interview them to determine the following:

a. How does their program define parent involvement? Do they have a policy statement in their handbook? What does their choice of parent involvement activities reveal about their philosophy of parent involvement?

b. Describe activities and strategies that are used to involve parents. How do staff members support these efforts?

c. What benefits do staff members perceive for children, families, and the program?

d. What challenges to participating do parents face that may prevent them from becoming actively involved? What has been or can be done to overcome these challenges?

2. In a small group, discuss the rationales for parent involvement in early childhood programs. By group consensus, determine the three most significant reasons for your community to promote involvement.

3. In multiple studies, researchers have discovered differences in parent involvement strategies used by programs for younger and older children. Conduct your own community research individually or in a team. Interview the parents of a child in preschool, of a child in kindergarten, and of a child in primary grades. Ask them:

a. What opportunities are available for parents to be involved in their child's program?

b. How does the teacher invite their support?

c. What activities have they been involved in?

d. What factors encouraged their participation?

e. What may have discouraged them from participating?

Analyze the similarities and differences among the parents, according to the age of their children.

4. Imagine yourself to be the parent of a young child; an early education teacher; and an early education administrator. What rewards and frustrations regarding parent involvment would you expect to encounter? Support your answers.

5. Identify federal, state, and community initiatives utilized in your area to promote family involvement. How long have these programs been operative? Are they selective or restrictive in determining eligibility for participation? What strategies or activities do they use that encourage parent involvement? How does the community perceive the value and effectiveness of the parent component?

REFERENCES

Berrueta-Clement, J., Schweinhart, L., Barnett, W., Epstein, A., & Weikart, D. (1984). *Changed lives: The effects of the Perry Preschool Program on youths through age 19.* Monograph, High/Scope Educational Research Foundation, No. 8. Ypsilanti, MI: The High/Scope Press.

Brandt, R. (1989). How to organize successful parent advisory committees. *Educational Leadership,* 44–45.

Braun, L., Coplan, J., & Sonnenshein, P. (1984). *Helping parents in groups.* Boston: Wheelock College Center for Parenting Studies.

Bronfenbrenner, U. (1974). Developmental research, public policy, and the ecology of childhood. *Child Development, 45,* 1–5.

Brown, P. (1989). Involving parents in the education of their children. ERIC Digest, EDO-PS-89-3.

Carnegie Corporation of New York. (1994). *Starting points: Meeting the needs of our youngest children.* New York: Carnegie Corporation.

Children's Defense Fund. (1994). *The state of America's children yearbook.* Washington, DC: Children's Defense Fund.

Consortium for Longitudinal Studies. (1983). *As the twig is bent.* Hillsdale, NJ: Lawrence Erlbaum Associates.

Council of Chief State School Officers. (1989). *Family support, education, and involvement: A guide for state action.* Washington, DC: Council of Chief State School Officers.

Curran, D. (1989). *Working with parents.* Circle Pines, MN: American Guidance Service.

Dunst, C., Trivette, C., & Deal, A. (1988). *Enabling & empowering families.* Cambridge, MA: Brookline Books.

Elkind, D. (Ed.). (1991). *Perspectives on early childhood education: Growing with young children toward the 21st century.* Washington, DC: National Education Association.

Epstein, J. (1986). Parents' reactions to teacher practices of parental involvement. *Elementary School Journal,* 227–293.

Epstein, J. (1987). Parent involvement: What research says to administrators. *Education and Urban Society, 19*(2), 119–136.

Epstein, J. (1989). Building parent teacher partnerships in inner city schools. *The Famiy Resource Coalition Report, 8*(2).

Fredericks, A., & Rasinski, T. (1989). Working with Parents: Lending a (reading) hand. *The Reading Teacher,* 520–521.

Galen, H. (1991). Increasing parental involvement in elementary school. *Young Children, 46*(2), 18–22.

Galinsky, E. (1988). Parents and teacher/caregivers: Sources of tension, sources of support. *Young Children, 43*(3), 4–12.

Goetz, K. (1992). *Programs to strengthen families: A resource guide.* Chicago: Family Resource Coalition.

Gordon, I. (1977). The application of infant research: Policy-making at the local level. *Current Issues in Child Development.*

Greenberg, P. (1989). Parents as partners in young children's development and education: A new American fad? Why does it matter?" *Young Children, 44*(4), 61–75.

Henderson, A. (1987). *The evidence continues to grow: Parent involvement improves student achievement.* Columbia, MD: National Committee for Citizens in Education.

Hester, H. (1989). Start at home to improve home-school relations. *NASSP Bulletin, 73*(513), 23–27.

Honig, A. (1979). *Parent involvement in early childhood education.* Washington, DC: National Association for the Education of Young Children.

Horowitz, J., and Faggella, K. (1986). *Partners for learning: Promoting parent involvement in school.* Bridgeport, CT: First Teacher Press.

Jones, J. (1989). Changing needs for a changing future. Keynote address June 14, Austin, TX. New York: National Center for Children in Poverty.

Keniston, K., and the Carnegie Council on Children. (1977). *All our children: The American family under pressure.* New York: Harcourt, Brace, Jovanovich.

Levenstein, P. (1988). *Messages from home: The mother-child program.* Columbus, OH: Ohio State University Press.

Liontos, L. (1992). *At-risk families and schools: Becoming partners.* Eugene, OR: ERIC Clearinghouse.

Lynch, A. (1991). Early childhood education: The parent's perspective. *Perspectives on early childhood education.* Washington, DC: National Education Association, 253–259.

Lyons, P., Robbins, A., & Smith, A. (1983). *Involving parents: A handbook for participation in schools.* Ypsilanti, MI: The High/Scope Press.

Miller, P., & McDowelle, J. (1993). *Administering preschool programs in public schools.* San Diego: Singular Publishing Group.

Powell, D. (1989). *Families and early childhood programs.* Washington, DC: National Association for the Education of Young Children.

Rich, D. (1987a). *Schools and families: Issues and actions.* Washington, DC: National Education Association.

Rich, D. (1987b). *Teachers and parents: An adult-to-adult approach.* Washington, DC: National Education Association.

Schaefer, E.S. (1973). Child development research and the educational revolution: The child, the family, and the educational profession. Paper presented at the annual meeting of the American Educational Research Association, New Orleans.

Schweinhart, L., Barnes, H., and Weikart, D. (1993). *Significant benefits: The High/Scope Perry Preschool study through age 27.* Ypsilanti, MI: The High/Scope Press.

Chapter 2

PARENTS AND TEACHERS AS PARTNERS: ISSUES AND CHALLENGES

READERS WILL BE ABLE TO:

- Recognize that all families have strengths.
- Analyze a family-centered philosophy in parent-teacher partnerships.
- Explain parental and professional prerequisites to engaging parents as partners.
- Identify demographic and societal factors influencing the family unit.
- Outline strategies for enhancing parent partnerships for "difficult to reach" parents (including parents challenged by economic stress, homelessness, lack of time, teen parenthood, single parenthood, and stepparenting).
- Explain supportive interactions for families in stressful situations (including separation and loss through divorce, death, and violence).
- Discuss what keeps fathers from being more involved and ways that teachers can facilitate their participation.

As explored in Chapter 1, the American family portrait has undergone significant change since 1960. Statistics on the changing demographics of American society provide dramatic evidence that families are facing continued and extraordinary lifestyle stresses. These complex changes of modern life affect children of all socioeconomic levels, in all areas of the country. Consequently, few children or families are immune to periods of social, emotional, or physical trauma. Because programs for young children increasingly reflect our society, early childhood educators can expect to work with greater numbers of children and families challenged by life's circumstances or in crisis as the result of them. There is no magic formula or prescription; however, the development by educators of personal and professional skills that reach and involve diverse families will be crucial in educating children in the years ahead.

ALL FAMILIES HAVE STRENGTHS

Each family possesses strengths that can help it respond to its needs. Family strengths are considered to be the family's abilities to meet the various needs of its members and maintain the integrity of the family itself. These abilities or strengths may lie in the values, attitudes, and beliefs that characterize the family's "lifestyle." Families may be committed to sticking together in difficult times, be willing to make personal sacrifices in order to help each other, take pride in members' accomplishments, or have a clear set of family rules and beliefs that define acceptable and desired behaviors. Strengths also may be reflected in the knowledge, skills, and capabilities of individual family members. For instance, some family members may be able to "look on the bright side" during troubling times, or know how to locate informal supports to help during a crisis. Families also develop mutually supportive behaviors in their interpersonal relationships, which promote positive family interactions. They may make time to be together, listen to an individual's points of view, talk about different ways to deal with problems, share feelings and concerns, and demonstrate a willingness to help each other (Dunst, Trivette, & Deal, 1994). Other strengths visible in families include (Swick, 1991):

1. *Love:* Strong emotional bonds of love between various family members—adults and children.
2. *Respect:* Helping responses that indicate members are concerned about each other's well-being.
3. *Communication:* Signs of active responsive listening, supporting family member projects, adjusting schedules, and listening to problems.
4. *Togetherness:* Sharing and support in carrying out roles to meet the family's needs.
5. *Consideration:* Sensitivity to the needs, feelings, and problems of various family members.
6. *Commitment:* A willingness to support the family and work through problems.

Interactive parent involvement strategies can reinforce parents' positive efforts in building family relationships and parenting. *Whatever the form or degree, all families have strengths.*

No family is completely self-sufficient, however. Because of this, many professionals who work with families concentrate on "weaknesses," not strengths. This results in a biased view that sees only what is not working well for the family and encourages a tendency to "do for them" rather than promoting the family members' ability to do for themselves. If teachers hope to develop a true partnership with parents and families that will foster the holistic development of children, they must learn to recognize the strengths inherent in every family system.

FAMILY SYSTEMS

A family's members and characteristics are considered part of the family system. Each family's system includes different people who have certain roles and functions. Each system utilizes various methods of meeting needs and sustaining the family. Since the days of cave dwellers, the reality of raising children

Family systems broaden the parenting network.

and meeting the needs of the family unit has required a group effort. Today's supportive contacts may require long-distance phone calls to grandma, a babysitting cooperative organized by neighborhood mothers, a class on parenting young children offered through the early childhood program, or financial assistance from the government for basic needs.

Naturally, the parents are the family's greatest assets. That is not to imply that all parents possess every skill to survive in these often-trying times or to respond appropriately to all the dilemmas that arise in raising children. Parenting isn't an instinctive skill and, unfortunately, babies don't come with instructions. Most parents at one time or another require resource information—whether from the extended family, from parenting literature, or from an early childhood professional.

PARENTS AS FIRST TEACHERS

Early childhood professionals must give parents credit for knowing their own child. By acknowledging parents as the first teachers of their children, it is recognized that parents teach, model, and guide their children. Logically, parents also have the most intimate knowledge of their child's history, personality, needs, and abilities. This parental insight can be an important resource for teachers in understanding a child.

FAMILY RESOURCES

Parents are resources—to themselves, to other families, and to the early childhood professionals working with their children. Families typically have some formal or informal networks in place. These supportive resources can be family, friends, church, or community organizations. They may be imbedded within the value system of the family and may appear within a religious or cultural context. Families under stress may not recognize supports that are already in place, such as the extended family or local service organizations. A caring professional can assist them in recognizing, accessing, and maximizing resources available to them. Different families find different solutions to similar problems and needs, yet the experience developed by one family may benefit another. Given options for self-help, peer support, and other network linkages, parents can make decisions most appropriate for them.

FAMILY-CENTERED PHILOSOPHY AND PRACTICE

Chapter 1 documented the positive connection between the home and school as a learning environment and a child's progress and achievement. To work most effectively with young children, the sensitive teacher recognizes the importance of family systems and understands the circumstances at home. The teacher also must personally reflect a commitment to parent involvement through a strong personal outreach and a nonjudgmental attitude (The Parent Institute, 1992). This is the groundwork for a family-centered approach to parent involvement. To say that parent involvement is an indicator of best practice in early childhood education doesn't make partnerships happen. There is a critical gap between theory and practice. Establishing and maintaining parental contacts may sometimes be challenging or even quite difficult for educators because of the complexity of family issues.

DANGERS OF DISTANCING

In the gap between theory and practice, the biggest obstacle can be the distancing that appears between parent and professional. The concept of accepting parents as "experts" can be confusing, even threatening, to the professional. Yet within the context of a family partnership, professionals are resources, not authorities who "know what is best" for families with young children. The professional can assist parents to develop a nurturing learning environment at home, and even may help parents identify options and develop strategies to solve the problems that affect the children and adults within the family. Powell (1989) states, "A program is what happens when parents and staff come together, not what staff 'do to or for parents.'" Professionals who undertake any type of parent involvement program must first, in their minds and hearts, understand their role in their dynamic relationships with parents.

FOUNDATIONS OF RESPECT

The professional's philosophy concerning parents can underscore or undermine the framework of trust and respect in the parent-teacher relationship. As the diversity of families increases, the understanding and appreciation of cultural and ethnic backgrounds and the acceptance of dissimilar value systems and lifestyles will become increasingly important for the early childhood educator who values parent involvement. (Cultural diversity is explored further in Chapter 3.) Families are sensitive to the economic, language, structural, cultural, or ethnic differences between themselves and others, whether they be other parents or the teacher. Consistent efforts should be made to communicate family strengths, to give consideration to unique problems or concerns, and to respond to them in a compassionate manner. Through responsive listening and by "tuning in" to parents' verbal and nonverbal messages, teachers can project an openness to parents' ideas on their child's development and learning. Controlling the impulse to talk too much, to "talk down," to correct or advise in a pushy manner, or to move too fast in parent-teacher communications is also critical to rapport. When a teacher demonstrates credibility as an early childhood professional (through confident, nurturing, child-centered behaviors; knowledge of teaching; good classroom management skills, etc.), parents gain assurance that the teacher is reliable. These qualities encourage a comfortable climate for building a partnership (Swick, 1991).

One initial strategy toward parent partnership is to learn about the families of the children, as Table 2.1 illustrates. Become familiar with the family's

TABLE 2.1

Identifying Family Needs, Strengths, and Solutions

CHILD	ADULTS IN FAMILY SYSTEM	POTENTIAL BARRIERS AND STRENGTHS, AND IDEAS TO OVERCOME BARRIERS
Lindsey	Mom, Aunt Betty	Single mom, works days, needs child care for 4 sibs. Aunt single and may help. Dad visits occasionally. Wants to "help Lindsey." Provide daily routine home activities. Meet at work during lunch? Send announcements to Dad, too.
Misha	Pat and Jim foster parents	Misha may be returned to biological mother within three months. Has visitation every other week. Two other foster children in the home. Meet with Mom? Involve caseworker.
Luke	Sarah	Luke was born when Sarah was 16. Both live with grandparents, have financial and emotional support. Sarah finished GED, works at Hardees, likes aerobics. Maybe will do a movement class with the 4-year-olds?

composition, interests, situations, and values. Sharing cultural, family, and school concerns is one way to broaden and strengthen the partnership. This process also can identify potential barriers to involvement. Often this can be documented through an interview and social history when the child enters the program. It can also be done individually on a home visit or as part of an orientation meeting at the center. Carefully done written or verbal surveys can communicate to parents that staff members are flexible and are sincerely interested in encouraging a "needs-fit" involvement match for each family. Making a simple chart like Table 2.1, with information on the children and adults, may help identify special family needs, strengths, and potential solutions to barriers.

ENGAGING PARENTS: PREREQUISITES TO PARTNERSHIPS

Professionals do get discouraged when families fail to respond to their best efforts to encourage a partnership. Sometimes a lack of transportation or child care stand in the way of involvement, but sometimes there does not appear to be an obvious reason. At these times, the teacher must have an honest, heart-searching look at his or her attitudes and behaviors. A courageous teacher can approach a colleague or a parent with whom there is good rapport to ask for assistance in analyzing the situation.

There are some hard yet simple truths to the business of parent partnerships. In order to actively participate in a parent-teacher partnership, parents must have some degree of readiness, or the capability to respond to the requirements of that partnership. These abilities center on four themes: parent self-image, parent self-control (optimism and sense of control over one's relationships and actions), parent development/maturation, and interpersonal skills. By consistently reinforcing the importance of parents as first—and best—teachers and recognizing positive parenting behaviors, teachers can communicate respect for the inherent value of each parent. Teachers can empower parents to view themselves as capable people by honestly helping them see family strengths, potential options, and choices.

PARENT SELF-IMAGE

How parents view themselves (positive or negative self-image) is reflected in all of their actions, especially in their acceptance of the parenting role and in how they interact with authority figures, such as teachers. Some parents may think they have nothing to contribute to their child's education because they do not see themselves as first teachers.

PARENT SELF-CONTROL

In life, people tend to see themselves as a victor or a victim—or a combination of both. This is sometimes referred to as the locus of control. When circumstances are difficult (and always have been), parents may feel that they have no control over what happens to them. Eventually, it becomes difficult to believe that they have the power of self-determination. Parents who are overwhelmed with simply meeting basic needs may feel they cannot undertake a less crucial obligation—that of meeting with a teacher.

PARENT DEVELOPMENT/MATURATION

As educators, we sometimes forget that development continues throughout a lifetime. As people mature—as individuals and as parents—they learn to cope with changes in relationships, and they develop a perspective about life experiences. Just because two people are physically mature enough to conceive a child does not mean that they have the emotional maturity to parent.

INTERPERSONAL SKILLS

Interpersonal skill building is related to self-confidence and the belief that "I can support others." A parent's life experience may not have empowered him or her to develop these types of skills, and this "disability" is brought into the parent-teacher encounter. Parents arrive at various points of development in relation to these four abilities in various ways and at different times in their lives. Nurturing experiences between parents and teachers in the early years offer opportunities for individual growth and success in interpersonal skill building that can reap benefits for both children and their parents (Swick, 1991).

CHALLENGES FOR EARLY CHILDHOOD PERSONNEL

In addition to the internal limitations that may hinder parent involvement, most families face increased stresses from the rapidly changing political, economic, and societal forces around them. Inflation, unemployment, and job insecurity jeopardize dreams for a better life. A tidal wave of poverty, substance abuse, increased violence, abuse, neglect, and disease have washed over an increasing number of families with young children. Inadequacies in employment, child care, housing, and health care threaten parents' hopes for their children's future. Most early childhood professionals will work with children and families facing many types of crises, and they need to be aware of how these situations affect families.

It isn't surprising that a great many families have special needs. These needs may include the basic requirements of food and shelter, or may involve intensive intervention during a crisis of homelessness or family violence. Some families may be looking for guidance in helping their children during the adjustment to a new baby, a divorce, or the death of a grandparent. Many families may need assistance in understanding the joys as well as the normal challenges of having a rapidly growing and developing preschooler in the household. It is critical to remember that, just as each family has a composite of needs, it also possesses unique abilities to respond to those needs.

Insights and Strategies for "Difficult to Reach" Parents

Some families have strong skills and come to the program ready to become involved; however, as described earlier, more families than ever before are influenced by societal and economic factors that affect their capacity to become full partners with their child's teacher. Teachers must understand where parents are developmentally, and respond with sensitivity to their life circumstances. By labeling parents "difficult to reach," educators often alienate them.

In a 1988 survey of parents, Don Davies of the Institute for Responsive Education examined the relationship between "hard-to-reach parents" and schools. The study concluded that most parents in the survey were indeed "reachable" and had a strong desire to be involved, but the schools were not really trying to involve them, were not knowledgeable of strategies, or were not sensitive enough to overcome cultural and social class barriers (Warner, 1994). Parents revealed the following obstacles to school involvement:

- The perception that non-middle-class children were viewed and treated differently.
- Communication from schools to parents was mostly negative.
- The perception that their families were deficient and that the fault lay with the parents. The focus was only on their problems.
- Among poverty-level families, parents revealed a low assessment of their ability to be involved in their children's schooling.

Research varies greatly in drawing specific conclusions about the groups of parents whom teachers may categorize as "difficult to reach." Outcomes for their children may be reported to be positive or negative depending on the study, the researcher, and the decade in which the research was done. Parents are very much aware of their circumstances and also may be aware of society's views of families like theirs. Sensitivity to these assumptions will color parent interactions with the early childhood program.

Unfortunately, teachers can be influenced by societal biases. The presence of certain characteristics (teen parent, divorced, low income) does not imply that a family will demonstrate particular attitudes or behaviors (e.g., low self-esteem, mistrust of the system). Each family is a unique group of individuals, with a unique history, support structure, and set of resources. The best source of information about a family is the family itself.

SUPPORTING FAMILIES IN CRISIS

No family is immune from crisis. Some crises (a grandparent's death or a separation) may be anticipated; others (a shooting or an act of domestic violence) may happen suddenly. Whatever crisis occurs, it frequently brings additional stress to a family's already stressful situation. Sometimes teachers can provide supportive interactions with parents, especially those with whom a trusting relationship has already been built.

Parents and professionals often encounter limits to parental involvement during crisis situations. When a family enters a crisis, individual members may need the intensive resources of family preservation and support services. Educators should know who provides these and where in the community they are located. Still, there are many things the teacher can do within the program to help the family. Teachers should:

- Provide a structured and predictable classroom environment. Children affected by constant stress and upheavals at home can find security and relief in a supportive classroom routine.
- Maintain continuity with the home. Supporting parents as well as children can be a goal of an active parent involvement program.
- Assist parents and children alike in interpreting and adjusting to life transitions; conversation, sharing books and materials, and modeling can help.
- Encourage positive coping and make referrals when appropriate.

FAMILY STATUS AND STRESS: IMPLICATIONS FOR EARLY CHILDHOOD TEACHERS

The identity of parents and the context of parenting has become increasingly diverse over the past 20 years. Piece by piece, statistics reveal a complex picture puzzle for the families of young children. This puzzle is composed of dual-income families, single parents, stepfamilies, and families subject to the multiple risk factors created by poverty or crisis. Not all parents will find themselves influenced by these lifestyle forces at one given time or even during their early parenting years. These factors that affect family status and well-being, however, are not necessarily isolated experiences for many families. One situation can be juxtaposed upon another. For example, parents may divorce and the mother may become a single parent struggling with the economic realities of minimum wage or unemployment. Families of young children in preschool programs and in elementary schools throughout our country are the statistics that are collected and analyzed by sociologists and economists. It is the teacher working with them who sees the faces behind the numbers.

Many facets of changing family lifestyles have become commonplace (dual-income families, for example); consequently, the stress that accompanies them may be underestimated. Families that have small children typically are headed by younger parents. As adults, they are establishing their unique family structure, while simultaneously developing career and other life goals. This is a common family dynamic that places many families and children under stress.

The sections that follow are not intended to make generalizations or predict outcomes for particular groups of families. There are too many individual variables within families and overlapping characteristics among groups to do that. Research does, however, offer some consistent guidance for educators and others in the helping professions in working with parents in special circumstances.

WORKING PARENTS

In 1993, according to the Children's Defense Fund, 60% of mothers with children younger than 6 were in the civilian work force. By the year 2000, it is estimated that 7 in 10 preschool-age children will have mothers employed outside the home. An increase of mothers in the workplace reflects the declining earning power of men and an increase in families headed by single mothers.

It's a fact of life in many families today that both parents work. When a mother has a job, she must deal with many new issues. The conflict between her roles of provider and nurturer, along with social disapproval of working mothers, can negatively affect a mother's attitudes and self-esteem. A woman's satisfaction with her dual roles often hinges on the degree to which her husband shares in the household chores and child care, her job satisfaction, how comfortable she is with child-care arrangements, and the perception of how her employment affects her children. Naturally, a mother's job outside the home mangnifies the problem of time—there's never enough of it. Fathers, too, are affected when the mother is employed. They often must step into roles (housework, child care) that are traditionally "women's work."

IMPLICATIONS FOR EARLY CHILDHOOD TEACHERS

A family's satisfaction with the organization and harmony within a single- or dual-income family will play an important role in the parent-teacher relationship. Potential concerns may include time management, child-care arrangements (before/after program, transportation, quality, cost), attitudinal conflicts, overwork, financial concerns, stress, and health-related issues.

Because of work schedules, opportunities for communication may be limited. A zip-top plastic bag used only for home-center communication may simplify message transfer and help children be more responsible for carrying special "mail." Telephone calls, notes, meetings scheduled for times convenient for the parents, and library loan materials may foster ongoing communication. Tape-recorded messages left on the school's answering machine after school hours (often called "warm lines") can keep working parents in touch with school events and classroom activities. Announcements of meetings and events should be given far enough in advance so that parents will have ample time to make arrangements. Likewise, care should be taken in canceling school at the last minute due to bad weather, as this may leave working parents with no place to take their children.

Flexibility in scheduling parent events is typically appreciated by working parents. Conferences could be scheduled in the early morning, during lunch, in the evening, or on weekends. Evening events may be preferred, possibly with child care provided at the site. Meetings before school or in the early evening could include a meal and child care.

To feel involved, working parents may need alternatives to traditional classroom volunteering. Make an effort to offer opportunities that benefit the program and are feasible for working mothers and fathers. (See Chapter 10 for additional ideas on program volunteers.) Encourage learning activities that are tied to the parents' home routine. When you look at parent involvement from the perspective of the working parent, it will be easier to find solutions.

DIVORCE, REMARRIAGE, AND STEPPARENTING

As divorce becomes more commonplace, researchers continue to study the effects of separation and divorce on the family unit and on children at different ages. The events that lead to divorce, and the arrangements made when one is agreed upon, are unique to each family. The divorce affects each family member differently, both at the time of the parents' breakup and later. How well adults handle their personal issues and assist their children in making the necessary transitions often determine how long the disharmony lasts. All members of the family are affected by the adjustment to new family configurations, possibly new homes, new routines, and other new life patterns. Joint custody arrangements can help create positive structures for the transition to new lifestyles. There may be a downside when parents, stressed by interpersonal upheaval, temporarily put parenting on a back burner. Children may be affected by inconsistent parenting as the custodial parent juggles the responsibilities of being a single parent and, sometimes, the sole provider.

In time, most divorced people remarry, frequently to other parents with children. Children in these blended families have a great many adjustments to make: new parents, new siblings, and new sets of extended families, including grandparents. Stepparents may find it difficult to establish a satisfactory relationship with their stepchildren, despite their eagerness to be accepted. Fathers may feel guilty about not living with their own children, while stepmothers may have a difficult time shaking the "wicked stepmother" image. Stepparents may be concerned about developing a strong marital bond while at the same time developing bonds with an "instant family." Developing a workable parenting arrangement is an ongoing task. Noncustodial parents also may harbor anger and resentment about the divorce, which can influence their relationship with the children and their participation in the children's education.

IMPLICATIONS FOR EARLY CHILDHOOD TEACHERS

Teachers should remember that children and parents will all react differently to separation and divorce. Divorce is a major change, and the family may need extra support, patience, and reassurance from the stable school environment. During a family upheaval, aggression and noncompliance on the part of their children are typical but troublesome issues that parents must deal with. Helping the parent understand what is happening with the child and offering practical support would be a probable partnership response. Teachers could suggest professional and parent resources on divorce, including contacts at local support services that specialize in family counseling (Procidano & Fisher, 1992).

Teachers should be kept informed of the legal and informal agreements regarding child care, and whether there are any restrictions to family visitation at school or special transportation arrangements. Parents who are on an emotional roller coaster may need to vent their anger and frustrations; teachers should be careful to remain professional and refrain from taking sides.

All parents should be included and made welcome in the program's parent involvement activities. Noncustodial parents should receive invitations to meetings, conferences, field trips, and other school events. Teachers should be sensitive to parental desires to be involved and aware of differences in last names. When making gifts or cards, children should be encouraged to make as many as they need for their families. Teachers should also be sensitive to visitation patterns for weekends, holidays, and vacations in order to understand why a child is acting a certain way.

A teacher who shares information about stressors and typical situations in remarriage/stepparent relationships can help a family adjust. The teacher can be a reassuring link for families and can assist them in recognizing their new strengths. Many excellent books can help children and parents talk about the concerns of a new lifestyle. Although books are no replacement for counseling, teachers can help families by making books or a bibliography of titles available. Care should be taken in selecting books for use with children. Children's "classic" tales often portray negative images that are confusing to young children. Stepparents, especially stepmothers, have suffered from a stereotypical image. Family-sensitive literature and curriculum materials now available for early childhood classes may become classic tales of children's literature in years to come (ERIC Digest, 1988, Procidano & Fisher, 1992).

SINGLE-PARENT FAMILIES

In single-parent families, one adult usually undertakes all the parental roles typically shared by two persons. These include economic support, child care, housekeeping, recreation and leisure time management, emotional support, and companionship. Consequently, the single parent is at risk for task overload and strain—both physical and emotional. Often the psychological stress and distress of the parenting situation are related to the age, educational level, parenting style, individual capability, and values of the parent. Typically the single parent is female. Single-parent fathers are also subject to role strain, although fathers seldom acknowledge serious child-rearing difficulties (Pruett, 1993).

Single parenthood can occur for many reasons. Although separation or divorce is the most common reason, other possibilities include a mother who never marries or death. When parents divorce or when one parent dies, the family must confront emotional and economic loss; relocation and the accompanying loss of friends and family support networks; and health and security concerns. The children's reaction and adjustment to these issues may add to the difficulty of the situation.

Single-parent households and low income do not necessarily mean low-quality parenting. Studies show that low-income single, working parents often spend as much time helping their children as do middle-class parents (ERIC Digest, 1988). However, if there isn't a father in the home, many mothers are concerned about the lack of a male role model, and noncompliance in young boys often creates problems for their mothers.

IMPLICATIONS FOR EARLY CHILDHOOD TEACHERS

Single parents may depend upon children's programs to provide a needed stable environment for children, and respite for them. Educators may provide valuable guidance, reassurance, and support during the adjustment process and beyond. Practical and emotional problems (child care, housing, limited education, child management difficulties) may be overwhelming. Requests for classroom donations or volunteers should be made with a sensitivity to a parent's feelings and his or her capacity to respond. Some mothers and fathers may feel guilt or remorse about being single parents. Some may shield their discomfort with a smoke screen of indifference.

Concerns common to other working parents may be heightened for single parents. Because work and school schedules may not coincide, there may be a concern about who's watching the child when a parent isn't available. Often, older children are given the job of supervising younger ones. A positive action on the part of a teacher would be to investigate nearby before- and after-school care and make that information available to the parent. Single working parents may want more contact and consultation with teachers. They also might be receptive to a parent-to-parent group. Teachers should make sure that all events appear open to parents who may not fit a typical family structure. Parents may feel left out if events are obviously geared to one parent or one type of family member (e.g., Mother's Breakfast, Dad's Saturday with Me, Grandparents' Day).

FAMILIES IN POVERTY

As the number of positions in manufacturing and management decline and those in service industries increase, many wage earners may find themselves working for less. The median income of young families (headed by someone below age 30) dropped 32% between 1973 and 1990. Consequently, two incomes may be needed to maintain a standard of living equal to preceding generations.

The realities of daily existence continue to undermine many families' hopes for a better life. The minimum wage has not kept pace with inflation. In 1993, full-time, year-round, minimum-wage earnings fell well below the annual poverty line for a family of three. Despite the fact that one parent is employed, the family still may live in poverty. The poverty rate was 40% among all children in families headed by someone under the age of 30. It is predicted that, unless an action plan is instituted to slow poverty in America, one in every four of our children will be poor by the year 2000. Additional statistics from the Children's Defense Fund indicate that not only is poverty increasing in America, but the poor are getting poorer. Contrary to popular myth, the majority of poor children are not black and are not on welfare. They are members of working families, and they live in small towns and in the rural and suburban areas of our country, as well as in the cities (Children's Defense Fund, 1994).

Poor families face more risk factors than do members of other groups mentioned in this section, although parents from any of those groups may also be economically deprived. Multiple risk factors subject children and families to developmental and dysfunctional problems. Lifestyle risks include inadequacies in housing, environmental safety, and sanitation. Poor neighborhoods are prone to a higher incidence of violence and crime. Poor working parents may be exposed to monotonous or hazardous working conditions and hazardous substances and chemicals. Health care may be inadequate or nonexistent. Hunger, poor nutrition, and child abuse are major, related problems. Family beliefs about child development, adult interaction, and discipline vary greatly. The emotional stress on children may manifest itself in behaviors similar to posttraumatic stress disorder: short attention span, weak impulse control, speech delays, sleep disturbances, depression, or aggression. Parents may have difficulty responding with sensitivity to these behaviors and may have behavior management and guidance problems. Economically deprived families often focus on basic survival needs, and classroom involvement becomes a low priority.

IMPLICATIONS FOR EARLY CHILDHOOD TEACHERS

Poverty-level parents may need additional help from churches and social service agencies. Parents may respond best to individual invitations and personal contacts. Frequent, informal contacts and visits may be important links for home-school connections, if the family is receptive. Poverty, illiteracy, and poor health tend to reduce the parents' ability to respond to stress in their lives and respond to expectations for parent involvement. Parent ownership and leadership of the partnership process is crucial. Opportunities should be provided for parents to "invest themselves" in the classroom environment by making or locating learning materials, giving classroom assistance, etc. Collaborations with community programs and agencies serving these same families can provide linkages for literacy and employment. The center library and bulletin boards should include resource information on family welfare issues such as nutrition, shelter, clothing, health, child care, and employment, and appropriate application forms if possible. Many families may be struggling for the first time with low-income issues. Parent programs and activities can focus on empowering strategies to deal with healthy meal planning, easy home repairs, job application and interview tips, or even a schoolwide clothing swap supplemented by clothing from community donations.

Parents may appreciate short, positive, regular reports about their child. Take and share snapshots of their children (especially of children and parents together), as these may be the only pictures the family will have. Because parents in poverty may have had few nurturing parent models, they may have a difficult time parenting and encouraging their own children. Parents need specific information about their children and general information about typical development and behaviors during these years. Suggestions for encouraging a positive learning environment at home should be shared in an individualized, sensitive manner.

Families may also find it helpful to talk with other parents at the center. Refreshments in a special area for parents and at meetings is one way to foster trust and communication. Parenting information in short, easy-to-read pamphlets or flyers should be available. Holiday activities and cultural events provide teachers with additional opportunities for positive parent contact (Klein, Bittel, & Molnar, 1993).

TEEN PARENTHOOD

Being a teen parent brings its own special problems. Only about half of teen moms finish high school, putting both mother and child at risk. Support systems may include parents, extended family, or friends; however, teen parents often need help from programs that assist with literacy, GED preparation, employment, family planning, and life skills.

Adolescent pregnancy is a major contributor to the increase in single-mother families. Two out of every five American girls become pregnant, and one in five bears a child before the age of 20. Most aren't married. Much of this has to do with poverty and a lack of achievement. Regardless of race, teens from poor families with below-average academic skills are about five to seven times more likely to become parents than are teens with solid skills from non-poor families (Children's Defense Fund, 1992). Often grandparents assume the role of parent and become primary contacts for early childhood professionals.

IMPLICATIONS FOR EARLY CHILDHOOD TEACHERS

Teens may be especially uncomfortable in unfamiliar settings—such as the early childhood center—and may lack the confidence or initiative to ask questions.

Teens may need transportation and on-site child care in order to participate in center events. Teen moms (and dads) respond best in special groups of other young parents. They are usually interested in learning about their child and may learn best by observing or practicing skills in a role-play setting. Incentives for attendance and participation may encourage involvement. Personal contact by a "big sister" or by someone from a parent-to-parent network at the center may also help (Nickel & Delany, 1985).

HOMELESS FAMILIES

Homelessness is a reality for many families in communities large and small, urban and rural. Statistics provided by the Children's Defense Fund (1994) are alarming: Families with children are the fastest growing segment (43%) of the homeless population in America. Leaders at the U.S. Conference of Mayors (1991) reported that one in four homeless people in their cities is a child. There is great concern about the lack of progress in assuring that all families have decent and stable housing, which is recognized as vital to children's development. Without a stable home in which to grow, these children typically develop more severe health, developmental, and nutritional difficulties than other poor children, and are more vulnerable to the effects of lead poisoning, educational dysfunction, emotional stress, and family separation.

The trauma of homelessness also includes the loss of stability, security, social and family networks, routines, and the emotional grounding that comes from "going home." It produces anxiety about the uncertainty of each day, and fear of the violence that may arrive at any moment in the parking lot or in the shelter. These places cannot offer children the safety, comfort, and security they need, nor provide age-appropriate opportunities for exploration and stimulation they require for healthy development.

Because the world of homeless children is chaotic, the early childhood center may offer them the only place where they can participate in the "normal" activities of childhood. These children may participate in public or private programs, or receive services in a special shelter program. Typically, shelter programs have limitations on how long families can stay and on the types of services and programs offered. The conditions that produce homelessness often are the same ones that contribute to a short enrollment in a single early childhood program.

IMPLICATIONS FOR EARLY CHILDHOOD TEACHERS

Parents who live in emergency housing are struggling with overwhelming demands. Teachers working with these families can best assist parents by:

1. Helping parents appreciate and understand their children. Provide information about their child's abilities, interests, play patterns, communications, and behaviors. Short, regular reports, especially about the positive things their child does, can be reassuring to parents. Share photographs of their child enjoying the program activities. Whenever possible, include parents in making decisions about their child's care and education. Help them to feel they are decision makers in their child's life.

2. Respecting and supporting the unique needs of the parents. Many parents of homeless children are vulnerable individuals in need of nurturing and care themselves. The parent space should have refreshments, and parents can be encouraged to join their children for breakfast, snack, or lunch. The center may also stock extra clothes, toys, books, or food for emergency use. Pamphlets on child rearing and child development issues can be available. Around holidays, teachers should be especially sensitive to the parents' need to provide positive memories for their child. Parent activities such as simple gift-making centers can be part of the parent program, as can fun outings with other parents, such as picnics, sports days, etc.

3. Providing information and/or support services to families. Encourage a trusting atmosphere where parents can share their concerns, stresses, and problems. Host or provide access to support groups for parents with similar concerns and be informed about local services or sources of support that may be needed by families. Schools and programs may also collaborate with shelters and offer services to children being served there (Klein et al., 1993).

FAMILY VIOLENCE AND NEGLECT

Many kinds of violence affect the lives of young children and families each day. Domestic violence takes place each hour in America, with staggering consequences. Women of childbearing age face the highest risk of violence by a male partner, especially during pregnancy. After a baby is born, many abused women experience postpartum depression, which affects the health and well-being of their newborn (Carnegie Corporation, 1994). Exposure to other violence—both in the media and in the neighborhood—also has a major impact on children.

Too often, young children are victims of abuse. The statistics are sobering. Of all children who experience physical abuse and neglect, one-third are infants under 1 year. Often, maltreatment of children under 3 years results in permanent injury or death. In 1990, almost 90% of the children who died as the result of abuse were under age 5. Reported cases of abused and/or neglected children increase each year. As a result, the numbers of children in foster homes, group homes, or institutional settings in the child welfare system are growing; sadly, infants make up the largest percentage of children entering care. Although many states have family preservation programs in place, for many children, foster parents and other caregivers are also part of the changing definition of "parent" (Children's Defense Fund, 1994).

Children's exposure to media violence concerns social scientists, public health experts, and many parents. Studies show that exposure to violence on television and in video games is associated with increased aggression, desensitization to violence, depression, and fear in children (Children's Defense Fund, 1994). Gun violence is also increasing. In 1994, an American child died of gunshot wounds about every two hours. Children growing up in violent neighborhoods may feel helpless and fearful. They often have difficulty sleeping, demonstrate increased anxiety or depression, and may withdraw or have difficulty paying attention. Parents too are affected. They often lose confidence in their parenting abilities and are so traumatized that they find it difficult to be emotionally responsive to their children (Carnegie Corporation, 1994).

IMPLICATIONS FOR EARLY CHILDHOOD TEACHERS

When children and families have been victims of violence, a teacher's expression of personal feelings and condolences can help the survivors in their efforts to reconstruct their lives. Families should be coached to respond sensitively to children's grief, which can manifest itself in anxiety, hyperactivity, fears, sleep disturbances, and bedwetting. Survivors may benefit from the local and national support groups formed expressly to assist others experiencing a similar crisis. These include Parents of Murdered Children National Headquarters, 1739 Bella Vista, Cincinnati, OH 45237, (513) 721-LOVE; Families and Friends of Missing Persons and Violent Crime Victims, 8421 32nd St. SW, Seattle, WA 98126, (206) 362-1081; and Compassionate Friends National Headquarters, P.O. Box 1347, Oak Brook, IL 60521, (312) 323-5010 (Steele & Raider, 1991). Victims of abuse should be directed to local shelters for women and children, where counseling and other support services are available. Local police departments or toll free numbers (available in telephone directories) can provide other assistance. Crises often require special counseling skills, and teachers should be prepared to direct families to appropriate local services.

UTILIZING COMMUNITY RESOURCES

In addition to early childhood education programs, professionals may be working with family support initiatives that promote healthy child development, improve family literacy, prepare children for school, reduce child abuse and neglect, and support teen parents. These support services may include home visits or drop-in centers that provide child care and preschool programs for parents participating in classes, group meetings, and social activities. Often these services have a variety of trained personnel who connect with other support agencies and programs within the community. These programs provide excellent resources and can refer teachers to additional sources of assistance for families. Programs serving young children and families should obtain or develop a directory of these services.

Family involvement is for fathers too.

INVOLVING FATHERS

Fathers have long been neglected when parent involvement is considered. Minimal participation by fathers has been almost expected. Fathers report that teachers are often shocked by their interest in participating actively in their child's educational life. As family-centered practices have become more common in early childhood education, sensitive professionals have increased the opportunities to empower fathers, stepfathers, and boyfriends as active participants in a child's life.

According to May (1991), men and women parent differently. Gender differences may be attributed to opportunity (time and proximity), encouragement, and cultural conditioning, rather than a biological difference. Pruett reports, however, that when mothers are present, fathers tend to defer to the mother's caretaking wishes. Fathers who are primary caregivers for their infants and children have demonstrated competency in that role, which has provided clear benefits for the children. Pruett reported that these children are active, vigorous children who are interested in the external environment. They also have performed above norms on standardized developmental tests.

Fathers (and those in fathering roles) need to recognize ways to make positive contributions in all facets of their child's life. According to May (1991), men's strengths lie in areas such as playfulness, leadership, adventure, independence, and responsibility. Fathers can be encouraged to play with and teach their child one-on-one.

Many programs target fathers, such as those for dads of Head Start preschoolers, for fathers of children with disabilities, and for teen or minority fathers. The most successful have provided a chance for men to participate in parenting or other educational programming, to discuss their feelings with other fathers in groups led by men, and to interact with their children in a play setting. These programs are designed around the interests of the fathers and have resulted in improved communication and a closer, richer relationship with their child (Levine, 1993).

The Advance Family Support and Education Program, which primarily serves Latino fathers, has seen positive changes in the men who have become involved in the project. Men interact with wives and children more gently and with greater respect. Family conflicts are handled in more positive ways, and both parents are likely to share in decision making (Children's Defense Fund, 1992).

Often program activities for men limit father participation to traditional "male jobs," such as construction projects. But many men may prefer to make videotapes, develop support systems for other men in the program, or advocate for the needs of young children in the community or at the state or national level.

Fathers, grandfathers, stepfathers, and stepgrandfathers all have a role to play as a new model of fathering is emerging. Men are often ignored or neglected because of a prejudice against their willingness to take a nurturing role with their child. Special programming for dads and adaptations to the parent involvement program can be made that are sensitive to the father's integral role in the family and his importance as parent as first teacher. By respecting the father's knowledge of his child and downplaying the professional as expert, a teacher may find it easier to draw fathers into the parenting program.

Because most early childhood personnel are female, teachers must learn how to work positively with men, making an effort to overcome any fears or preconceptions about male stereotypes. Welcoming and encouraging fathers (and other male family members) may take a conscious effort, but it will pay off. Here are some ideas:

- Project the expectation that it is normal for men to be involved and be supported in the fathering role.
- Get to know the fathers as well as the mothers and siblings of children in your class.
- Make phone calls home (especially those positive "warm calls") at a time when both parents are home and available to talk.
- Write information in program records so that it is respectful to both parents.
- Don't neglect fathers not living in the home. Copies of permission agreements, program information, and other materials should be sent to the father as well as to the home where the child lives.
- Schedule appointments and program activities to accommodate the father's work schedule, when possible.
- Hold special events for men. "Our Special Saturday" breakfast and an activity center program can include dads and children.
- Alert families to support programs for men in parenting roles. Try to locate those led by men for men.

TABLE 2.2
Family Support Professionals

TYPE OF PROFESSIONAL	SERVICES PROVIDED	PROFESSIONAL ORGANIZATION
Marriage and Family Therapists	Counseling for family members having difficulty coping with life situations.	American Association for Marriage and Family Therapy 1717 K St. NW, Suite 407 Washington, DC 20006
Pastoral Counselors	Counseling for families within a religious context.	American Association of Pastoral Counselors 99508A Lee Highway Fairfax, VA 22031
Registered Nurses	Help with medical concerns.	American Nurses Association 2420 Pershing Road Kansas City, MO 64108
Home Economists	Information on issues concerning family and children, such as nutrition, child care, housing, and money management.	American Home Economics Association 1555 King St. Alexandria, VA 22314
Social Workers	Information about community services that assist children and families. Some also may do counseling.	National Association of Social Workers 7981 Eastern Ave. Silver Springs, MD 20910

SOURCE: Coleman, 1991

■ Include materials for men in the parent space at the center, and keep informed about other options for involving men in early childhood programs.

The Minnesota Fathering Alliance (1992) has published a guide to working with fathers, and James May (1992) is a leader in developing supports for fathers with children who have special needs. Both are excellent resources for the development of parent involvement programs directed to fathers. (See Table 2.2.)

SUMMARY

This chapter has investigated some of the many issues facing families today and has explored some of the implications for building parent-teacher partnerships. Working with children and families facing personal challenges requires great dedication and concern—prerequisites for early childhood teachers in today's world.

Working with families in crisis may trigger strong emotions: pity, anger, control, rescue fantasies, etc. Determining the source of these feelings may help a teacher keep them under control. Teachers also must anticipate being the target of strong feelings expressed by parents, and must maintain an objective viewpoint. They should pay particular attention to the needs and feelings of the parents, and keep them separate from those of the children.

The more parents are stressed, the more dependent they may appear to become. This tendency can be recognized and accepted, although parents should be encouraged to develop the skills and confidence to solve their own problems. Educators need to realize that parents under stress will have difficulty making commitments and organizing their lives. Teachers should become knowledgeable about the range of special services available to parents and be a resource and referral for parents. They shouldn't underestimate the ability of parents to help one another by securing assistance through their own support networks (Braun, Coplin, & Sonnenschein, 1994).

ACTIVITIES FOR DISCUSSION, EXPANSION, AND APPLICATION

1. Interview teachers, directors/principals, and social workers from programs in your community. Using their input and your personal observations, discuss the demographic and societal factors affecting families in your area. How do these impact the early childhood programs and services available for families?

2. Consider a family with which you are familiar. Determine its strengths and possible areas of concern. As an early childhood professional, how would you approach family members, respond to their concerns, adapt the parent involvement program, and encourage their involvement?

3. Develop a checklist or chart that could be used in either the development or evaluation of an early childhood parent involvement program. It should include (a) quality statements to evaluate activities, and (b) indicators to determine the degree to which a teacher/program has integrated a family-centered philosophy of parent involvement into the early childhood program.

4. Select one group of parents whose involvement in your program could present a challenge. Outline the group's characteristics and potential barriers to involvement. What could a teacher do to adapt the parent involvement program to the group's unique needs?

5. What type of family would be most challenging for you to engage in a parent involvement program? Why? How would you have to adjust your attitudes, responses, etc., to make the partnership successful?

ADDITIONAL RESOURCES

Clay, J. (1990). Working with lesbian and gay parents and their children. *Young Children, 45*(3), 31–35.

Derman-Sparks, L., & the A.B.C. Task Force. (1989). *Anti-bias curriculum: Tools for empowering young children.* Washington, DC: National Association for the Education of Young Children.

Henslin, J. (1989). *Marriage and family in a changing society.* New York: The Free Press.

Jewett, C. (1982). *Helping children cope with separation and loss.* Boston, MA: Harvard Common Press.

Liontos, L. (1992). *At-risk families and schools: Becoming partners.* Eugene, OR: ERIC Clearinghouse.

McConkey, R. (1985). *Working with parents.* Cambridge, MA: Brookline Books.

McCracken, J.B. (Ed.). (1986). *Reducing stress in young children's lives.* Washington, DC: National Association for the Education of Young Children.

Miller, P., & McDowelle, J. (1993). *Administering preschool programs in public schools.* San Diego: Singular Press.

National Commission on Children. (1991). *Speaking of kids: A national survey of children and parents.* Washington, DC: National Commission on Children.

Rich, D. (1987). *Schools and families: Issues and actions.* Washington, DC: National Education Association.

Rich, D. (1987). *Teachers and parents: An adult-to-adult approach.* Washington, DC: National Education Association.

Robinson, B. (1990). The teacher's role in working with children of alcoholic parents. *Young Children, 45*(4), 68–73.

Schaefer, E.S. (1973). Child development research and the educational revolution: The child, the family, and the educational profession. Paper presented at the annual meeting of the American Educational Research Association, New Orleans.

Schweinhart, L., Barnes, H., and Weikart, D. (1993). *Significant benefits: The High/Scope Perry Preschool study through age 27.* Ypsilanti, MI: The High/Scope Press.

Yawkey, T.D., & Cornelius, G.M. (Eds.). (1990). *The single parent family.* Lancaster, PA: Technomic Publishing Co.

REFERENCES

Allen, M., Brown, P., and Finlay, B. (1992). *Helping children by strengthening families.* Washington, DC: Children's Defense Fund.

Braun, L., Coplin, J., & Sonnenshein, P. (1994). *Helping parents in groups.* Boston: Wheelock College Center for Parenting Studies.

Carnegie Corporation of New York. (1994). *Starting points: Meeting the needs of our youngest children.* New York: Carnegie Corporation.

Chafel, J. (1990). Children in poverty: Policy perspectives on a national crisis. *Young Children, 45*(5), 31–37.

Children's Defense Fund. (1994). *The state of America's children 1994.* Washington, DC: Children's Defense Fund.

Coleman, M. (1991). Planning for the changing nature of family life in schools for young children. *Young Children, 46*(4), 15–20.

Dunst, C., Trivette, C., and Deal, A. (Eds.). (1994). *Supporting and strengthening families: Volume 1: Methods, strategies and practice.* Cambridge, MA: Brookline Books.

Epstein, J. (1987). Parent involvement: What research says to administrators. *Education and Urban Society, 19*(2), 119–136.

ERIC Digest. (1988). Improving the school-home connection for low-income urban parents. *ERIC Digest, 41.*

Klein, T., Bittel, C., & Molnar, J. (1993). No place to call home: Supporting the needs of homeless children in the early childhood classroom. *Young Children, 48*(6), 22–31.

Levine, J. (1993). Involving fathers in Head Start: A framework for public policy and program development. *Families in Society 74*(1), 4–19.

May, J. (1991). *Fathers of children with special needs: New horizons.* Bethesda, MD: Association for the Care of Children's Health.

May, J. (1992). *Circles of care and understanding: Support programs for fathers of children with special needs.* Bethesda, MD: Association for the Care of Children's Health.

Minnesota Fathering Alliance. (1992). *Working with fathers.* Stillwater, MN: Nu Ink Unlimited.

Nickel, P., & Delany, H. (1985). *Working with teen parents.* Chicago: Family Resource Coalition.

The Parent Institute. (1992). What's working in parent involvement. *Newsletter, 2*(4), *2*(7), *3*(2). Fairfax Station, VA: The Parent Institute.

Pooley, L., & Littell, J. (1986). *Family resource program builder.* Chicago: Family Resource Coalition.

Powell, D. (1989). *Families and early childhood programs.* Washington, DC: National Association for the Education of Young Children.

Procidano, M., & Fisher, C. (Eds.). (1992). *Contemporary families.* New York: Teacher's College Press.

Pruett, K. (1993). The paternal presence. *Families in Society, 74*(1), 46–50.

Steele, W., & Raider, M. (1991). *Working with families in crisis.* New York: Guilford Press.

Swick, K. (1991). *Teacher parent partnerships to enhance school success in early childhood education.* Washington, DC: National Educational Association.

U.S. Conference of Mayors. (1991). *A status report on hunger and homelessness in America's cities: 1991. A 28 city survey.* Washington, DC.

Warner, C. (1994). *Promoting your school.* Thousand Oaks, CA: Corwin Press.

Chapter 3

WORKING WITH FAMILIES FROM DIVERSE CULTURES

THE READER WILL BE ABLE TO:

- Define diversity in the early childhood setting.
- Identify ways in which families differ from one another.
- Discuss the role of the teacher's attitude in parent involvement.
- Identify educational practices that present barriers to parent involvement.
- List common barriers to parent involvement from the parents' perspective.
- Describe strategies and techniques that help remove barriers between families and schools.

In early childhood education, diversity means more than racial differences. Educators encounter families from diverse backgrounds, cultures, and family structures. Because today's family is changing, educators and administrators find it increasingly important to redefine strategies that establish and maintain lines of communication between home and school. Teachers must examine their attitudes and eliminate any biases so they can fully accept each child and his or her family network.

In the context of this text, **diversity** refers to children and families of any cultural background or religious origin who are a part of family configurations that include those headed by a single parent of either sex, blended families, teen parents, families headed by gay or lesbian parents, children in the custody of adults other than biological parents, and foster parents. Diversity, then, is the blending of many separate and unique families. Toward the goal of building partnerships with schools, each family possesses individual strengths that deserve to be recognized and tapped.

This chapter will focus on four main topics. First, the ways in which families differ from one another will be described. Issues such as family structure and pattern, value systems and socialization, perceptions of authority, degree of isolation, and degree of permanence in the community all impact a family's attitudes and beliefs toward schools. Second, practices related to teacher attitudes will be discussed and the effect they have on how well families are accepted by teachers and staff. Third, barriers to parent involvement—from the parent perspective—will be explored. Research has shown that parents often perceive invisible walls to parent involvement that may exist despite written policy to the contrary (Cockrell, 1992). Concluding this chapter is a discussion of methods to overcome barriers, from both the parents' and the teachers' perspectives.

VIEWPOINT ON DIVERSITY

Numerous articles and books that explore issues related to diversity focus solely on the multicultural aspects of education. A great deal of attention is paid to these issues, especially as they relate to curriculum and their effect on young children's attitudes. Often a chart or graph is created that categorizes information about group values, family structure, and attitudes toward education. While cultural issues are often the most noticeable and, in some cases, problematic because of language barriers, there are similarities in the concerns and needs of all children whose background or family structure differs from the mainstream community in which they live. Many families share feelings of isolation, a lack of awareness of expectations, and concern that their child's needs to ensure school success will be met. Such a "recipe approach" promotes stereotypical attitudes.

As educators, we must broaden our definition of diversity and utilize the same strategies to reach *all* parents. Without such efforts, many families "fall through the cracks," and opportunities for involvement are wasted. For this reason, the authors have chosen not to simplify the attitudes, beliefs, and values of diverse groups of people into a few words or phrases. Instead, we will discuss the universal strategies and techniques that apply to *all* parents, and will explore methods of increasing parent involvement based on individual family needs.

WAYS IN WHICH FAMILIES DIFFER

Basic differences exist among all families, across all socioeconomic and racial lines. Differences may have more to do with family heritage and life experiences than ethnicity. In addition to the more visible differences of socioeconomic level, there are other criteria that distinguish families from one another, including the degree of permanence in the community, family configuration, values socialization, and perceptions of authority.

DEGREE OF PERMANENCE

Central to establishing parent involvement is an understanding of the degree of permanence each family has within the community. Employment status, reasons for living in the area, and length of time in this country all impact the commitment parents feel to a school, neighborhood, and community. Families

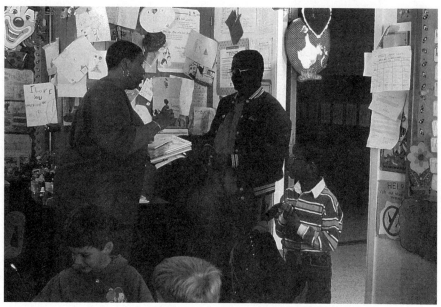

Teachers must incorporate a variety of resources to meet family needs.

may be educated, employed, and permanent citizens of the United States. They may be recent immigrants, employed, and working toward citizenship by adopting the new traditions and values of the current culture, yet continuing to embrace some cultural traditions. Families may be refugees who fled their homeland under duress and are continuing to live under enormous amounts of stress and poor economic conditions. Parents who are migrant workers may be part-time members of a community that serves as a place of temporary employment for weeks or months.

Teachers should resist forming preconceived ideas about any parent based on name or race; doing so creates invisible walls to participation. Rather, parent needs for involvement should be determined *after* meeting families and discussing mutually desired goals for their children.

FAMILY CONFIGURATIONS

As described in Chapter 1, families of the 1990s are more complex than at any other time in history. The 1950s version of the nuclear family (two-parent families in which the father is employed full time, the mother does not work outside the home, and all of the children are born after the parents' marriage) is becoming rarer. Recent statistics show that only 11% to 16% of America's children now reside in two-parent, one-wage-earner families (Hernandez, 1993). It is estimated that more than 59% of children born in 1983 will reside, for some period of time, in a single-parent household before age 18 (Norton & Glick,

1986). In addition, demographic studies indicate that the majority of children born in the industrial era (1920–present) have lived in families that experienced at least one of the following: parental separation, divorce, or death; sibling born out of wedlock; a period of unemployment or part-time employment by the father; or a mother in the work force (Hernandez, 1993).

How do these trends affect parent involvement in the schools? Teachers must devise new strategies that will reach *all* parents, including nonliterate parents, adults with limited English proficiency, noncustodial parents who wish to remain involved in their child's education, extended families with two or three generations of a family under one roof sharing responsibility for the children, blended families, single parents of both sexes, and teenage parents.

Educators also must be open to developing relationships with adults who may be significant in the child's life but are not biological parents, such as foster parents and grandparents (Clay, 1990). These conditions can and will occur across all socioeconomic and racial lines. To make assumptions based on stereotypical information is not serving parents fairly. Rather, educators need to take responsibility for making face-to-face contact with families *before* interpreting their needs for communication, involvement, and assistance.

SOCIALIZATION AND VALUES

Socialization refers to the qualities and attributes that families encourage in their children, ones that are required for adult roles in a particular society or ethnic orientation. Socialization deals with such issues as level of independence, cooperativeness vs. competitiveness, individuality vs. group goals, tactility (comfort levels of touch from another person), and aggression (Soldier, 1992; West, 1992). Families are not the only agents assisting children in adapting to their environment—schools assume a large degree of the responsibility as well. Historically, one of the school's primary roles has been to perpetuate society's knowledge, skills, customs, and beliefs (Kliebard, 1987). The difficulty lies in the conflict between these two sets of knowledge. Children who come from a family outside of the mainstream, dominant culture may experience dissonance when integrating what is taught at home and at school (West, 1992). This applies to children in ethnically different as well as in nontraditional families. Children often are caught in a struggle to meet the expectations of family and school.

Some of the more general ways in which families differ include:

1. *Work ethic:* Standards for industriousness, level of ambition expected of children, value placed on competition both in school and in personal relationships, degree of emphasis on cooperation within peer groups. All vary within cultures and may impact student or parent response to school expectations.
2. *Communication style:* Appropriate communication styles vary according to cultural standards. This includes how children may address adults verbally, maintenance of eye contact, silence, distance, emotional expressiveness, and body movements (Randall-David, 1989).

3. *Basis for ascribed status:* Cultures differ in their methods of assigning status to individuals. Level of education, occupation, class of birth, and family heritage are common criteria for assigning high, middle, or low status within a culture (Berns, 1993).

4. *Value of achievement vs. heritage:* Cultures may place more value on the heritage, or family line, than on individual accomplishments. Children from these cultures may be expected to achieve for their families and not for themselves.

5. *Role definition in family and community:* Some cultures place equal value on the child's responsibilities at home and school; others value school performance as a reflection of the family honor (Shen & Mo, 1990). Gender roles in the home may be specifically prescribed and may conflict with philosophies of gender equality in the schools.

Within a culture, there may exist tremendous variations between subgroups. For example, Soldier (1992) points out that while there is a population in the United States identified as Native American, it is made up of more than 250 federally recognized tribes, each with unique beliefs, customs, and languages. While it is difficult to make generalizations about all groups, there may be certain core beliefs that are shared by many. Gaining familiarity with these core attitudes, values, and behaviors can aid teachers in discovering basic sociocultural orientations.

Another factor to consider is that some minority families may be in a state of transition. It is critical that educators avoid stereotyping families by any single criterion such as race or economic level.

> Cultures change through the years, so the degree of cultural orientation that children bring with them into the classroom will vary contingent on the strength of their ethnic identification and how acculturated their parents are. (Soldier, 1992)

As Soldier points out, many families fall between the two extremes of traditional orientation and full assimilation. By addressing each family individually, without preconceived notions, educators make it possible for each set of parents and children to have their needs met realistically and fairly.

PERCEPTIONS OF AUTHORITY AND THE ROLE OF THE SCHOOL

Educators may gain insight into parent attitudes toward involvement by discovering how strongly they feel about their culture's traditional views of education. Cultures differ on the appropriate role parents are to assume in their child's education. In some groups, formal schooling is reserved for the elite. Parents who have never been part of the educational system have difficulty understanding the roles and responsibilities of parent involvement in this society. In other groups, the school and its teachers are highly respected, but not viewed as having a collaborative relationship with parents. School assumes a role of authority in the culture similar to the position of the church (Cryer, 1989).

There are also families who, because of chronic poverty, unemployment, and poor school experiences, have negative attitudes toward education and teachers. These are parents who have little to do with their children's schooling, and they offer minimal support for the teacher's efforts to communicate. Included in this group may be parents who have had difficulties obtaining special education services or meeting immunization requirements so their children can enter school.

DEGREE OF ISOLATION

Another factor that affects parents' willingness to become involved is their degree of isolation within the school community. In some cases, isolation occurs because the parents are not residents of the community (e.g., special needs students are bused into neighboring communities to receive services). Parents are limited in their opportunities to socialize with other parents and are likely to receive less communication from the school.

There is also the isolation that exists for parents who are not connected to other parents in their situation. For example, teenage mothers are often socially isolated from their peers and from other teen parents. They may also feel excluded from the mainstream of school parents once their child enters school. New immigrants may experience a great sense of isolation when they are separated from extended families and are unable to locate families of similar background with which to bond.

Families also experience isolation if the community is not accepting of their lifestyle or culture. "Conditions of cultural difference, prejudice, and the unequal distribution of economic and political power extends to all institutions in the community, including the educational institutions" (Cockrell, 1992). It is apparent, then, that to encourage parent and family involvement, schools must be accepting of the diversity within their family population.

TEACHER ATTITUDES AND SCHOOL PRACTICES INFLUENCING PARENT INVOLVEMENT

TEACHER ATTITUDES

In creating opportunities for parent involvement, educators must look at their own practices and attitudes to examine how, if at all, existing biases, beliefs, and prejudices affect their ability to nurture involvement. We are all greatly influenced by the culture in which we were raised; attitudes, beliefs, and values stem from this environment. In order to provide a welcoming atmosphere for families from cultures or family structures different from one's own, there are two steps to take:

1. Develop an awareness of your own cultural and family values and beliefs, and a recognition of how they influence your attitudes and behaviors.

2. Develop an understanding of the cultural values and lifestyle choices of your students' parents and how those values and choices influence their attitudes and beliefs. To do this, consider the questions in Table 3.1 as a springboard to acknowledging individual cultural heritages. Answers may help professionals clarify their attitudes and serve as a starting point when considering other family situations.

Many of the difficulties that are experienced stem from the outmoded idea of the United States as a melting pot. In reality, it is a rich, diverse mix of people resembling a "quilt, rich in colors, textures, and patterns that make up the fabric of our society" (Randall-David, 1989). In order to address such diversity, it is critical to examine some of the unintentional ways in which educators discourage parents from participating in their children's education.

1. Teachers may believe they're not prejudiced.   Even when a teacher believes he or she is not biased against people of other races or lifestyles, it is possible for biased beliefs to sneak into everyday language. Phrases like "running around like wild Indians" or "throwing like a girl" have become a part of our everyday language; little thought is given to how the words will affect impressionable children (Greenberg, 1992). Whether intentional or not, prejudice hurts, and it builds walls that impede communication.

TABLE 3.1
Acknowledging Your Cultural Heritage

1. What ethnic group, socioeconomic class, religion, age group, and community do you belong to?

2. What experiences have you had with people from other ethnic groups, socioeconomic classes, religions, age groups, or communities?

3. What were those experiences? How did you feel about them?

4. When you were growing up, what did your parents and other significant adults in your life say about people who were different from your family?

5. What do you find embarrassing about your ethnic group, socioeconomic class, religion, age, or community? What would you like to change? Why?

6. What sociocultural factors in your background might contribute to your being rejected by members of other cultures?

7. What personal qualities do you have that will help you establish interpersonal relationships with persons from other cultures? What personal qualities may be detrimental?

SOURCE: Randall-David, 1989

Awareness and acceptance of cultural diversity is critical.

2. Some teachers are proud of being "color blind."   Many teachers, in an effort to display openness to all children, espouse the belief that "all children are the same to me." Sociologists have found that "all the same" generally refers to the Euro-American culture and that this is the standard of acceptable sameness. Refusal to acknowledge the evident differences between children's cultures and traditions does not allow the opportunity to explore ways of coping with diversity in the real world.

3. Teachers may employ the "tourist approach" to introducing multicultural activities into the classroom.   The tourist approach, while once thought to be an ideal way to expose children to various holidays, foods, and customs, usually perpetuates stereotypes. Children focus on the exotic differences between people and tend not to see the similarities of life experiences, family, and day-to-day problems common to everyone. This approach also lends itself to a one-time exposure to a culture and therefore, variety is not integrated into daily curriculum in a meaningful way (Koeppel & Mulrooney, 1992).

4. Teachers believe that Caucasian children are unaffected by diversity. All children, whether exposed to diversity through a classroom mix or not, need to be aware of our society's cultural richness and diversity in order to adequately prepare them to cope with the real world. Curricula and books that perpetuate stereotypes do children a disservice by reinforcing myths and biases (Jones & Derman-Sparks, 1992).

5. Teachers of Euro-American descent often believe that children from minorities are "culturally deprived."   Children who are not of the dominant culture and who are assumed to be deprived may not be allowed to experience the respect and value their individual heritage deserves. It is necessary to a child's self-esteem that his family's traditions, customs, and holidays are regarded with equal importance to others celebrated. Maintaining pride in one's heritage is an important key to helping children bridge the gap between home and school (Jones & Derman-Sparks, 1992).

6. "At risk" does not mean "deficient."   Each child brings experiences and thoughts to school about which she can talk, write, and read (Walker-Dalhouse, 1993). Pellegrini (1991) summarized that children labeled at-risk who experience school failure do so because of "unfamiliarity with the rules governing the learning context of the school." Success can be achieved, in part, by the use of curriculum materials that reflect a child's heritage and offer opportunities to express language.

EDUCATIONAL PRACTICES

Several educational practices promote the concept that minority children are less capable learners. This perception creates a self-fulfilling prophecy: Diversity creates lowered expectations, which result in lower levels of academic achievement. Teachers need to become advocates for their students' parents to ensure that, based solely on diversity issues, the students are not being unfairly placed in remedial classes or special education rooms, or labeled as slow learners. Seeking ways to draw out parents who might otherwise feel unwelcome in a school system is a beginning. What should follow is the commitment on the part of the staff to developing and maintaining a working relationship with families for the benefit of the child.

EDUCATIONAL PRACTICES THAT LIMIT CHILDREN FROM DIVERSE BACKGROUNDS

The following is a partial list of educational practices that tend to have a lasting impact on low-income and minority students. Some of theses practices persist when "different" is seen as "deficient."

1. Kindergarten retention, academic tracking, and ability grouping convey a message of limited worth to children who belong to a minority group or who are economically disadvantaged (Walker-Dalhouse, 1993). Children who do not match the social expectations of the schools tend to become labeled as low achievers and do not receive the same encouragements to succeed as other children. In fact, labels often follow children into subsequent grades. Parents of children so labeled tend to be less involved and feel their presence and opinions are less desired in the schools. When this occurs, negative feelings and damaging stereotypes persevere and are likely to return, full circle, in the next generation.

2. Programs designed for English as a Second Language students often operate on a "deficit philosophy."   When such programs are viewed as compensatory in nature, a child's ability to maintain a native language suffers at the expense of acquiring English (Soto, 1991). It is generally believed that language learning and cultural enhancement occur when the emphasis is on preserving the bilingual capabilities of young children rather than substituting one language for another (Garcia, 1986).

3. Schools that fail to acknowledge the changing composition of families and family life restrict many parents from full participation in their child's education.   Educational practices of each school need to be continually revised and updated to meet the unique needs of the population being served. When schools adhere to outmoded practices such as daytime classroom volunteering, daytime conferences, limited phone access to both teachers and administrators, and daytime registrations, orientations, and screenings, it is logical that many parents will be unable to participate in their child's education. Acknowledgment of changing lifestyles and parenting needs presents to educators the challenge of creating new, more accessible channels of communication and opportunities for teacher contact (Epstein, 1986).

4. Lack of emphasis is placed on teacher training about family stresses and family structures.   Teachers need accurate, practical information about the kinds of stresses that many kinds of families endure (Coleman, 1991). Cultural differences may require background knowledge and training so that trusting relationships can be created. An increasing number of diverse families, along with the many stresses all families face, make it necessary for teachers to have additional training in order to create "family friendly" schools.

5. School policies that restrict access to the school.   Concerns about violence and security have forced educators to adopt rules restricting school visitors, requiring students to sign out, and other security measures. To some parents, especially those from other cultures, this may give the impression that they are not welcome in their children's school.

PARENT PERCEPTIONS OF BARRIERS TO INVOLVEMENT

An examination of practices within individual schools often can uncover the barriers to parent involvement. Parents may perceive difficulties in developing a relationship with or an interest in their schools for the following reasons.

1. Poor language and communication efforts between the school and the home.   Without meaningful, understandable communication, families with a language or reading barrier are less likely to feel a part of their child's education (Salerno & Fink, 1992). Parents who sense that the school is uninterested or biased toward their family structure also may find it difficult to maintain an interest in the school (Coleman, 1991). Written, spoken, taped, individual, and group communication should be developed. Face-to-face contact; group meetings with other parents; and printed information covering relevant areas of curriculum, conferencing skills, school policies, evaluation methods, and discipline are necessary for transmitting available information to the greatest number of parents.

2. Parents often feel that schools do not value their input on important matters.   Many parents, especially those who represent minority cultures or who are themselves uneducated, feel that their opinions about the school are not valued by teachers or administrators. Common complaints include the attitude that teachers want parents to only do menial tasks and that decision making is better off in the hands of educators. Clerical work, fundraising, and being a room parent are the typical roles that parents in general are assigned.

3. Parents' previous negative experiences with schools, whether as a student or parent, impact willingness to participate.   Adults who have experienced prejudice, unfair treatment, or poor support for educational problems are less likely to initiate communication with their child's teacher (Berger, 1987; Swick, 1991). For example, parents who have had difficulty receiving appropriate services for their special needs child may transfer that frustration to teachers.

4. Parents from minority cultures or migrant populations, or those who are illiterate or do not have jobs, may have feelings of inadequacy that can inhibit the growth of positive relationships between home and school.   Parents who have low self-esteem may find it overwhelming to take an active role in their child's education. Because many cultures assign the responsibility of formal education to teachers alone, those parents often view parent involvement as an unfamiliar concept (Salerno & Fink, 1992; Mallory & New, 1994). A more general explanation of feelings of inadequacy stems from the immediate life concerns that occupy the thoughts and actions of many families. Such necessities as food, shelter, child care, and medical care often take precedence over long-range goals of education. Teachers who are aware of individual family stresses can more realistically plan for acceptable levels of involvement.

When parents are unable to assist or observe in the classroom, they are also unable to gain expertise from modeling the teacher's methods for working with children. This can be especially crucial in early childhood environments and special education classrooms where parents may lack confidence in handling children's behavioral and educational problems.

5. Barriers to parental involvement can also make it extremely difficult for parents to become active participants in school-related activities. Obstacles such as lack of child care for siblings, lack of transportation, and inability to afford to take time away from work to attend conferences or meetings are very real barriers for many parents. Employers who penalize absenteeism or

A welcoming atmosphere begins at the door.

withhold pay may cause a parent to miss an event scheduled during school hours. Participation may be limited by cost of transportation and distance to the school (special needs children, for instance, often must attend a school outside their neighborhood). Embarrassment over clothing or mastery of English can make a parent reluctant to enter the facility and meet with other parents.

6. Lack of a welcoming atmosphere in the schools.   Staff members who are inconsiderate of language barriers or cultural differences can send the message that some families are not truly welcome in the school. Parents view the lack of adequate directions in locating various areas of the building, an absence of storage areas for personal items, and negative attitudes on the part of the office staff toward language barriers as conveying a less than welcoming atmosphere. Often classrooms have only one adult-sized chair—and it belongs to the teacher. Inflexible policies that make such routine tasks as registration and orientation difficult for single working parents, for example, also influence future relationships between home and school.

STRATEGIES USED TO OVERCOME BARRIERS TO PARENT INVOLVEMENT

The challenge that diversity presents to educators is amplified when one considers that for parent involvement across all educational levels there is, on the average, one full-time position per 500,000 students in public schools

(Nardine & Morris, 1992). This translates into very little support for individual classroom teachers. The classroom teacher and building principal generally are charged with the responsibility for devising strategies to improve communication and involvement that meet the needs of the school's families.

The following suggestions are meant to be starting points. To be successful, ideas and techniques should be tailored to individual needs. While there is no limit to the types of strategies that can be developed, some general categories bear attention. These suggestions are based on Joyce Epstein's five levels of parent involvement. (See Chapter 1.)

TYPE 1: PARENTING

1. Information about parent education classes or workshops may assist families unfamiliar with a new community or whose children are having problems at school. Teachers can collaborate with each other to provide classes for parents. Many state-funded programs, such as prekindergartens, require linkages with existing programs in making such information available.

2. Teachers aware of the needs of member families can serve as a resource for local parent support groups. These groups may be specific to a particular culture or may provide emotional support for single parents, teen parents, adoptive families, or blended families.

3. Schools should make an effort when the school year begins to offer workshops on topics of particular interest to parents, such as "A Day in the Life of Your Preschooler," "How to Help Your Child with Homework," or "Handling TV Superheroes." This may be the first time that parents have attended a school function. It is important that the first meeting be a positive one and generally on a neutral topic. Meeting about the school performance of a child often will create feelings of anxiety and concern; these are not the ideal conditions under which to begin a relationship.

4. Teachers need to become familiar with the customs of the various cultures represented in their classroom and develop some working knowledge about their students' situations at home.

5. Parent education in the workplace is an increasingly popular method for reaching parents who might otherwise have difficulty attending evening classes. Forging a link between employers, unions, and the schools is an effective way to bring parenting information to parents and meet their needs for involvement (Zager, 1989).

TYPE 2: COMMUNICATING

1. School handbooks and policy statements should be examined to determine whether the information they give is complete. Families from different cultures may take offense at, or may misunderstand, the need for certain types of information and may feel that their privacy has been intruded upon (Herrera & Wooden, 1988). Available services may not be fully explained and may go unused by qualifying families. Paperwork about common school policies, such as the free lunch program or speech and language services, may be difficult for a parent with low literacy skills. Often, feelings of embarrassment at this lack of understanding discourages the parent from seeking help.

2. Written communication from school should be available in several languages, where necessary, in order to ensure the distribution of important news from school. School newsletters and notices should be monitored for readability.

3. For parents who cannot read, school calendar events can be broadcast on local radio stations. For non-English-speaking parents, use a radio station that broadcasts in their language.

4. A bilingual parent can serve as a liaison between the school and the home of new parents who may need assistance with registration, conferences, etc. This liaison could serve as a mentor, accompanying parents to evening meetings to acquaint them with school groups such as the PTA or PTO. A mentor can serve in this capacity until a family's transition into the school allows its members to participate on their own.

5. Multimedia approaches are valuable in disseminating important information from the schools into the community. For an annual early childhood screening, for example, advertise on local stations that reflect the languages spoken in the community, print flyers in those languages, and ask local churches and day-care centers to contact parents.

6. Educational slang and jargon obstruct communication. Parents of all backgrounds and educational levels will feel intimidated if the school staff is unable to communicate in a way they can understand.

7. Consider alternate sites for parent conferences or home visits if a parent is reluctant to enter the school or have a staff member in the home. Local restaurants, churches, libraries, or the workplace can serve as meeting spots. Indicating a willingness to accommodate parents may be the first step toward breaking down attitudinal barriers to school involvement and building a trusting relationship.

Type 3: Volunteering

1. Parent involvement that is encouraged by "showcasing" families of diverse ethnic backgrounds could put unfair demands on a family's time and resources. English-speaking limitations or cultural beliefs about schools and teachers may inhibit a parent from speaking to the class. Do not assume that membership in a racial class imparts a great expertise in that culture. A family may be third or fourth generation Americans with few ties to the original culture. Extend an open invitation for speakers and enlist the help of those who volunteer their services.

2. Parents experienced in classroom and school volunteering can be encouraged to serve as mentors for new parents unfamiliar with the concept of school volunteering. Many cultures regard school as a place for the elite only, and where teachers are the experts (Swick, 1991). Before they will freely volunteer, parents may have to be convinced that they have something to contribute to the school. Lack of familiarity with the staff and school policies may make them unwilling to offer services. Again, an experienced volunteer or aide can provide assistance in understanding the routines and needs of the classroom teacher.

Type 4: Learning at Home

1. Opportunities for parent-child interaction can come from parent meetings that focus on a specific curriculum area. Modeling occurs when teachers can demonstrate appropriate practice and materials with young children.

2. Take-home learning activities that emphasize a science, math, or literacy game or experience can be shared by the parent and child (Spewock, 1991).

3. Home visits can be excellent backdrops for individualized teaching experiences between the teacher, parent, and child. Building parent confidence in the role of first teacher will allow more interaction and will encourage the parent to participate in school functions (Fox-Barnett & Meyer, 1992).

4. It is helpful to send information home that explains new curriculum concepts and how they affect the children. For example, parents may be concerned about the child's ability to maintain the native language skills, and may have questions about integrated curriculum and their child's chances for success. Share with parents material that will enable them to better understand the teaching philosophies of the school staff (Rose & Smith, 1993; Diamond, Hestenes, & O'Connor, 1994).

5. Teachers need to create an atmosphere of open communication so that concerns about the curriculum and any other area can be discussed. Parents who are mistrustful of the school or who are angry because their concerns are not heard will be less likely to participate.

Type 5: Representing Other Parents

1. Advisory councils that are recruiting new members should seek to include a diverse group of parents. This "widening of the circle" ensures full representation.

2. Mentoring programs that focus on developing leadership roles help bring parents into positions of governance. Ownership of a school begins when each parent feels included in the decision-making process.

SUMMARY

Educators, administrators, and families will strengthen partnerships when each person feels valued and an integral part of a child's education. To be successful in meeting the challenges that all types of diversity present, teachers must first commit to setting goals for themselves. They need to learn more about today's complex family structures and stresses. They need to examine school practices and policies that restrict full involvement. Practices such as daytime conferences, restrictive phone access to teachers, and volunteer opportunities that are limited to classroom hours must be reshaped to allow full participation from busy families. Lastly, educators and administrators need to be open, both philosophically and practically, to the changing complexities of today's American family.

> We know that children feel respected when their families are respected—which means reaching across diverse cultural lifestyle and economic differences, using all of our resources outside the classroom, including family life professionals, to create linkages between family and school environments. (Coleman, 1991)

ACTIVITIES FOR DISCUSSION, EXPANSION, AND APPLICATION

1. Interview an early childhood professional about his or her experiences with diversity in the classroom and in the school or center. Discuss the ways that diversity is addressed in the curriculum, holiday celebrations, socialization practices, and parent involvement in the facility.

2. Examine several textbooks from a primary reading and social studies curriculum to determine how diversity is presented to young students. Look at pictures, wording, and areas of emphasis.

3. Visit an elementary school library and the children's section of a public library to review children's literature from the perspective of multicultural balance.

4. Interview a school librarian and a children's librarian at your local library about recent trends in educational videos, programming, and children's books related to issues of diversity. How accurately do library holdings reflect the population being served? What attempts are made to include a balanced cultural viewpoint when purchasing new resources?

5. What personal qualities do you have that will help you establish a relationship with parents from other cultural groups? What personal qualities may be detrimental?

6. When you were growing up, what did your parents and other family members say about people who were different from your family?

REFERENCES

Berger, E.B. (1995). *Parents as partners in education.* Englewood Cliffs, NJ: Merrill.

Berns, R. (1993). *Child. family, and community* (3rd ed.). Fort Worth, TX: Harcourt Brace.

Clay, J. (1990). Working with lesbian and gay parents and their children. *Young Children, 45*(3), 31–35.

Cockrell, K. (1992). Voices of native America: A native American community's perception of home/school communication. A paper presented at the annual meeting of the American Educational Research Association. San Francisco, CA.

Coleman, M. (1991). Planning for the changing nature of family life in schools for young children. *Young Children, 46*(4), 15–20.

Cryer, R. (1989). The language barrier and family stress: Taking the extra step. *Family Resource Coalition Report, 8*(2), 8.

Dean, C. (1989). Institutional change leading to greater parent involvement. *Family Resource Coalition Report, 8*(2), 3.

Diamond, K., Hestenes, L., & O'Connor, C. (1994). Integrating young children with disabilities in preschool: Problems and promise. *Young Children, 49*(2), 68–75.

Epstein, J. (1986). Parent involvement: Implications for limited-English-proficient parents. In C. Simich-Dudgeon (Ed.), *Issues of parent involvement and literacy.* Washington, DC.

Epstein, J. (1991). Parent involvement. *Educational Leadership*, 45–49.

Fox-Barnett, M., & Meyer, T. (1992). The teacher's playing at my house this week! *Young Children, 47*(5), 45–50.

Garcia, E. (1986). Bilingual development and the education of bilingual children during early childhood. *American Journal of Education, 11*, 96–121.

Greenberg, P. (1992). Teaching about native Americans? Or teaching about people, including native Americans? *Young Children, 47*(6), 27–30.

Hernandez, D. (1993). *America's children.* New York: Russell Sage Foundation.

Herrera, J., & Wooden, S. (1988). Some thoughts about effective parent-school communication. *Young Children*, 78–80.

Jones, E., & Derman-Sparks, L. (1992). Meeting the challenge of diversity. *Young Children, 47*(2), 12–22.

Kliebard, H.M. (1987). *The struggle for the American curriculum: 1893–1958.* New York: Routledge.

Koeppel, J., & Mulrooney, M. (1992). The sister schools program: A way for children to learn about cultural diversity when there isn't any in their school. *Young Children, 48*(1), 44–47.

Mallory, B., & New, R. (1994). *Diversity & developmentally appropriate practices.* New York: Teachers College Press.

Nardine, F., & Morris, R. (1992). In A. Salerno and M. Fink (Eds.), *Home/school partnerships: Migrant parent involvement report.* Washington, DC: Office of Elementary and Secondary Education.

Norton, A., & Glick, P. (1986). One-parent families: A social and economic profile. *Journal of Family Relations, 35*, 9–17.

Pellegrini, A.D. (1991). A critique of the concept of at risk as applied to emergent literacy. *Language Arts, 68*(5), 380–385.

Randall-David, E. (1989). *Strategies for working with culturally diverse communities and clients.* Bethesda, MD: Association for the Care of Children's Health.

Rose, D., & Smith, B. (1993). Preschool mainstreaming: Attitude barriers and strategies for addressing them. *Young Children, 48*(4), 59–73.

Salerno, A., & Fink, M. (1992). *Home/school partnerships: Migrant parent involvement report.* Washington, DC: Office of Elementary and Secondary Education, Migrant Education Programs.

Saracho, O., & Spodek, B. (1983). *Understanding the multicultural experience in early childhood education.* Washington, DC: National Association for the Education of Young Children.

Shen, W., & Mo, W. (1990). *Reaching out to their cultures—building communication with Asian-American families.* Information analyses (070)—Viewpoints.

Soldier, L. (Sept. 1992). Working with Native American children. *Young Children, 47*(6), 15–21.

Soto, L. (1991). Understanding bilingual/bicultural young children. *Young Children, 46*(2), 30–36.

Spewock, T. (1991). Teaching parents of young children through learning packets. *Young Children,* *47*(1), 28–31.

Swick, K.J. (1984). *Inviting parents into the young child's world.* Champaign, IL: Stipes Publishing.

Van Deusen, J. (1991). Community schools: A vision of equity and excellence for young children. *Young Children, 46*(5), 58–60.

Walker-Dalhouse, D. (1993). Beginning reading and the African American child at risk. *Young Children, 49*(1), 24–29.

Zager, R. (1989). Linking the home and school through the workplace. *Family Resource Coalition Report, 8*(2), 9, 26.

READERS WILL BE ABLE TO:

- Recognize common responses, concerns, and issues of families of children with special needs.
- Describe the circumstances that may surround the identification of a child with special needs.
- Identify historical milestones of parent involvement in special education.
- Outline parent involvement required by special education law.
- Describe the philosophy and practice of inclusion.
- Analyze particular challenges and concerns of families of children with special needs.
- Explain the special value of a family systems approach to parent involvement.
- Analyze the helping relationship between parents, teachers, and service providers.
- Identify unique barriers to parent involvement when the family includes a child with special needs.
- Outline strategies to enhance communication, support, and advocacy within special education service structures.

Why include a chapter on involving parents of young children with special needs? Not long ago, that information could only be found in materials geared to special education teachers. Today, segregated educational opportunities, like other practices that insulate individuals with disabilities from their communities, are being challenged. No longer can teachers prepare to teach only "regular" kids. With more infants and young children being born with developmental disabilities (due to such factors as prenatal exposure to drugs and medical advances, for example), teachers almost surely will have children with some degree of exceptionality in their classes and programs. Providing increased opportunities for children with special needs to be with other children their age brings everyone together—often for the first time. Exciting inclusive programs are developing in communities nationwide, and early childhood is taking a lead in fulfilling the

Inclusion will shape the future for all children.

promise of the law. Special education has promoted the development of many tenets of parent involvement, while research on children with exceptionalities and their families has supported many changes in all types of educational and social services. Much progress has been made since 1950 concerning parent involvement in special education, and the vision of continued change will shape the future of education for all children.

This chapter deliberately differs in style from others in this book. It places less emphasis on things to do and forms to use than in later chapters. It is perhaps less of a "how to" chapter, because parents of children who have special needs respond to all the wonderful strategies explored in this book, just like *any* group of parents. A teacher who works with a child with special needs and successfully involves his or her family succeeds for the same reasons a teacher succeeds with *any* child and family. (In all probability, parents who have a child with a disability also have children without disabilities as well!) Although many teachers can relate to the parenting experience because they are parents themselves, few have had the experience of parenting a child with a disability. This chapter provides insight into the issues of parenting a child with special needs and special rights. For as the Little Prince said, "That which is essential, is invisible to the eye" (Saint-Exupéry, 1943).

CHILDREN WITH SPECIAL NEEDS: FAMILIES WITH SPECIAL NEEDS

The dynamic system we recognize as "family" is continually changing with life experiences and the development and maturity levels of its members. Yet, few changes impact family relationships as profoundly as the introduction of a child with special needs. Parent, sibling, and extended family relationships are uniquely influenced by the immediate and long-reaching implications that accompany the birth or adoption of such a child, or the change in a young child's development brought on by an accident or illness. Barraged with feelings and questions ("Why us?", "What was the cause of this?", "How will we cope?", "How close to normal will our child be?"), parents frequently struggle with intense emotions as they face new problems and make adjustments. The process frequently isolates families and may cause marital stress, modified family relationships, and the ongoing challenge of balancing family needs. Families enter a new world of professionals and services that may cause them to feel dependent for information, care, and educational interventions.

Familiar interactions with school systems often become transformed by the unique procedures of "special education." In the midst of the disequilibrium, parents struggle to meet their individual needs and maintain some sense of hope for a sometimes uncertain future. For many mothers and fathers, their experiences border on the "twilight zone" of parenting. Despite this, children with special needs are children *first* and have strengths and needs common to *all* children. Likewise, their parents are parents *first*, subject to all the strengths and foibles of *any* parent. Families of children with disabilities are not "handicapped families."

FAMILIES MAY HAVE DIFFERENT BEGINNINGS

Each family of a young child with special needs has its own special story. The timing, circumstance, severity, and implications for each member varies with each family, and becomes part of the history they share with scores of professionals. With the frequency and sophistication of prenatal testing, parents may be aware of a potential difficulty before their child is born. Other parents learn at birth, or shortly thereafter, of a condition that threatens the expectation of a "normal" baby. Children with special needs may be born with a medical, physical, or developmental difficulty stemming from identifiable causes, such as prematurity, genetic deviations, intrauterine trauma, or prenatal exposure to substances (alcohol, drugs, or environmental toxins) that cause medical or developmental problems. Some children develop special needs as the result of a postnatal illness, injury, or environmental influence, such as lead poisoning. Chronic illnesses, diseases, or medical conditions also require some children in their early years to receive special services or programs.

Several factors of our modern society have had a dramatic impact on early childhood special education. First, sophisticated medical technology has allowed more infants who are premature, at risk, or who have severe disabilities to survive than in any other time in history. Second, more babies are being born to mothers who exposed them to drugs prenatally, and those babies often have disabilities (Alper, Schloss, & Schloss, 1994).

For many children, especially those with developmental delays, it is not always possible to determine the source or the long-term impact of the difficulty. Consequently many parental questions about their child have answers that are hidden in the future. With so many potential origins and the variability in determining when a child's delay qualifies him or her for special services, parents may have limited awareness of a child's need for services. Parents may be unaware that children developing normally demonstrate particular skills at certain ages, or may dismiss slow development (speech and motor skills, for example) as a familial characteristic. Child Find is a common name for an initiative to heighten public awareness of early intervention for children who may benefit from special services. These efforts are mandated by federal law to advertise typical developmental milestones and the availability of infant, toddler, and preschool developmental screenings and programs. As these efforts become more noticeable in both large and small communities, it is hoped that parents will become more sensitive to the ongoing development of their young children.

PARENT INVOLVEMENT PROTECTED BY LAW

Each child with special needs is unique. A single diagnosis or the categorization of a disability does not define a child's potential for development or the need for specific services or programs. There is a multifaceted spectrum of qualities to the concept of "special needs." Whether it be cerebral palsy, mental retardation, deafness, or spina bifida, there is no one prognosis or program placement. This is required to be individualized to each child and each family's needs and abilities. When special education programming is determined to be needed, the rights of parents and of the child are ensured by federal laws.

HISTORICAL MILESTONES OF PARENTAL INVOLVEMENT IN SPECIAL EDUCATION

The guarantee of special education is actually quite new. In the United States, there has been a dramatic and radical progression of philosophical changes toward involving children with special needs and their families since the 1900s. Although some states had visionary programs in place early on, as a rule during the years from 1900–1950 many parents who had children with developmental delays were encouraged to relinquish their role as caregivers and send their children to institutions. In the 1950s and 1960s, parents were encouraged to *not* institutionalize their children, because it was more commonly believed that these children could learn and did deserve a right to more educational opportunities. The National Association for Retarded Citizens was formed during this decade, and it began exerting pressure on the government to include children with special needs in educational policy decisions. It also increased support for research and training in special education. During this era, early childhood education was based on general sensory stimulation theory. Programs grew from the assumption that by stimulating a child's development at a young age, secondary disabling conditions could be prevented. Parents often attended intervention or therapy sessions, but most frequently they were observers of activities conducted by professionals. There also was heightened interest in helping parents deal effectively with their "feelings of grief that resulted from having a child with a disability" (Harbin, 1993). In 1968, the Handicapped Children's Early Education Program (HCEEP) began. HCEEP was a federally sponsored initiative to develop innovative models of early intervention and increase the availability of services. Parent involvement, a requirement for receiving one of the grants, was believed to improve the child's development. Parents would influence their child for life, whereas teachers and therapists had only transient impact. In this way, federal policy preceded widespread practice of parent involvement in early intervention.

THE 1970S USHERS IN AN ERA OF CHANGE

The federal policy for HCEEP programs laid the foundation for the importance of parent involvement and the perception during the 1970s that parents should have knowledge of their child's disability, emotional support, and skills to cope with the demands of daily life. Parent meetings were typically designed by professionals based on the professional's impression of parent needs. As research from the HCEEP pilot programs emerged, the positive results of parent involvement provided new impetus for change in the teacher's view of families.

In the mid-1970s, parents were encouraged (or required) to carry out intervention actions designed by professionals. In order to do this, parent training programs emerged, allowing parents to become more formally involved in their child's education and to participate as "teacher" or "therapist." Parents of school-age children had been asking for more educational services and more participation in their child's program plan, including the right to be a member of their child's multidisciplinary team. Significant legal victories were won in the courts as parents battled the states for legal rights to public education. Parent involvement ultimately led to a major victory in 1975 with the Education for All Handicapped Children Act, also known as Public Law 94-142. This marked a fundamental shift in the teacher's view of the family. Previously, teachers and other professionals were in control of the education plan; with PL 94-142, that role was to be shared with parents.

In the mid- to late 1970s, a new philosophical concept of human development and home interaction prompted investigation into the complexities of working with families of children with special needs. Because of early intervention and parent research conducted by Dunst, Bailey, Gallagher, Simeonsson, Turnbull, Fewell, and others, there has been a dramatic increase in family-focused research since the 1980s. Studies have examined the effects of "parent as first teacher," mother-child interactions, child abuse, and parent stress. These and other studies propelled early intervention services into law in the 1986 passage of the Education of the Handicapped Act Amendments (Part H of Public Law 99-457) and the Individuals With Disabilities Education Act. Both laws require that early interventionists from all disciplines view families as both planners and recipients of services, and that infants and toddlers with developmental delays and their *families* are eligible for services. These legal protections were not given, but were earned by parents and professionals advocating for the child's needs within the educational system and philosophy of the day. It has meant angry confrontations and legal battles. It has also underscored the importance of positive communication and partnerships between the educational system and the parents (Harbin, 1993; Bricker, 1989).

This overview offers a sketch of how parent involvement has been defined for children with special needs. At times, it sounds very similar to what services are commonly available for families with children in regular education; at other times, visionary. In many ways the research, legal definitions, and family-centered programs of special education are leading parent involvement into the next century.

SERVICES AND SAFEGUARDS GUARANTEED BY LAW

What specifically do these laws mean in terms of services for young children and their families? PL 94-142 gives individuals with disabilities ages 3 to 21 years access to a free, appropriate public education. Called the Education for All Handicapped Children Act, this includes such protections as:

- An individualized educational program (IEP) written according to the child's particular educational needs when special education or related services are required. This must include an assessment and reporting of the child's educational performance; a statement of annual goals and short-term instructional objectives; a statement of specific special education and related services to be provided and the extent the child will be able to participate in regular education; a date for initiating services and the anticipated duration of the services; and objective criteria and evaluation procedures for determining the effectiveness of the program.
- Parent participation in the development, approval, and evaluation of their child's IEP. Parents are also to participate in assessments of their child's progress, to contribute to placement decisions, and to be involved in program evaluations. Parents also can participate in their child's educational program by carrying over instruction and therapies at home.
- Services are to be provided in the least restrictive environment necessary to meet the child's educational needs.
- Related services that help a child benefit from special education can include speech, physical and occupational therapy, audiology, psychological services, diagnostic medical services, school health and social work services, early identification, and transportation. Parents also may receive counseling and training as a related service.

This law also assures that schools must provide opportunities for parents to consent to or object to their child's educational identification, classification, program, or placement. The procedures to contest any of these is called **due process.** Before 1975, there were no federal laws protecting the rights of children with disabilities to receive an education, although some states provided limited special services under whatever provisions the state legislatures designed. Once federal monies were available to support the education of children with special needs, states could institute these programs at their discretion, and most, but not all, began offering services through their local public schools.

In 1986, Public Law 99-457, reauthorized Public Law 94-142, mandated services to 3- to 5-year-olds with disabilities in all states, and allowed special provisions for children from birth to age 3 years and their families. Infants who show developmental delays (as defined by the state) or have a diagnosed physical or mental condition which has a high probability of resulting in a developmental delay are assured of services through an Individualized Family Service Plan (IFSP). Children who are "at risk" for developmental delays also may qualify, at each state's discretion. The IFSP is designed to help a family enhance the child's development in the areas of cognitive, physical, language and speech, psychosocial, and self-help. Services are selected in collaboration with parents and usually are free or are provided on a sliding scale. An IFSP can include:

- Services such as audiology, case management, family training, counseling and home visits, health services, diagnostic medical services, nursing and nutrition services, speech, occupational, and physical therapy, psychological and social work services, special instruction and early identification, screening and assessment.
- A statement of the child's current levels of development, based on a multidisciplinary evaluation of the child.
- A statement of the family's concerns, priorities, and resources related to enhancing the development of the child, based on the assessment of the family.
- A statement of the major outcomes expected for both the child and family, the criteria, procedures, and time lines to determine progress for achieving the outcomes and modifications or revisions of outcomes or services.
- A statement of specific early intervention services necessary to meet the needs of the child and family, as determined by the identified outcomes. This includes the frequency, intensity, location, and method of delivering services, payment plans if applicable, and other services needed by the child, and the steps outlined to secure the services.
- The initiation date for services, the anticipated duration of those services, and the name of the case manager from the profession most relevant to the child's or family's needs who will be responsible for the IFSP and coordination with other agencies or services.
- Specific steps to be taken to support the child's transition to another program at age 3, including parent training and discussion regarding the transition.

The IFSP process is built upon the philosophy that families are systems, and no one member (the infant/toddler) can be helped unless all members are involved. This has the potential for strengthening and empowering families of young children with disabilities by helping them to develop expectations for their child and themselves and become active participants in contributing to their child's progress if they choose; discover their strengths and learn how to develop others; analyze their concerns and learn effective coping skills; and develop valuable networks and strategies to reach professionals and service providers. Families can learn how to become self-advocates, assume leadership in coordinating services they need, and enter into the next educational program with a better understanding of what they want.

In 1991, amendments were made to these laws with Public Law 102-119 which changed the language of "Education of the Handicapped" to the Individuals With Disabilities Education Act (IDEA). Children could be eligible for programs serving children aged 3 to 5, at the state's discretion, if they had a developmental delay in one or more of the areas of physical, cognitive, communication, social/emotional, or adaptive. At local or state discretion, the family may use the IFSP instead of the IEP, if IEP requirements are met. The eligibility requirements for infants and toddlers were changed to be the same as those listed earlier for 3- to 5-year-olds. In services, infants and toddlers could now receive vision services, assistive technology devices and services, and transportation and related costs in their IFSP. The IFSP would allow a family-directed assessment of their resources, priorities, and concerns, instead of "strengths and needs." Families now are required to provide informed, written consent before services in an IFSP are provided and services are "to the maximum extent appropriate" to be provided in natural environments such as the home or community in which children without disabilities participate.

In addition to the provisions already described, there are safeguards concerning access to and confidentially of student records, child evaluations, notices, and consent to services. Families have the right to examine all relevant records relating to their child's identification, evaluation, placement, and education. Parents must be notified in their native language if information that identifies their child is on file and that they have access to this information.

Parents can request copies of records and may challenge the information they contain. Federal law also provides for the confidentiality of student records. Parents of children ages 3 to 21 are also entitled to an independent educational evaluation given individually by a qualified examiner to determine eligibility or the extent of services needed. Schools must give written notice to parents of children ages 3 to 21 receiving services whenever they propose to initiate or change the student's identification, evaluation, or placement, and for infants and toddlers, when changing the provision of services to the child or family. Parental consent must also be given for the initial evaluation and for the child's placement in a special education program.

The Americans With Disabilities Act of 1990 (Public Law 101-336) addresses the needs of adults with disabilities, but has some interesting implications for young children. This piece of legislation had heightened public awareness of the segregation and discrimination against people with disabilities in our society. The assurances of "equality of opportunity and full participation" affect the acceptance of children with disabilities into child-care facilities and community programs for preschoolers, and the accessibility of public facilities and services in general. This has created a new push for the concept of including children with disabilities in regular preschool programs. Parents who themselves have disabilities now have increased opportunity to more fully participate in their community and in their child's education in many ways. They can, for example, visit schools that are more accessible for the physically disabled and have increased access to interpreters and special accommodations for enhancing communication.

Additional information on special education law can be found in Shea and Bauer (1991); Smith, Rose, Ballard, and Walsh (1991); Turnbull and Turnbull (1990); and Alper, Schloss, and Schloss (1994).

A GREATER PARENTAL VOICE IN ADVOCACY

The existence of special education law is largely due to the persistent efforts of parents who desired a better education for their children. Like parents of children with special needs before them, parents today are finding their voices and questioning the policies and practices of all aspects of education that impact their child. This creates new and better opportunities to develop partnerships and collaborations that can greatly enhance outcomes for each child and family. Although not all parents of children with disabilities have or need a strong voice, the empowerment of parents to participate in all aspects of their child's program and life within the community may more strongly impact other groups within the school or program. Parents of infants with special needs are sometimes coming to schools with the message, "My child will be in your program in two or three years, I know this may take time, so I'm telling you now this is what I want for him." Often these young parents are telling schools and communities, "I want my child to belong here." As a result, children with special needs are increasingly included in regular child care, community preschools, recreation programs, sports teams, and other activities. Empowering parents to fully participate can have the added benefit of broadening their advocacy for children with disabilities from the local community to state legislatures and to Congress.

OPPORTUNITIES FOR INCLUSION: REALIZING A DREAM

Case by case, child by child, the vision of belonging not only in the family, but in a regular class in the neighborhood school and community has become a reality for over one-third of American children in special education (LRP, 1994b). The practice of considering *appropriate* programs for children with special needs to be only *segregated* programs has brought parents, professionals, legislators, state boards of education, and the public to question policies that exclude children with special needs from regular school programs. Although *inclusion* is not mentioned in federal law, it is an interpretation of least restrictive environment that refers to placing children with disabilities in the school facility where they would typically be placed were there no disability with their age and grade peers for the full day. With inclusion, to the maximum extent possible, educational services are provided in the general education classroom with appropriate classroom supports. State and federal policies are appearing which uphold the placement of children with disabilities in these inclusive settings.

This has been the focus of much debate and confusion among educators and parents alike. Although the federal law has always required placement in the least restrictive environment, school districts have tended to segregate children who have special needs into isolated classes, programs, or buildings. Increasingly, parents have disputed this placement in the courts. Recent judicial trends support inclusive programming in neighborhood schools, but it is not impossible for school authorities to substantiate that the welfare of a child or his or her classmates would be jeopardized in the regular classroom (McCarthy, 1994; NASB, 1992).

The concept of inclusion has spread like wildfire across the country, igniting controversy at federal, state, and local levels. Within the education community, inclusion has had inconsistent support among special educators. Teachers of self-contained special education classrooms or resource programs are concerned for the educational outcomes of their students in another setting, as well as for their own job security in a changing system of educational services. Confusion surrounds the logistic and financial aspects of inclusion. The history and tradition of special education, pride in the expertise of being a special educator, and loss of control as many children are placed outside the segregated classrooms have contributed to "turf" issues that often surface in the inclusion face-off. Placement in "regular classrooms" requires that the Individual Educational Program be fulfilled—including the maintenance of special services, therapies, and other supports. The inclusion of some children may require additional personnel to assist with the class or with the child's special requirements. Regular educators may be afraid that children will be "dumped" in regular classrooms causing undue disruption of learning in the class, and they may fear that there will not be enough time to meet the needs of all students and that students will suffer. Regular education teachers who have not been professionally trained to work with children with disabilities are concerned about their abilities to do so and about receiving support from the school system. Many teachers, challenged by the numbers of children in their classes and the intensity of needs within "regular" education today, do not feel educationally, emotionally, or sometimes philosophically equipped to work with children with special needs.

Professionals aren't alone in objecting to inclusion. Some parents of regular education students may fear inclusion, because it may disrupt their children's learning and hold them back. Many families of children with special needs believe that a specialized class setting or even a residential placement is the most appropriate educational setting for their child and that without the specialized attention and program, their child would not make sufficient progress. These concerns can be aired and considered at the staffing and IEP meetings concerning the child's placement and program (Wilmore, 1994/95; LRP, 1994b; Rose & Smith, 1993).

Likewise, many parents have had opportunities to voice concerns about the implementation of IDEA when testifying before the National Council on Disability; they voiced objections that schools fail to inform parents of their rights, act only under the threat of due process, and exclude children with disabilities from the regular classroom because the schools have not planned for them and aren't ready. As consumers of the special education system, these parents were invited to share their stories and suggest improvements in the law and its implementation. Surfacing in their testimony was the need for teacher and parent training, requirements for adequate supports in inclusive placements, and a clarification that least restrictive environment begins with the regular classroom (LRP, 1994).

Proponents of inclusion have had success in destroying barriers that keep children apart. The law stipulates that all placement options must be considered, beginning with regular classroom placement and proceeding toward more restrictive placements. Parents and professionals are becoming aware of the need to revisit the concept of least restrictive environment and decide together as partners the most appropriate placement for each child. Many districts have made a sincere effort to accommodate children in regular classrooms. They have a strong philosophical belief that children belong together, that curriculum and methods can be adapted for the individual needs of all students, that students and staff can be successful with sufficient supports and inservice, and that an active partnership with parents is a priority. Many state initiatives, such as Project CHOICES and Early CHOICES in Illinois and the Minnesota Inclusive Education Technical Assistance Program, provide a continuum of supports in planning for and implementing inclusion in district programs. Parents, along with regular and special educators, community members, administrators, students, and board of education representatives may form a task force to initiate steps toward system change. Typically, this group will obtain technical assistance, conduct staff development activities, hold informational meetings for all parents, conduct building and classroom inventories, review individual student placements, and determine and provide necessary supports and aids (Minnesota Inclusive Education Technical Assistance Program, 1991; Project CHOICES/Early CHOICES, 1992).

Benefits for all children are enhanced when inclusion begins during early childhood. Children with disabilities are valued as children with skills and abilities and have a healthier self-esteem; learn and use social skills; attend a typical early childhood program with their age-peers and feel less isolation; expand their language/communication skills in typical early childhood contexts; become more independent and better able to work, live, and play in an integrated society; have fun, learn from, and make new friends. Children without disabilities make new friends, develop an acceptance of diversity and individuality, learn when and how to help others, grow up accepting people with disabilities as valuable members of society, and accept others as friends and coworkers regardless of labels, abilities, or disabilities. Professionals, parents, and the community at large learn that children are more alike than different, all children should be appreciated for their strengths and special gifts, acceptance springs from a positive and optimistic attitude, life situations are the best learning opportunities, and diversity and individuality of all kinds is to be celebrated (Project CHOICES/Early CHOICES, 1992; LRE, 1992; Minnesota Inclusive Education Technical Assistance Program, 1991; Institute for Educational Research, 1992).

In early childhood, the collaborations that create the best integrated programs, as with every other programmatic collaboration, are both parent-professional partnerships and collaborations among professionals. These are based on a shared vision of the family's hopes for the child's future and what professionals can do to help make that dream a reality. Professionals with expertise in special education share their knowledge with the family and other professionals to facilitate the child's success, whether it be in toilet training or augmented communication. Likewise, parents can offer information to teachers and staff about techniques that work well at home or that expand the professional's understanding of their child's abilities.

Parents may be faced with new challenges because of the inclusive experience and may need increased support from professionals as a result. Parents whose children are in inclusive settings are often as apprehensive as the teacher about their care, progress, and well-being. They may feel uncomfortable having to explain their child's disability to more people and may fear that their child will not be appreciated as part of this new group. The opposition from other parents, teachers, and administrators, as well as the need to work in a wider circle of partnerships, may cause parental stress. Parents may need to be more active in the classroom, attend more meetings, and choose which support services are worth fighting for and what can be compromised.

On the other hand, parents may feel more a part of the school community and participate more fully in events at the school, such as holiday programs and fundraisers. Inclusion means having more people with whom to problem-solve and share ideas. New hopes for a child living and working in the community as an adult may develop as young children take their place with others in neighborhood schools. Frequently, parents may not need extraordinary encouragement to attend IEP meetings or be active in a group such as the PTA. Often these parents have a clear concept of parent involvement and what it means for them (Holden, Kaiser, Sykes, & Tyree, 1993; NASBE, 1992).

Many parents believe that if their dream of having their child be a true part of the community is to come true, all children should be educated together. At a time of stressed finances within society, few, if any, educational programs are funded sufficiently. Inclusion is not an automatic reduction of services, or of costs, since many special services increase the cost of educating a child. Yet throughout the nation, young children with disabilities are being successfully included in community preschool programs. These pioneers are providing researchers with documentation that further substantiates that children with disabilities make significant advances in integrated settings, and that their peers benefit as well. It will take time and ongoing professional education to develop widespread administrative supports for inclusive programs, enhance teacher skills in classroom intervention strategies, and, overall, increase teacher comfort with accepting a child with an exceptionality. Despite the obstacles, parents across the country are finding placements for their children in community preschools, regular kindergartens, and public schools. The vision has become reality. The issues of inclusion will continue to be debated and decided at school board meetings and in the legal arena. The real issues, state Arnold and Dodge (1994), are based in tradition, values, and beliefs. Parents and professionals are reshaping those three dimensions in hopes of helping extraordinary children lead ordinary lives (Diamond, Hestenes, & O'Connor, 1994; Galant & Hanline, 1993).

CHALLENGES AND CONCERNS FOR FAMILIES OF CHILDREN WITH SPECIAL NEEDS: IMPLICATIONS FOR TEACHERS

With the age of inclusion upon us, teachers are more likely to have children with special needs in their classrooms. Accordingly, teachers and other professionals need to also become more aware of the challenges and issues confronting the parents of these young children.

PARENTAL RESPONSES

How a child with a disability affects a family has been characterized in many ways. Lyon and Preis (1983) and Powers (1993) reported the chronic sorrow response to disability. Austin (1990) proposed a stage-based bereavement process, similar to that for acceptance of life-threatening illnesses. Buscaglia (1983) and Powers (1993) both identify numerous emotions that confront parents of children with disabilities as they experience the loss of their "original" child, whether that was the "perfect" baby or the preschooler they knew "before." Initially, parents take in and evaluate what is happening to their child, themselves, and the rest of the family. They next search for answers, programs, professionals, and service providers to develop a different adjustment to life with their child and develop an awareness of making some sense of the life events—at least in the interim.

During these adjustments, families may face a myriad of emotions: disbelief, shock, sorrow, mourning, self-pity, anger, irritability, denial, envy, self-recrimination, guilt, shame, fear, uncertainty, anxiety, depression, apathy, acknowledgment, and hope. All of them are common, sometimes recurring, responses in adjusting to being a family with special needs. According to Powers, there is no "typical" length of time for working through the feelings accompanying a disability, just as there is no predetermined pattern for all parents. There will be as great a diversity for grieving as there are other diversities among families. Characteristics of the child's disability also impact a family's reaction to the exceptionality. The nature of the exceptionality, the severity, the time of onset, and the demands the child's needs place upon the family are all factors to consider in understanding the family's response (Turnbull & Turnbull, 1990; Shea & Bauer, 1991; Kroth, 1985; Association for the Care of Children's Health, 1990; Fine, 1991; Webster & Ward, 1993).

Some researchers have challenged the notion that having a child with a disability is a life of sadness or stigma. Singer, Irvin, Hawkins, Hegreness, and Jackson (1993) surveyed parents of children with special needs and reported such positive feelings as: My child is fun to be around, affectionate, kind, and loving, and that because of my child I have many unexpected pleasures. Parents report that they also have learned important life lessons because of their child and have an increased sensitivity and compassion for others. Parenting a child with exceptionalities can be rewarding as well as challenging. As teachers, we should remember that we serve children with special needs who live in families with unique and changing special needs.

Whether or not the disability is visible, whether it has a label of mild, moderate, or severe, or whether or not a precise diagnosis has been made, parents of children with special needs face unique emotional issues. Regardless of when parents learn of their child's condition or disability, the issues of acceptance of the disability are faced time and time again as the child arrives at typical developmental milestones: the age for walking, talking, starting kindergarten, beginning to read or ride a bike, getting a driver's license, first dance, graduation, career or college, etc.

For some families, there are increased tensions that may magnify any marital discord and feelings of inadequacy. Spouses and siblings alike may feel rejected or abandoned. Some statistics indicate that the divorce rate is higher when there is a child with a disability within the family (Alper, Schloss, & Schloss, 1994). Today, there are more single mothers parenting alone and a greater chance of blended families when there is a remarriage. Some children with special needs are in foster placements or adoptive families. There has been an increase in the number of children, many with medical or psychological problems, who do not find a lasting placement (Cobb & Reeve, 1991). Media attention has been drawn to the "border babies" left in the hospital by mothers incapable of assuming their care. These children, often HIV positive or substance exposed, are posing new challenges to the child welfare system. There are new concerns among social service providers that there will be a resurgence of residential placements, such as orphanages, for these and other hard-to-place children.

Many families with children with special needs must carefully consider issues that are unique either in their nature or the timing of when it must be addressed. One of these issues is the guardianship and the inevitable support for their child when they reach adulthood. Parents of young children may be troubled by these and similar concerns during their child's infancy, although they are years into the future. These premature stressors are common to some parents of children with disabilities (Mori, 1983).

It can be very valuable for the teacher to be aware of the various responses that have been identified, as it opens new avenues of understanding in parent-teacher communication. Regardless of which characteristics parents display, it is critical that the teacher recognize that each parent's response progression will be uniquely individual and impacted by adult developmental stages and life events which do not necessarily relate to the child. It is important for the teacher to understand and perhaps assist the parent in understanding their feelings in regard to their child. These multiple, complex feelings can change character and intensity in response to the often turbulent internal emotions and external experiences parents encounter. Self-doubt, embarrassment, social isolation, fears, frustration, and confusion may thrust parents into periods of uninvolvement with the school or program. Because the early childhood years may include the identification or diagnosis of a particular condition or disability, or present concerns of a potential difficulty, it is important for professionals to recognize that some families will need particular support and understanding.

EMOTIONAL STRESS

Caring for any young child can challenge the energy and patience of most adults. Families of children who have any type of special need, whether it be medical, physical, developmental, or social/emotional, all live with the stress and frustration of meeting the needs of one child while balancing (or compromising) the needs of the rest of the family. Many children with special needs are not developing on a typical schedule. Spoon feeding a 3-year-old with swallowing difficulties, diapering a 6-year-old, or communicating with a preschooler who is mute can cause endless modifications to a typical family routine. Sometimes the stress and fatigue of continuous care and the occasional crisis presents unhealthy patterns for parents. They may not get enough sleep or have enough time for leisure activities or to attend to personal needs.

Teachers should be aware of and sensitive to parents' unmet needs and allow parents to "use" the child's program for respite time if necessary. And, when parents sometime resist the "homework" assignments given by teachers and therapists, teachers should understand that it's not out of a lack of concern for their child's development, but from the frustration of wanting to be "just his Mommy sometimes." The school program can be a unique support system for families beyond the educational realm (Allen, 1992).

Tragically, there is evidence that children with disabilities are more likely to be the target of family abuse (Allen, 1992). Infants and preschoolers with developmental disabilities may behave in ways that are upsetting to parents. Babies who have a high pitched, inconsolable crying pattern try the nerves of sleep-deprived parents. With some disabilities and especially for infants prenatally exposed to drugs, this pattern of behavior is frequently coupled with other behaviors, such as rigidity, hypersensitivity, and feeding problems. Babies who have a difficult time retaining feedings may become failure-to-thrive or sick infants when caregivers are distressed beyond their ability to cope. A normal child living in a stressful environment with an abuse-prone parent can become disabled because of injury from abuse. Without adequate supports, the family of a child with disabilities may incur enough stress to cause parents to become abusive. Adequate support systems are a key factor for family well-being, especially for families of children with disabilities (Allen, 1992).

Social Isolation

Social isolation is a frequent concern of families with children who have special needs. Often the caretakers of children with medical needs must have some special training, which may make respite care difficult to locate. Child-care centers and even family members are sometimes reluctant to care for these children. Parents may be unwilling to entrust the child with another person. Yet, as the child grows and develops, this possessive sense of responsibility may ease, unveiling the obstacle of locating supplementary care. Parents of children with disabilities also face isolation. It can be difficult to face the stares or awkward questions from strangers and even family members. Restaurants, stores, and playgrounds can present emotional "tests" for the child and parent alike. Yet, it's not just the family of a physically disabled child that is confronted with these situations. Autism, seizure disorders, attention deficit, developmental delays, or similar conditions can make it hard for the family to go out in public. Consequently, parents may limit their visibility in the community and shelter the child (and themselves) from the outside world.

For children with limited physical abilities, transportation can create extraordinary stress for the family once they grow too large for their caregiver's ability to physically carry them. Few homes are wheelchair accessible inside and out. In addition to the more obvious ramps and door widths, furniture, fixtures, and other household features may need to be adapted as the child grows. Mobility issues in the home can initiate unanticipated remodeling or relocation for accessible housing. Vehicles adapted for wheelchair transport that would allow a more typical family mobility style are extremely expensive. Consequently, families may alter their lifestyle and choices of activities in a way that limits participation by the whole family. Going to the movies or out to eat in a restaurant as a family, for example, may not be possible. If families must reduce their involvement in typical community and life experiences for any reason and are unable to overcome the restrictions, family morale and sibling experiences can be affected.

Family acceptance of the child's disability mediates this issue, but can test the tolerance of friends and associates. Families of children with disabilities are sometimes shunned or unintentionally ostracized in a neighborhood or community. Schools, therefore, can offer a harbor of acceptance and understanding for the family as well as the child. Teachers can be sensitive to the needs to be accepted and encourage parent involvement that includes social events and parent-to-parent contacts that meets the need for parental support and understanding in a special way (Powers, 1993).

SPECIAL CHALLENGES RELATED TO MEDICAL/PHYSICAL DISABILITIES

Frequently the term "special needs" conjures up the image of a child who has a specific physical problem, or one who requires special medical care. When a child is physically or medically involved, there is the unique challenge of securing and adjusting to the medical recommendations for treatment. Although some conditions include anticipated surgeries (such as a child with Down's syndrome who requires cardiac surgery, or the child with spina bifida who requires surgery to close the exposed section of spine or place a shunt to drain fluid from the brain), some encounters with the medical establishment are few and relatively minor. There also are children who need continual monitoring, as their condition may change dramatically from "good health" to critical in the matter of hours. The families of medically fragile children must adjust to new lifestyles that include, and sometimes revolve around, the particular medical needs of the child. Frequent medical appointments, endless hours in waiting rooms, extended travel to be seen by specialists, therapy sessions, hospitalizations and surgeries, all tax the physical and emotional reserves of the family.

Concerns about time, money, insurance, transportation, and the stress of home responsibilities and relationships place additional strain upon parents already anxious about the well-being of their child. Some parents of medically involved children have categorized their life in two ways: their routine while the child is hospitalized and when the child is home again. Sometimes this requires one parent to temporarily live near the medical facility and delegate home responsibilities and care of children to the other parent or support persons. These crisis periods may be concentrated during the early childhood years, when particular procedures are recommended, or may be ongoing during childhood, as in the case of spina bifida, and cancers, like leukemia. When medically involved children are not hospitalized, they may require additional medical attention, medicines, special foods, or specialized equipment or care/procedures, which dramatically alter the home routine. Other children may be susceptible to chronic illnesses and may not be able to attend school regularly.

It is important for teachers to be flexible and understanding when the child is absent frequently or for long periods of time. Parents of these children may feel stressed by the past, present, or anticipated medical procedures or illnesses. Friendly contact from the teachers during these absences just to keep in touch and inquire how the child *and* the family are doing is typically appreciated. Teachers often visit their hospitalized students if it is possible and appropriate. Children with physical disabilities, including hearing and visually impaired, may require special training for signing or mobility, which usually involves parental training also. Life does go on, and both children and families often demonstrate remarkable resilience.

APPREHENSION OVER PROGRAM TRANSITIONS

Families that have built a relationship with the service team of the early intervention program will "lose" that support to a large degree when the child moves into another program. This transition causes many concerns for families (Rosenkoetter, Hains, & Fowler, 1994). Concerns include changes in the focus of services (family to child), in the types and location of services (home to school), in discrepancies in eligibility and labeling, and in personnel. Families of children with special needs will continue to bring with them the complexities and challenges of their lives. The invitation is to grow *together*, to focus on the vision of schools by meeting each other's needs, and develop the skills and sensitivities the process demands.

NEW OPPORTUNITIES VIA TECHNOLOGICAL ADVANCES

Computers, microprocessors, and other electronic advances have brought many changes to the world of special education. Communicative and assistive devices, together with medical advances, have permitted children and adults to more fully participate in life. Assistive technology can refer to low technology adaptations (putting a sipper top on a cup or using a padded support or footrest) or high technology electronic devices (a portable computer with a speech synthesizer). Depending on a child's abilities and needs, the child will be evaluated by a team often composed of an occupational therapist, physical therapist, speech language pathologist, or a specialist in assistive technology. This assessment will include reviewing medical and educational records and rating the child's language and cognitive abilities, and skills in the sensory areas of motor, vision, and hearing. If a child will be using a computer or other electronic device, the team will carefully evaluate the child's range of motion, pointing accuracy, speed of pointing, and other response skills. Parents are often consulted in the assessment.

Undoubtedly, computers and electronic technology have offered the greatest promise to the greatest numbers of children. Many regular computers can be adapted with special internal cards or boards, adapted screens, or alternative keyboards. The assortment of internal adaptations permit the use of particular programs or peripherals. The huge variety of adapted touch screens or tablets and alternative keyboards permit a child with physical limitations to utilize the attractive software programs available for young children as well as adapted programs. Alternative keyboards can be used instead of a mouse or joystick and may have specialized keys or switches to replace or supplement the standard microcomputer keyboard. Keys may be enlarged, have alternative stickers, or regulate particular keyboard functions. With special finger access software, a child can control the regular keyboard with a single finger, pointing device, or mouthstick. High tech communication aids are basically computers with dedicated programs and special capabilities like synthesized speech. These utilize any number of pictographs, symbols, letters, or words to actualize prestored messages or individual words. Many toys can be adapted with activating switches (some actuated by an eye glance or a puff of air into a tube) to stimulate the attention and reinforce the attempts of young children to interact with their environment.

Not all assistive technology involves such complex materials. Adaptives also include wheelchairs and picture communication boards. Parents and teachers can often adapt regular toys to facilitate play in young children with disabilities. These adaptations may be *physical supports* that utilize strategies to stabilize materials to allow the child to play independently. Children with a limited grasp can use wristbands with toys attached to them or wear gloves with Velcro or magnets attached to them to assist the child in holding on to playthings. Playboards or toy bars can be used to affix toys to a surface so the toys won't move or fall off. Wheelchair trays can be lined with a special tacky-surfaced mat or have Velcro strips attached so that toys with Velcro at their base (such as toy dishes, dolls, or other smaller toys) can be more stable. Parts such as handles, knobs, or textured surfaces can be added to toys to make them more accessible. Markers, paintbrushes, and spoons can have foam attached to the handle to also promote an easier grasp. Larger toys and toys with clear, familiar features can be selected to enhance visual perception. Together, teacher and parents can create playthings and utensils that allow children to more fully experience the world around them. Technological advances are offering increased opportunity to develop every child's potential. Some of these high tech aids are expensive, and locating sufficient funding for them may be a challenge. This too may be a focus of the parent-teacher partnership.

A FAMILY SYSTEMS PERSPECTIVE

The concept of family systems is crucial to understanding and effectively working with families with children who have special needs. The family is a unique "system" in which its members establish roles and relationships, and grow, develop, and change in interaction with one another. Any change, like a wind gust upon a hanging mobile, will impact both its individual members and the family as a whole. Family systems have rules for affection, communication, and power, and ways of dealing with stress and problems. A child with a disability influences many aspects of the family system, from economics to social relationships to interpersonal relationships between the parents and other children. Understanding the family system framework requires an analysis of the family resources, family interactions, family functions, and the stage of family development.

The family itself is its one best resource. The characteristics of the exceptionality (age of child, sex, type and severity of disability/condition) will prompt a different response from each parent. Other considerations, like the structural and personal characteristics of the family members, the number of parents, ages, maturity levels, their parenting and coping style, the physical and emotional health of family members, number and birth order of children, and family stability and harmony factor into this life equation (Turnbull & Turnbull, 1990). The presence or absence of employment/financial security, insurance coverage, the extensiveness of the extended family/friend support network, and religious beliefs, also affect the impact a child with special needs has upon the family (McWilliam & Bailey, 1993). Many family characteristics impact the coping response to the adjustments which arise with the addition of a child with special needs and the professional family partnership. Family functions include who earns the family income, how affection is demonstrated, and to whom and to what degree members provide guidance to the family and pursue educational goals for the child (Fine, 1991; Turnbull & Turnbull, 1990). How family members secure rest and recuperation and how the domestic and health-care concerns of the home are handled are also factors of family functioning. Cultural differences may factor into how family is valued and how comfortable the family members are with outside service providers. Family traditions, values, and standards for raising children as well as family preferences to accept help or "handle their own problems" all reflect the individual differences between each family system (Alper et al., 1994). Research has indicated that mothers tend to be more accepting than fathers, and that parents of lower socioeconomic class are more accepting than parents of higher status (Alper et al., 1994). Geographic location and mobility also influence the number of stressors, as well as the availability of services and the continuity of the program. Sometimes the family life cycle changes in response to financial or work-family issues: Mom stops working outside the home, which provides more time for child care, but less income, for example. Chronological changes occur as each member of the family grows older and structural changes occur with births, deaths, marriages, and divorce.

Each parent will probably reevaluate his or her self-image and sense of self-worth. This process of reevaluation will occur in the husband/wife dyad as well and may prompt conscious and unconscious decisions for the couple. Relationships within the extended family may also face readjustment, depending upon the strength of those relationships and the frequency of family contact. The relationships among the family's children may be different, in some ways reflective of the attitudes and actions children observe in adults, peers, and others in the broader community (Powers, 1993; Hazel et al., 1988; Stayton et al., 1990).

PARENT INVOLVEMENT AND THE HELPING RELATIONSHIP

Many young children with special needs are involved in some type of early intervention or preschool program. Families frequently become involved with professionals, service providers, and educational programs and systems while their child is quite young. Consequently, early childhood teachers may expect to have children with special needs at some time. Recognizing that family stresses and emotions impact the relationship teachers have with parents helps teachers develop a sensitive partnership with these families. Parents bring heightened concerns for their child's physical care and development mixed with the need to keep some semblance of normalcy about their child's early years and their family life. Schools often provide a much needed support and respite for these families. It is imperative that a trusting relationship is built between family and teacher. Partnerships can be built upon an openness to information shared with the family and a sensitivity to the changing needs and concerns within each family system.

The helping relationship between a parent and a professional is a powerful yet delicate relationship. The quality of that parent/professional relationship must be a concern to anyone working with children and families during these early years. These partnerships may have great meaning, reflect a range of emotions, and change over time as the child, parent, and professional grow and develop. Each partner wants to feel capable and effective, yet the pressure to "do something" is offset by the fear of not always knowing the "right answer" or being able to carry through. Some professionals want to control too completely, or try too hard to fix the problems; in those cases, the ultimate objective of a partnership is forgotten.

In the helping relationship between parent and teacher, one goal is to increase family involvement and empower parents to become informed family members and effective service coordinators for their child. Despite the legal protection of parent involvement, many parents of children with disabilities do not become actively involved in their child's program.

Dunst, Trivette, and Deal (1988), in recognizing this dilemma, offer suggestions from research. Working with families is a dynamic, fluid process that includes the art and craft of developing positive outcomes in the partnership. The relationship is the key, and every contact with the family counts toward establishing trust and respect. Confidentiality must be maintained and preserved at all times. Honesty is critical and effective help-giving requires an understanding of a family's concerns and interests. Emphasis should be placed on solutions, not causes. Effective interactions focus on positive, proactive strategies that promote the use of informal supports as the main way of meeting needs.

Family involvement is developmental, and parents may not be ready to begin a parent/professional helping relationship. Professionals may not yet be skillful in the craft of working with parents and should make a sincere effort in developing "people skills." Suggestions for promoting positive relationships with parents include:

- Allow the family to tell its own story and listen carefully to parents and family members. Respect their history. Don't minimize what they have to say.
- Help families to identify and process unresolved issues that are bothering them. Use reflective listening and effective questioning. Don't make premature judgments or moralize.
- Avoid hasty, patronizing attempts to solve problems, offer advice, or give information. Empathy, not advice, may be the real need.
- Provide accurate, honest information in response to parent queries, or assist parents in securing such information. Use language that parents and family members can understand. Avoid jargon.

- Provide parents with many variations and individualized alternatives for working appropriately with their child, including suggestions for functional skill building and parent goals.
- Do not attempt to produce or use guilt to motivate parents and family members. Don't threaten, ridicule, or blame.
- Inform parents and family of community resources that may help them meet their child's or family needs.
- Treat parents as adult partners who care about their child, and never assume that your training or experience has given you more knowledge than the parents about their child.
- Assist families in recognizing that their needs will change over time as will those of their child. Strive for realistic optimism.
- Be accepting of yourself and of the parents and family members with whom you work. Demonstrate warmth and sensitivity.
- Learn whatever family skills you need to work effectively: family assessments, home strategies for skill building, etc.
- Be open to parents' questions and concerns and be available to talk with them. Don't be afraid to say "I don't know" and suggest someone who can assist, or seek answers and get back to the parents.
- Examine your attitude toward children with disabilities. Remember, they are children first. Focus on their strengths, not on what they can't do.
- Respect the parents' right to choose their level of involvement and participation.
- Find other parents who have children with disabilities who would be willing to talk with your student's family. Parent-to-parent networking is a great resource.

These suggestions have been gleaned from the works of Turnbull and Turnbull (1990), Simpson (1990), Mori (1983), Rundall and Smith (1985), Linder (1983), and Fenichel and Eggbeer (1990).

FAMILY-CENTERED COLLABORATIONS

Many developments regarding early childhood described in this chapter have served to create opportunities, and occasionally conflicts, for families of children with special needs. Legislation has brought parents into focus as consumers of educational programs and services. As more families develop communication and advocacy skills from participation in early intervention programs, and a general awareness of best practices, the schools will see more parents who are comfortable in the role of advocate/service coordinator for their child. Programs for 3- to 5-year-olds will be challenged to adapt and work with parents as real partners in the process of education. Laws have challenged states and communities to "catch up" to recommended practices for family-centered involvement at minimal levels. As programs continue to develop and refine this concept, and as new programs are created based upon family-centered and family-guided approaches, this philosophy will continue to spread within the state and community social services. Agencies, once autonomous, are thrust together on interagency councils to work out how to achieve maximum outcomes with limited dollars. Collaborations that once were inconceivable are emerging with new energy, opening the door to more comprehensive services for families.

INCREASED FAMILY SUPPORTS

The focus on comprehensive services has resulted in an increase in the services and supports offered to families with children who have special needs, often through collaborations at state and local levels. Many states have passed family support legislation, increasing the availability of respite and child care, adaptive assistance, transportation, financial assistance, and such family services as support groups, parent training, and information centers (Exceptional Parent, 1993; Ziegler, 1992). State agencies (such as public health), local agencies, and programs are making information services about disabilities and parent-to-parent linkages more commonplace. May (1991) reports an increase in awareness of men's needs in the parenting of children with disabilities and an increase in the number of support groups especially for fathers. The PTA has a special division to encourage the involvement of parents who have children in special programs. Advocacy initiatives with varied state and local sponsorships are reaching out to families with questions and are heightening the awareness of disability issues. Both individual and group efforts have promoted family supports throughout the nation. However, even the best constructed program is not without potential difficulties.

BARRIERS TO PARENT INVOLVEMENT

BARRIERS WITHIN THE SERVICE SYSTEM

Many barriers to parent involvement for parents of children with special needs are identical to those identified in this book for all parents. Yet because special education interventions in early childhood often take place during times of stress, professionals must have a heightened sensitivity to the possible origins, prevention, and resolution of any difficulties. The source of the problem may lie with the professional, the system of services and how they are delivered to the family, or with the family system itself. Professionals may lack the experience or training to work with parents of children with special needs and may feel uncomfortable. Different philosophies or a resistance to accepting the parent as a respected partner may present obstacles. As well, many colleges and universities fail to offer adequate coursework in family-centered approaches in their teacher preparation requirements.

Systems themselves can create obstacles in policies, regulations, or procedures. Special education protocol is perhaps the most regimented system within the school setting. This can result in a lack of flexibility that is frequently coupled with a shortage of resources, including money for program extras like parent involvement, and a shortage of professional time to build partnerships with families. Parent involvement in the form of active partnerships is a relatively new concept fostered through the family-centered programs in early intervention and by sensitive early childhood professionals and service providers. The current trends in early childhood are a radical change from some past attitudes toward parents. Family support services and parent advocacy are quantum leaps of philosophy for schools that exclusively served the child for their daily program, considered parent contact solely in terms of compliance with legal requirements for signatures and meetings, and viewed parents who expressed their views with an advocate's voice as troublemakers.

BARRIERS WITHIN THE FAMILY

The emotional and physical complexities of raising a child with special needs is itself overwhelming for parents. Yet, when the child becomes eligible for early intervention or special education services or programs, parents need to become aware of the variety of service providers, the language of special education, and their legal rights in a fairly complex educational system—all while continuing to function as a family during an often-turbulent early childhood period. As professionals share knowledge of services, programs, and service systems with parents, parents typically increase their participation. Often parents do not desire to take on the responsibilities of active involvement because they are unclear about their child's needs, or believe there will be a time as their child gets older to become more involved. Until then it is important that the teacher concentrate on the child and attempt to overcome the problems. Parents can be so overwhelmed with survival issues and family responsibilities that there is no time or energy left to participate in meetings where they do not feel comfortable or needed. There are enormous differences in parents, and some obstacles are within the dynamics of the particular family system (Bailey, Buysse, Edmondson, & Smith, 1992).

Lynch (1981) reported nine barriers to parent participation in special education programs. As identified by parents, they were problems with communication, transportation, and babysitting; a lack of time; a lack of understanding of the system; feelings of inferiority; a feeling that problems won't be resolved; language and/or cultural differences; and realistically accepting their child's disability. While many potential solutions to these difficulties already have been proposed in previous chapters, there are many additional strategies to enhance communication, support, and advocacy within special education service structures.

STRATEGIES TO ENHANCE PARENTAL COMMUNICATION, SUPPORT, AND ADVOCACY

Parents who are stressed by life events and circumstances that accompany caregiving for a child with special needs may be extremely sensitive to a professional's response to them or their child. They may feel vulnerable and anxious about situations where major decisions are made about them and their child. Confronted with traditional authority figures from the school, parents may   feel powerless, incompetent, and angry. It is of utmost importance, therefore, that teachers utilize strategies that create positive communication patterns, provide individualized supports, and empower families to become knowledgeable and active participants in their child's school or program (Markel & Greenbaum, 1981).

STRATEGIES TO ENHANCE COMMUNICATION

Most families have a strong need to be informed about their child's program and progress. Early childhood programs frequently have large numbers of service providers interacting with special needs children. All members of the instructional team should make an effort to help parents understand who works with their child, including names, titles, and responsibilities. Communications that are sent home by various individuals should be coordinated, perhaps on a single "daily news" form, to provide an easy way to keep track of notes and requests.

Initial contacts with parents should be as comfortable and as positive as possible. Parents should be informed about *why* information is needed, *what* procedures are ahead, and *who* will be involved. One of the best ways to enhance parent participation is to help demystify the system. Parents may need help developing open communication skills when talking with professionals, practice in asking questions, and practice in sharing their knowledge, their experiences, and their hopes. Techniques for tracking observational data at home for health, behavior, or other concerns should be shared so that parents can become more active participants in their child's program.

Parents also will need assistance in deciphering the code of special education terminology. The initials, the assessment instruments used with the child, and technical terminology used in the diagnosis or educational program should be explained. There are a variety of books and tapes available to specifically help parents (see Additional Resources section); however, the most helpful information may be in a handbook created by parents for parents. Teachers should offer to share explanations, materials, or reading material on particular aspects of a disability or program. Parents may be interested in attending meetings on such topics as home therapy techniques and strategies, the IEP process, parent rights and responsibilities, advocacy training, or the program's assessments for children and families (Lynch, 1981; McGonigel, Kaufmann, & Johnson, 1991).

Sharing experiences with other parents can provide useful information and emotional support.

STRATEGIES TO ENHANCE SUPPORT

During their involvement with an early childhood program, parents determine what supports they feel are valuable. It is up to the teachers and support staff to provide access to and awareness of supports that make a "needs-fit" for the families. Family needs inventories or other types of family assessments can assist individual families in identifying the issues that concern them most. With this information, the parent-teacher team can work together to identify resources, either within the family system or outside. For example, a family may express a need for child care. Several options would be an extended family member or friend, a student from the local college nursing or education program, the local child-care center that takes children with disabilities, or the child-care referral agency that could assist in locating a day-care home. Families should be empowered to actively pursue their own choices without undue assistance from the professional.

Conferences and meetings may cause extraordinary stress for the parents. This may overwhelm a parent who may not be able to respond to the suggestions during the meeting or accurately recall all the details to relate to the absent parent. An excellent support strategy is to suggest that both parents attend together, or that the parent ask a family member, friend, or advocate to attend with him or her. If there are two parents in the family structure, provide opportunities for both parents to have input in the child's program.

Professionals cannot assume that they know what a family is undergoing, unless they themselves have a child with a disability. Teachers can provide valuable assistance by helping families locate, through a parent network, other families that share a similar situation. Often these networks are sponsored by organizations for individuals with disabilities and are found through local or state agency programs. The state department of public health may offer special counseling and support services for families of children with genetic disorders. The National Organization for Rare Disorders (NORD) or a disability-specific organization at the national, state, or local level can be a valuable referral for a family. Community resource guides, available through social workers, service organizations, or community consortiums, can help families locate resources to meet other needs. The teacher can locate potentially helpful telephone numbers and agency contact names and share them with families. Many programs host a parent-to-parent program, which may become a support for all families, or just those entering the program or leaving it. Parent-to-parent programs offer an individualized and personal response by another parent to the unique challenges these families face. These programs provide emotional support, information/education, social activities, and advocacy. They may also have a group structure which enhances the social supports for parents. Parent-to-parent programs may be organized through the school or program, a hospital, or other agency offering supports to families. Information on this type of program may be available through a state government office or through national organizations like the Beach Center on Families and Disability, the National Center on Parent-Directed Family Resource Centers, Technical Assistance for Parent Programs, or the National Parent Network on Disabilities (Family Resource Coalition in Santelli, Turnbull, Lerner, & Marquis, 1993).

STRATEGIES TO ENHANCE ADVOCACY

Parents have become empowered through the federal and state laws that protect their rights and establish responsibilities for involvement. Advocacy efforts on the behalf of children with special needs and their families are flourishing at the national, state, and local levels. Parents are coming to schools less passive and "humbly grateful," and are more likely to advocate for the most effective services for their children. The means to achieving this is not necessarily adversarial. In order for schools and parents to have a respectful and sensitive relationship, all parties must be knowledgeable of the facts, needs, rights, and options. Professionals should be aware of generalizations about parents of special needs children and focus on the individual relationship built as a team. Watch for attitudes of defensiveness or intimidation within the relationship. Parents may have the impression that the school/program staff are against them or their child. This creates negative emotions that spill out into legal advocacy actions, such as due process. Strong parent involvement and communication empower a working relationship in which differences can be mediated amiably. This problem-solving, communicative process develops from a consultative, helping relationship that is reflected in the intervention plan devised by the parent-professional team. Developing and practicing the positive partnership-building skills mentioned earlier can assist the teachers (and the school) link with nontraditional families and multicultural families. These skills contribute to the effectiveness of any advocacy efforts.

By monitoring the effectiveness of a child's program, teachers can be important allies in assisting parents. (Do the services meet the child's [or family's] needs? Would something else work better?) Working within the system to ensure that quality programming is in place for the child, and that parents are participating members of the team, may avoid or reduce any future conflicts. This child—and now family—centeredness is the focus of the changing system of special education and is a vital piece of advocacy.

Good communication skills are basic to any advocacy effort. Through schools/programs, parents can learn social support advocacy skills such as how to write and visit with their legislator or congressional representative, what legislation has been proposed that may affect families and children with special needs, and how to meet with local officials in order to positively impact community changes. Schools and programs also can provide parents with public relations skills that can be used when working with the community at large, or with medical service providers, social services providers, and others. By sharing information and building skills within the system, there is a greater likelihood that parents will develop as allies, not adversaries (Alper et al., 1994).

SUMMARY

The magnitude of change in both the philosophies and practices of involvement for parents of children with special needs has created new and individualized strategies. Nationwide, programs are emerging that reflect these changes. Most visible are programs serving children from birth through 2 years of age and their families, and inclusive programs that accept all children, regardless of ability. No longer are people complacent with the philosophy of isolating and segregating children who need special services, whether in the schools or in the community. New attempts at collaboration at the state and local levels are broadening the support networks into grassroots communities. Compliance with federal policies requires philosophies that view families as planners as well as recipients of services. Throughout a growing number of special education programs, parents are accepting the position of system-change agent by more fully exercising their rights under special education law. Government is developing family support policy with input from families, communities, business, education, and social services, and is discovering new collaborations to most effectively meet needs. It is an exciting time, a challenging time, for families, service systems, and policymakers. Most exciting of all is that professionals working with young children and their families are key facilitators of this change.

ACTIVITIES FOR DISCUSSION, EXPANSION, AND APPLICATION

1. Research and list public and private agencies, schools, support groups, and other service providers in your area that provide assistance to parents of children with special needs in coping with the emotional and physical challenges of parenting. Create a resource list that includes title of the resource, contact person, address, phone number, and type and cost of service.

2. Interview someone working in an early intervention program that serves infants and toddlers with disabilities, and someone working with older preschoolers with disabilities. How does each view parent involvement in his/her program? Describe each worker's contacts with parents. Compare and contrast the following: frequency of contacts with parents, the nature of the interaction (typical location, length of contact, typical topics, support materials typically shared, etc.), and the type of parent education or advocacy programming provided. Compare your research with that of others in your group. Discuss the philosophies, services, and the impact upon parents.

3. Interview a parent of a child with special needs. Ask the parent's permission to share the responses with your group. Ask the parent to tell the story of parenting his/her child. What was the reaction when the child's difficulties were first realized? How did family and friends react? What were their frustrations, sorrows, joys? How is the parent involved in the child's program? What are the parent's dreams for the child? Share what you have learned with your group. What are the similarities and differences? Why?

4. Interview a social worker, psychologist, therapist, teacher, or administrator for a special education program. What do they say are the challenges and rewards of working with parents of children with special needs? What are the most sensitive issues for professionals to discuss with parents? Why? What would they wish parents would do more or less of? What can teachers do to encourage parent involvement? Discuss your findings with your group.

5. Use ideas collected by your group in activity number 4 and other research to develop a usable resource, such as a checklist, article, or guidebook for teachers and other professionals. Include strategies, suggestions, and guidelines for working in partnership with parents of children with special needs.

6. Interview a parent whose child with special needs is in elementary school or high school. Investigate how time has changed what services are available to preschoolers with special needs. What were the issues the parent felt were important when the child was young? What issues does the parent perceive to be important for parents today? How and why are they different? Discuss with your group what you've learned.

7. Interview an adult with a disability. How is growing up now different for children with special needs than it was for him or her? In what ways is it the same? What are the critical differences for people with disabilities today? (Excellent contacts can be made through your area disability services organizations.)

8. Are young children with special needs being included in regular school and community programs in your area? Contact elementary schools, preschools, child-care centers, local YMCAs, library programs, sports organizations, churches, etc. If you were a parent of a child with a disability, what would your response be? If possible, contact the parents of a child who is included in regular programs. Ask them to share their story of how their child was included. What has been the most difficult, and the most rewarding, aspects of the child's experience? What fears did they have? What are their dreams for their child? Share with your group what you have learned. Discuss the school and community environments. Are they open to inclusion? Why or why not?

ADDITIONAL RESOURCES

Beckman, P., & Boyes, G. (1993). *Deciphering the system: A guide for families of young children with disabilities*. Cambridge, MA: Brookline Books.

Coleman, J. (1993). *The early intervention dictionary: A multidisciplinary guide to terminology*. Rockville, MD: Woodbine House.

Cutler, B. (1993). *You, your child, and "special education": A guide to making the system work*. Baltimore: Paul H. Brookes.

Downey, P. (1986). *New directions for exceptional parenting*. Washington, DC: Association for the Care of Children's Health.

Featherstone, H. (1982). *A difference in the family: Life with a disabled child*. New York: Penguin.

Gallagher, J., Trohanis, P., & Clifford, R. (1989). *Policy implementation: Planning for young children with special needs*. Baltimore: Paul H. Brookes.

Glidden, L. (1989). *Parents for children, children for parents: The adoption alternative*. Washington, DC: American Association on Mental Retardation.

Goldfarb, L., Brotherson, M., Summers, J., & Turnbull, A. (1986). *Meeting the challenge of disability or chronic illness: A family guide*. Baltimore: Paul H. Brookes.

McCarthy, J., Lund, K., & Bos, C. (1986). *Parent involvement and home teaching*. Denver: Love.

Meyer, D., & Vadasy, P. (1987). *How to organize workshops for grandparents of children with handicaps*. Seattle: University of Washington Press.

Meyer, D., Vadasy, P., & Fewell, R. (1987). *Living with a brother or sister with special needs: A book for sibs*. Seattle: University of Washington Press.

Moore, C. (1990). *A reader's guide for parents of children with mental, physical, or emotional disabilities*. Rockville, MD: Woodbine House.

Perske, R. (1988). *Circles of friends*. Nashville, TN: Abingdon Press.

Reynolds, K., & Shanahan, V. (1981). *The parent to parent program organizational handbook*. Athens, GA: The Parent to Parent National Project, University of Georgia.

Routberg, M. (1986). *On becoming a special parent: A mini-support group in a book*. Chicago: Parent/Professional Publications.

Segal, M. (1988). *In time and with love: Caring for the special needs baby*. New York: Newmarket Press.

Simons, R. (1987). *After the tears: Parents talk about raising a child with a disability*. Orlando, FL: Harcourt Brace Jovanovich.

Taylor, S., Bilken, D., Lehr, S., & Searl, S. (1987). *Purposeful integration . . . inherently equal*. Boston: Technical Assistance for Parent Programs.

Vergason, G. (1990). *Dictionary of special education and rehabilitation*. Denver: Love.

Warger, C., Tewey, S., & Megivern, M. (1991). *Abuse and neglect of exceptional children*. Reston, VA: Council for Exceptional Children.

Wilson, N. (1992). *Optimizing special education: How parents can make a difference*. New York: Insight Books/Plenum Press.

REFERENCES

Allen, K. (1992). *The exceptional child: Mainstreaming in early childhood education.* Albany, NY: Delmar.

Alper, S., Schloss, P., & Schloss, C. (1994). *Families of students with disabilities: Consultation and advocacy.* Boston: Allyn & Bacon.

Arnold, J., & Dodge, H. (1994). Room for all. *American School Board Journal, 191*(10), 22–26.

Association for the Care of Children's Health. (1990). *Your child with special needs at home and in the community.* Bethesda, MD: Association for the Care of Children's Health.

Austin, J.K. (1990). Assessment of coping mechanisms used by parents and children with chronic illness. *Maternal and Child Nursing, 15*, 98–102.

Bailey D., Buysse, V., Edmondson, R., & Smith, T. (1992). Creating family-centered services in early intervention: Perceptions of professionals in four states. *Exceptional Children, 58*(4), 298–309.

Bricker, D. (1989). *Early intervention for at-risk and handicapped infants, toddlers, and preschool children.* Palo Alto, CA: Vort.

Buscaglia, L. (1983). *The disabled and their parents: A counseling challenge.* Thorofare, NJ: Slack Inc.

Church, G., & Glennen, S. (1994). *The handbook of assistive technology.* San Diego: Singular Press.

Cobb, H., & Reeve, R. (1991). Counseling approaches with parents and families. In M. Fine (Ed.), *Collaboration with parents of exceptional children.* Brandon, VT: Clinical Psychology Publishing Co.

Cook, R., Tessier, A., & Kline, M. (1992). *Adapting early childhood curricula for children with special needs.* New York: Merrill.

Diamond, K., Hestenes, L., & O'Connor, C. (1994). Integrating young children with disabilities in preschool: Problems and promise. *Young Children, 49*(2), 68–73.

Dunst, C., Trivette, C., & Deal A. (1988). *Enabling and empowering families: Principles and guidelines for practice.* Cambridge, MA: Brookline Books.

Exceptional Parent. (1993). Family support programs growing. *Exceptional Parent, 23*(6), 36–40.

Family Resource Coalition. *Starting and operating support groups: A guide for parents.* Chicago: Family Resource Coalition.

Fenichel, E., & Eggbeer, L. (1990). *Preparing practitioners to work with infants, toddlers, and their families: Issues and recommendations for the professions.* Arlington, VA: National Center for Clinical Infant Programs.

Fine, M. (1991). *Collaboration with parents of exceptional children.* Brandon, VT: Clinical Psychology Publishing Co.

Galant, I., & Hanline, M. (1993). Parental attitudes toward mainstreaming young children with disabilities. *Childhood Education.* 1993 Annual, 293–297.

Hazel, R., Barber, P., Roberts, S., Behr, S., Helmstetter, E., & Guess, D. (1988). *A community approach to an integrated service system for children with special needs.* Baltimore: Paul H. Brookes.

Harbin, G. (1993). Family issues of children with disabilities: How research and theory have modified practices in intervention. In N. Anastasiow & S. Harel (Eds.), *At-risk infants: Interventions, families, and research.* Baltimore: Paul H. Brookes.

Holden, L., Kaiser, M., Sykes, D., & Tyree, R. (1993). *Quilting integration: A technical assistance guide on integrated early childhood programs.* Columbus, OH: Early Integration Training Project/Ohio State University.

Institute for Educational Research. (1992). *Teacher Today, 8*(2), 2–6.

Kroth, R. (1985). *Communicating with parents of exceptional children: Improving parent-teacher relationships.* Denver: Love.

Linder, T. (1983). *Early childhood special education: Program development and administration.* Baltimore: Paul H. Brookes.

LRP Publications. (1994a). Developmental factors in preschool inclusion outcomes. *Early Childhood Report, 5*(11), 4–5.

LRP Publications. (1994b). Parents, advocates rail against programs that thwart education and inclusion. *Inclusive Education Programs, 1*(12).

Lynch, E. (1981). *But I've tried everything! A special educator's guide to working with parents.* State of California Department of Education.

Lyon, S., & Preis, A. (1983). Working with families of severely handicapped persons. In M. Seligman (Ed.), *The family with a handicapped child.* New York: Grune & Stratton.

Markel, G., & Greenbaum, J. (1985). *Parents are to be seen and heard: Assertiveness in educational planning for handicapped children.* Ann Arbor, MI: Greenbaum & Markel Association.

May, J. (1991). *Fathers of children with special needs: New horizons.* Bethesda, MD: Association for the Care of Children's Health.

McCarthy, M. (1994). Inclusion and the law: Recent judicial developments. In *Research Bulletin,* Center for Evaluation, Development, and Research. Phi Delta Kappa. November, No. 13.

McGonigel, M., Kaufmann, R., & Johnson, B. (Eds.). (1991). *Guidelines and recommended practices for the individualized family service plan.* Bethesda, MD: National Early Childhood Technical Assistance System, and the Association for the Care of Children's Health.

McWilliam, P.J., & Bailey, D. (1993). *Working together with children and families: Case studies in early intervention.* Baltimore: Paul H. Brookes.

Minnesota Inclusive Education Technical Assistance Program. (1991). *Inclusive education in Minnesota: What's working.* Minneapolis: Minnesota Inclusive Education Technical Assistance Program.

Mori, A. (1983). *Families of children with special needs: Early intervention techniques for the practitioner.* Rockville, MD: Aspen.

National Association of State Boards of Education. (1992). Winners all: A call for inclusive schools. The report of the NASBE Study Group on Special Education. Alexandria, VA: National Association of State Boards of Education.

National Resource Coalition. *Starting and operating support groups: A guide for parents.* Chicago: Family Resource Coalition.

Oster, A. (1985). Keynote address at Comprehensive approaches to disabled and at-risk infants, toddlers and their families. In *Equals in this partnership: Parents of disabled and at-risk infants and toddlers speak to professionals.* Washington, DC: National Center for Clinical Infant Programs.

Powers, L. (1993). Disability and grief. In G. Singer & L. Powers (Eds.), *Families, disability, and empowerment: Active coping skills and strategies for family interventions.* Baltimore: Paul H. Brookes.

Project CHOICES/Early CHOICES. (1992). Project CHOICES/Early CHOICES inservice materials. Springfield, IL: Illinois State Board of Education.

Rose, D., & Smith B. (1993). Preschool mainstreaming: Attitude barriers and strategies for addressing them. *Young Children, 48*(4), 59–62.

Rosenkoetter, S., Hains, A., & Fowler, S. (1994). *Bridging early services for children with special needs and their families: A practical guide for transition planning.* Baltimore: Paul H. Brookes.

Rundall, R., & Smith, S. (1985). *Parent readiness levels: A developmental approach to parent intervention.* Training module. Illinois Governor's Planning Council on Developmental Disabilities.

Saint-Exupéry, A. de. (1943). *The little prince.* New York: Harcourt Brace.

Santelli, B., Turnbull, A., Lerner, E., & Marquis, J. (1993). *Parent to parent programs: A unique form of mutual support for families of persons with disabilities.* In G. Singer & L. Powers (Eds.), *Families, disability, and empowerment: Active coping skills and strategies for family interventions.* Baltimore: Paul H. Brookes.

Simpson, R. (1990). *Conferencing parents of exceptional children.* Austin, TX: Pro-Ed.

Singer, G., Irvin, L., Irvine, B., Hawkins, N., Hegreness, J., & Jackson, R. (1993). Helping families adapt positively to disability. In G. Singer & L. Powers (Eds.), *Families, disability, and empowerment: Active coping skills and strategies for family interventions.* Baltimore: Paul H. Brookes.

Shea, T., & Bauer, A. (1991). *Parents and teachers of children with exceptionalities: A handbook for collaboration.* Boston: Allyn & Bacon.

Smith, B., Rose, D., Ballard, J., & Walsh, S. (1991). *The preschool (part B) and infant/toddler (part H) programs of the Individuals With Disabilities Education Act (IDEA) and the 1991 amendments (P.L. 102-119): Selected comparisons.* Paper.

Stayton, V., Allred, K., Cooper, C., Kilbane, K., & Whitson, V. (1990). *A family systems approach for individualizing services.* Training module for Illinois Technical Assistance Project. South Metropolitan Association, Flossmoor, IL, and the Illinois State Board of Education.

Turnbull, A., & Turnbull, H.R. (1990). *Families, professionals, and exceptionality: A special partnership.* New York: Macmillan.

Webster, E., & Ward, L. (1993). *Working with parents of young children with disabilities.* San Diego: Singular Press.

Westman, M. (1991). A great beginning: Early intervention services. *Inclusive education in Minnesota: What's working.* Minnesota Inclusive Education Technical Assistance Program, Spring/Summer.

Wilmore, E. (1994–95). When your child is special. *Educational Leadership, 52*(4), 60–62.

Ziegler, M. (1992). Parent advocacy and children with disabilities: A history. *OSERS News in Print.* Summer 1992, 4–6.

PART TWO

Communication

Chapter 5

WRITTEN CORRESPONDENCE

READERS WILL BE ABLE TO:

- Describe strategies and techniques utilizing written communication that facilitate home-school communication.
- Describe the roles of a newsletter and a parent handbook in improving communication between home and school.
- Identify strategies used to create a welcoming atmosphere for families in schools.
- Discuss methods used to collect information and opinions from parents.
- Identify the role of portfolios and alternative assessments in establishing clear communication between teachers and families about student progress.

Communication is a critical element in the formation and maintenance of successful partnerships. Clear, concise, and direct messages convey respect for the questions parents have about issues regarding their children. In this fast-paced decade of the '90s, it has never been more important that parents and teachers understand each other's motives, feelings, and concerns. It is for this reason that educators need to approach each parent relationship with an open-minded attitude, the willingness to learn, and a spirit of cooperation (Swick, 1991).

Educators taking that first step will find that there are numerous ways of conveying messages to the home. This chapter will detail the many written communication strategies that are available for school-to-home use. Methods of one-way communication include Individual Teacher's Communications to Parents, and Schoolwide/Group Communications to Parents.

Strategies described are:

notes	parent handbooks
letters	yearbooks
happy-grams	parent bulletin boards
report cards	suggestion boxes

brochures	surveys
passport systems	daily logs
parent contracts	newsletters
informational packets	

The impression made on families by the wording, timeliness, and subject matter of written materials chosen can influence their feelings toward the school or center, principal or director, and teachers (Swap, 1987). Some considerations to keep in mind are:

- Are printed materials sent home in enough time to allow parents to schedule and plan for upcoming events?
- Is everything spelled correctly? Check for good sentence structure and grammar.
- Is the wording readable and jargon-free? Is feedback sought in a regular manner?
- Are the efforts at communication sporadic, or regular and reliable?
- How is information communicated to parents with limited-English proficiency?

In an effort to help schools and centers review the level of effectiveness of their written communications, have a committee of teachers complete the chart Home-School Communication Assessment (Figure 5.1), identifying strengths and weaknesses so that appropriate changes can be made where necessary.

Creating true partnerships in education involves outreach to parents by the administrators and teachers. Some will participate by invitation alone; others will be more passive until they are comfortable enough with the personnel and building to take an active role (Honig, 1979). Whatever the level of involvement, communication is at the cornerstone of each relationship.

■ BARRIERS TO EFFECTIVE WRITTEN COMMUNICATION

One of the greatest barriers to the individual teacher is time. Traditionally, the school schedule does not permit a true commitment to the purpose of communicating with families (Swap, 1993). Teachers are given little, if any, planning time for curriculum tasks and less for communicating with parents outside of the standard parent-teacher conference. Many early childhood teachers in day-care situations are on duty almost every hour the children are in the facility. Teachers frequently use breaks, lunch hours, and personal time after school to put together newsletters and notes. Understandably, many educators perceive the efforts spent on additional forms of communication as a burden, especially when administrators do not allocate appropriate amounts of time for that purpose (Swap, 1987). It is possible, then, that home-school communication could vary within a school, dependent on the individual teacher's commitment to devote the time necessary for written dialogues with parents.

A second barrier is the lack of sufficient funds to maintain an ongoing publication, such as a newsletter. This lack of funds also contributes to the limited availability of office machines, such as duplicating machines and copiers, used

FIGURE 5.1
Home-School Written Communication Assessment

Written Communication

Mark (X) the appropriate boxes on this chart to indicate the kinds of written communication used in your school.

CHARACTERISTICS OF COMMUNICATION

Communication Media	On Time	Frequent	Easy to Read	Focus on Academic	Encourage Responses	Important Information	Adequate Distribution	No Distribution	Does Not Apply
Letters Home									
Notes									
Report Cards									
Success Reports									
School Newsletters									
Class Newsletters									
Progress Reports									
Parent Surveys									
Parent Handbook									
Passport System									
Meeting Notices									
Activity Calendars									
Brochures									
School Menu									

to reproduce materials for parents. Teachers often are forced to choose between a weekly newsletter or a parent survey, for example, if paper supplies and copying access are severely restricted. Again, the lack of commitment, in the form of time and money, toward improving home-school communication can complicate the efforts of motivated teachers.

Schools and teachers frequently fall into the trap of doing things the way tradition dictates—"It's always been done this way" (Swap, 1987). The majority of today's families are anything but "the way they've always been," and maintaining communication means finding and using innovative ways of keeping the channels open in both directions. Consider the ever-expanding variety of families that schools encounter each year: single-parent families, children under the guardianship of relatives, students in foster care, two-mother/two-father families, blended families, families with children who have special needs, and interracial families (Wickens, 1993). The need for flexibility and sensitivity becomes apparent (Wardle, 1990). It is no longer desirable to think in terms of only mothers and fathers. For many children, there are other significant adults in their lives who desire a connection with the school (Corbett, 1993; Patterson, 1992). In order to feel involved in a child's education, the methods used to communicate must acknowledge parents and other adults' commitment to the child.

The following sections will describe specific techniques and strategies that will assist early childhood professionals in improving the quality of communications between home and school.

INDIVIDUAL TEACHER'S COMMUNICATION TO PARENTS

An important key to building successful relationships with parents is through frequent, positive kinds of communication (Shea & Bauer, 1991; Baskwill, 1989; Cataldo, 1987). Each type of correspondence has specific applications depending on the topic and purpose. Examples of letters, notes, report cards, contracts, and surveys will illustrate the variety and purposes of each type of communication.

LETTERS

Letters are an excellent vehicle for the transmission of lengthy or detailed information that parents need about their children, the school, or policies. A letter can serve the entire group of parents or be written for a specific few. It can also replace lengthy phone conversations or parent meetings, especially if attendance is apt to be poor.

There are a variety of purposes for a parent letter. Often a teacher will send a letter to students in August as a method of introduction, and perhaps to relay registration information or supply lists for the first day of school. This is especially appreciated by parents who are anxious over their young child's adjustment to a new school or program. A warm welcome from the teacher sets a positive tone for the year and is the first step toward creating a relationship with parents and children (Baskwill, 1989). See Figure 5.2.

Letters often accompany the explanation of a new or revised policy that applies to the students, such as library check-out policies, field trip procedures, homework policies, and parent-teacher conference formats. In the case of

FIGURE 5.2
Kindergarten Welcome Letter

August 1996

Dear _____,

Hello! My name is Mrs. Baker and I will be your kindergarten teacher this year. I am very excited about meeting you and your family when you come to Bradley East School for Orientation Day!

Please come to Room 100 on Monday, August 24th, at 9:30 a.m. for a tour of your new classroom, some delicious snacks, and the chance to meet all of the friendly faces here at your new school. You will meet the bus driver, Mr. Martin, and the principal, Mr. Garry.

Please bring your school supplies with you that morning so that we can put them in your cubbie and label it with your name.

* a large box of 64 crayons
* a large box of tissues
* six regular pencils
* one bottle of glue
* one roll of tape

I hope that you will enjoy the rest of your summer, and I will see you on Orientation Day!

Your friend,

Mrs. Baker

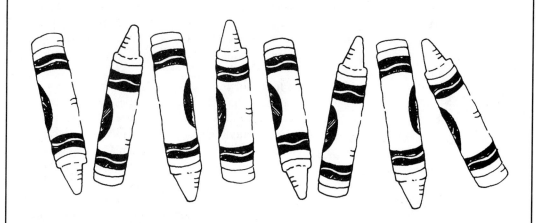

curriculum changes, a letter may be an appropriate tool to explain new information to parents. In the area of language arts, for example, many educators are moving from the traditional basal, workbook, and phonics approach of teaching reading to the more holistic philosophy of whole language. Whole language teachers find it valuable to send letters to parents in order to explain portions of the language arts curriculum as it relates to the whole language philosophy (Fisher, 1991). Such curriculum restructuring typically raises parent concerns that need to be addressed. It is unrealistic to expect parents to understand the philosophy and the attendant changes for day-to-day teachings, even if a parent meeting has been held for that purpose. A letter addressing a particular aspect of whole language—invented spelling, journal writing, or publishing of student books, for example—can be explained in a series of letters as the school year progresses.

One first-grade teacher who is introducing the whole language philosophy to her parents sends home an appropriate journal article reprint each Friday accompanied by a letter explaining how this topic relates to her classroom and its students. In this way she is hoping to increase their awareness of the many unique qualities of this reading/writing approach, and yet not overwhelm parents with too much information at any one time. Parent reactions are positive; they comment that they feel more confident when discussing their child's progress in school because the teacher has shared many of her practices with them as an ongoing project and has provided the necessary background information.

Confidentiality is another purpose of a parent letter. Mailing a letter about a sensitive topic can protect the privacy rights of parents and students. Teachers handling behavior or academic problems find that filing a copy of all correspondence sent home in the student's permanent file is a good way to document action taken on specific problems (Baskwill, 1989).

A parent letter also may serve as the primary method of communication between home and school for rural parents, parents with disabilities, noncustodial parents, and any parent reluctant to attend a conference at school. Often a parent will maintain a continuing "conversation" with a teacher through written letters. It is important to recognize this as an effective link worth the time and effort in order to encourage communication between the home and school (Shea & Bauer, 1991).

Since time is in short supply for most teachers, prewritten parent letters can make it easier to communicate about a variety of topics. Sample letters can be found in books about parent communication or in educational clip-art books. Often these letters can be modified to suit the individual teacher, and thus save the time required to compose an original letter. Companies such as Good Apple, Frank Schaeffer, and Gryphon House publish suitable model letters in books that are subject-specific and include graphics in a pleasing arrangement, ready for photocopying.

To make a letter effective and readable, care must be taken to use clear, jargon-free language that is concise and to the point. Limiting a letter to one page in length increases the chance that it will be read or, at the very least, skimmed. If it is any longer, busy parents are apt to put the letter aside for later reading. If the content cannot fit on one page, consider breaking the topic into two or more separate communications to be distributed at different times. Have a colleague read the letter to ensure the clarity of the message and to act as a proofreader. Teachers and administrators also find that the regular use of a specific color of paper and an identifying program or school logo help letters from school stand out from other materials going home.

WRITING DIFFICULT LETTERS TO PARENTS

One of the most unpleasant tasks a teacher faces is that of writing letters to parents about a behavioral or academic problem. Most teachers are reluctant to compose letters that relay bad news because they lack the confidence and skills necessary to do so without alienating parents. Letters of this nature require a measure of diplomacy so that the parent does not feel attacked or blamed by the school. "Children are parents' most vulnerable spot," and educators must take care not to create situations where sides are drawn between home and school (Hunter, 1991).

Encouraging mutual support is dependent upon the ability of a teacher to convince the parent of the school's genuine concern and its desire to collaborate toward a positive resolution of a problem. Hunter (1991) writes of four messages that become the structure around which every disciplinary communication is built: the message that the child can be successful; the child is not being successful; acknowledgment that the parent cares about his or her child's school performance; and the suggestion for planning together to remedy the situation.

When writing a letter concerning a problem, focus on the concept of collaboration between school and home, staff and family. This sends a positive message of belief in the child's adequacy and the reaffirmation of the parent's concern. The letter also should emphasize the school's willingness to plan with parents for problem resolution, inviting parents into this process. The following sample letters illustrate the incorporation of these four messages.

Dear _____,

Todd has shown leadership among the other boys in class. He is often the first to enthusiastically jump into a new game or center. Sometimes the ability to be the "first" to try new things causes other children to imitate Todd's actions. Todd's recent behavior in the cafeteria has created difficulties for himself and other students in following the rules set by the lunchroom monitor.

I would like to discuss with you ways to help Todd become more positive in his behavior at lunchtime. Please come to school on
_____ at _____. If this time is not convenient for you,
please call me at school between 8:00 and 8:30 a.m. in order to set up
a time.

Sincerely,

Mrs. Baker
555-8480

Dear _____,

Jeremy is an active, happy kindergartner who is energetic and
ready for our center activities each day. His enthusiasm often creates
great interest at the block center, where he especially enjoys spending
his worktime. I was surprised, then, by his use of markers on the
wooden blocks, because it closed the block/construction center for several days.

I would like you to come to school on _____ to discuss ways
to help Jeremy channel his actions toward the classroom materials more
positively. If you cannot be at school at this time please call me between
8:00 and 8:30 a.m. Monday through Friday to arrange a meeting.

Thank you.

Sincerely,

Mrs. Baker
555-8480

Notice the use of a positive opening remark in each letter. Imagine the
feeling a parent would have upon receiving this communication. Strategies
such as conveying appreciation for a child's strengths and attempts to enlist
the parent as a collaborator increases the likelihood of gaining parental support. The overall focus of any letter from school to home should emphasize the
responsibility that teachers and parents share for the child's best interests
and outcomes.

SPONTANEOUS NOTES

Spontaneous notes usually are written to convey less detailed, one-topic messages that involve daily activities in the classroom (Ball, 1985). Information such as conference time changes, minor accidents on the playground, lost books, or humorous anecdotes often are handled through a quick note and sent home with the student (Bundy, 1991). Again, it is important to remain brief when communicating through notes or the process will become impossible to maintain and an important means of communication lost. Clip-art books carry numerous short forms designed for spontaneous notes that are catchy and pleasing to the eye. Many carry headings to alert the parent to the primary message. For example:

"Wanted you to know . . ."

"Dropping a line to remind you . . ."

"_____ is having a great day because . . ."

Teachers who make a point of staying in touch with parents on a regular basis usually keep a supply of notes on a clipboard handy for playground or recess time, snack times, or free-reading time when they can complete a few notes for daily distribution. Quick response to a parent note or question will greatly improve the communication between home and school and, in the process, strengthen the relationship between teachers and families (Rick, 1987).

When using notes to share interesting anecdotes about individual students, it is important to keep a checklist to be sure that notes are written for each child on a regular basis. In this way, recordkeeping is simplified and use of notes increases because it is convenient for the teacher. The note can be an effective substitute, especially in schools where phone calls are difficult to complete due to a lack of private facilities or free time.

One Head Start program uses an observation log to help parents know what activities occupied their child during the day and to stimulate conversation between parent and child. See Figure 5.3. Parents accustomed to receiving good news will not regard communication from the school as a sign of a problem (Cataldo, 1987). When, and if, a problem does arise, the lines of communication and the establishment of a partnership will already be in place. Parents are more likely to work cooperatively with the school if they feel that the teacher has true respect and genuine concern for their child. Laying the groundwork early in the school year for a positive relationship will ultimately benefit everyone (Rich, 1985).

HAPPY-GRAMS

Happy-grams are very brief notes that generally have more graphics than words and convey a special message about improvement, good behavior, or cooperative acts (Autrey, 1989). The happy-gram is a nice "pat on the back" for a

FIGURE 5.3
Daily Activity Log

To help you talk
with your child about
his or her school day,
here is a brief description
of what your child did today.

CENTERS WHERE YOUR CHILD PLAYED: _____
_____

LANGUAGE: _____
_____

SPECIAL ACTIVITIES: _____
_____
_____

GYM: _____
_____

SNACKS WE ATE: _____
_____

MY JOB: _____
_____
_____

OTHER: _____
_____

FIGURE 5.4
Happy-Grams

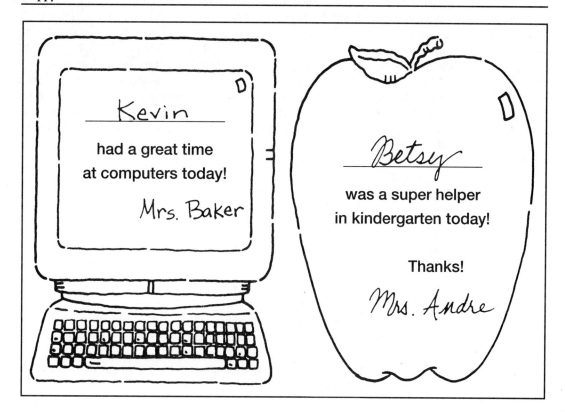

student and lets parents know that their child was noticed. Clip-art books and teaching supplement books often have several types of happy-grams that can be duplicated for use. A teacher can easily design her own using school logos, mascots, or student-drawn designs. The purpose of a happy-gram is to let parents see that small deeds or improvements are acknowledged and appreciated. As with spontaneous notes, a ready supply of these kept in a visible location make it fairly easy to complete a couple in just a minute or two. Generally, the simplest happy-grams require only that the child's name and date be filled in (see Figure 5.4). If a return response is desired, a space can be provided at the bottom of the happy-gram for that purpose (Carney, 1984). Make sure that happy-grams go home to all students periodically.

PARENT CONTRACTS

Home-school contracts demonstrate a commitment to parent involvement by requiring a planned promise of participation (Swap, 1993). Some schools or centers utilize a one-way contract, signed by parents, to agree to a minimum number of hours of volunteering, observation, attendance at conferences, or participation in parent education classes. Ideally, the contract would be a two-way document, signed by parents and school personnel, outlining each party's responsibilities toward the child's education. School personnel could agree to provide a range of resources for meeting a child's academic needs, appropriate methods of reporting student progress, and opportunities for conferences.

Swap (1993) suggests that the use of contracts should not reflect a deficit approach. Emphasis should be on what will be done by all parties involved instead of consequences of negative actions, should they occur. Contracts that specify punitive courses of action will not set a positive tone for the relationship.

PARENT SURVEYS AND QUESTIONNAIRES

Parent surveys and questionnaires are an efficient means of gathering information from large groups of people (Swick, 1984; Hunter, 1989). There are a number of reasons to do a needs assessment or survey of a group of parents (Swap, 1987):

1. To determine what parents want to contribute to the school, center, or program.
2. To determine what parents want to learn about or discuss.
3. To determine what service or programs parents want the school to initiate.
4. To determine what changes parents would like to make in existing programs and services.

Considering these purposes may help to channel thinking and to narrow down the specific information that is needed. Decisions on the focus of the questions should be based on input from teachers, principals, and parents (Biagini, 1991). Is the staff already investigating major program changes, an improved volunteer program, or the initiation of a new service? A needs assessment could provide valuable insights from the future participants that would be helpful in shaping the activity (App, 1991). See Figure 5.5.

A teacher may devise her own survey to gain information about a child's home environment and previous experiences. One kindergarten teacher utilizes a questionnaire, filled out by parents at orientation meetings, to provide background information about incoming students. Parents have the opportunity to share their views of their child as a learner and describe any areas of concern. See Figure 5.6.

Another kindergarten teacher surveys parents about the literacy environment at home and the child's previous experience with books (Baskwill, 1989). Baskwill finds that this information helps her design appropriate and realistic goals for incoming students and gives her an estimate on how much support for literacy exists in the home. See Figure 5.7.

FIGURE 5.5
Request for Basic Information about a Child

KINDERGARTEN INFORMATION QUESTIONNAIRE

CHILD'S NAME: _____

PARENTS' NAMES: _____

ADDRESS: _____

PHONE: _____

CHILD'S BIRTHDAY: _____

WILL YOUR CHILD RIDE A BUS? _____ NUMBER: _____

DID YOUR CHILD ATTEND PRESCHOOL? _____

NAME: _____

Does your child have any health problems of which the teacher should be aware?

Does your child require any special medicine?

Is your child allergic to anything? If yes, how does it affect the child?

Does your child have any speech problems?

Does your child have any vision problems? If yes, does the child wear glasses?

Does your child have any hearing problems or frequent ear infections?

What are any special interests of your child?

What do you see as your child's academic strengths?

What do you see as your child's academic weaknesses?

Would you be willing to help in the classroom?

Would you be willing to come to the classroom to share information?

___ Career (What?)_____

___ Hobbies or Interests (What?) _____

___ Other areas: _____

Specify other ways you might be interested in helping:

Would you be willing to help on projects at home if you are unavailable during the school day?

___ Cutting   ___ Sewing   ___ Donating Items

___ Other areas: (please specify) _____

LIST ANY AREAS OF CONCERN OR OTHER THINGS YOU WANT US
TO BE AWARE OF ON THE BACK OF THIS FORM.

WELCOME TO KINDERGARTEN!!!!

FIGURE 5.6
Request for Parent's Observations about a Child

HELP ME KNOW YOUR CHILD

Date _____

Dear Parent/Guardian:

I invite you to share with me the talents, interests, and habits of your child, _____ , so that I may be prepared to teach in the best way possible. Please share concerns about your child so we can have a cooperative team approach to education. Call and let me know when you would like to visit our classroom or just talk about your child. The best time to reach me during the day is from _____ to _____ p.m. at _____ (telephone).

1. My child learns best by _____

_____

2. Some things I do at home to help my child learn are _____

_____

3. Right now my child's goal/dream is _____

_____

4. You will know my child is having problems when _____

_____

5. The thing my child likes best about school is _____

_____

6. One difficulty my child has at school is _____

_____

7. When my child is having difficulty learning something, I find it works best to

_____

_____

8. Questions I would like to discuss at a parent/teacher conference include

_____

_____

Please return this form to   Teacher_____

FIGURE 5.7
Playgroup Survey

OPINIONNAIRE
PLEASE FILL THIS OUT IF
YOU HAVE ATTENDED PLAYGROUP

1. Playgroup is held at a time that works well for me. _____ (yes or no)

2. The physical facility is: poor   good   could be improved
If "poor" or "could be improved," please list suggestions:

_____

3. Activities and play opportunities fit the needs of my child:
        poor   very well   could be improved

4. Circle time is: don't like   ok   good   very good

5. Guidelines and procedures about the use of the facility, toys, children's behavior are:
        clear   unclear
        What I don't know is: _____
        My suggestion is: _____

6. Interaction sessions (playdough, fingerpaint) have been appropriate for my child's age and interests.   true   false

7. Handouts are of interest to me.   true   false
Other information I'd like to see offered:_____
Please include any suggestions, constructive criticism, or bright ideas that you may have on the back of this sheet. Thanks!

When the survey deals with parent opinion, it is important to follow up with the survey results so that parents see that their opinions were read and tabulated (Goetaski, 1983). A general summary of the information gathered and ideas about the future use of the data will communicate to the parents an honest attempt on the part of the school to incorporate their opinions into the planning of new programs.

Once a program or service is instituted, it is wise to do an annual evaluation survey to generate feedback from participants. Again, publish results in order to share findings with all parents. For example, in response to a survey of prekindergarten parents' interests in school-sponsored summer activities, a school could tell parents: "68% of parents requested a parent-child story hour to be held at the library weekly during the summer vacation. We are investigating the feasibility of beginning such a program with the help of the local library."

TIPS ON COMPOSING A QUESTIONNAIRE OR SURVEY

1. Determine what you need to know and why. Review question content carefully so that the data collected provides meaningful information. Answers to the survey questions should provide necessary facts to assist decision makers.

2. Identify who is conducting the survey, the purpose, and the goal of gathering the information. People are reluctant to take their time to fill out a survey without knowing the organization's name or the reason for doing the assessment. If the survey is to be sent to parents and community members instead of being filled out in a group, be certain that this information is clearly stated.

3. Keep the questionnaire or survey brief. One or two pages is the optimum length. Completion and return rates generally drop off if a survey is overly time-consuming.

4. Write clear, jargon-free instructions. Have a test group of parents complete the survey, checking for technical wording or confusing directions.

5. If a rating scale is used:

   ■ Limit the choices to no more than five. For example "excellent," "somewhat helpful," "fair," "not useful," and "did not apply" would be enough choices for parents filling out a workshop evaluation.
   ■ ask only one question at a time.
   ■ include an alternative indicating "don't know" or "does not apply."
   ■ make sure sentence stems grammatically and semantically fit the choices.

6. Include blank space for respondent comments and encourage individuals to add personal remarks.

7. Consider grouping similar topic areas together to simplify survey completion.

8. Create a visually appealing, easy-to-read survey that is free of spelling and grammatical errors.

9. Clearly indicate when and where the completed survey should be returned.

(List is adapted from Swap, 1987.)

PASSPORT SYSTEMS

Passport systems and dialogue journals are two effective means of maintaining daily communication between home and school. Research has shown that daily communication improves the quality of the parent-teacher relationship (Runge & Shea, 1975). A passport can be as simple as a notebook that travels with a student to school each day and allows the teacher to carry on a written conversation about the child's behavior or academic progress.

It is helpful to introduce the passport during a conference so that the method can be fully explained and a plan of action determined that is agreeable to both teacher and parents. It is important to the success of the passport system that the child be included in setting up this process (Shea & Bauer, 1991). Parents and teachers should explain the procedure and encourage the child's cooperation in transporting the notebook to and from school. Care should be taken to help the child understand that the messages are meant to help, not exist as a source of punishment. Emphasis on a positive reward system instead of a punitive one will encourage the child to participate (Popkin, 1987).

A passport system can be as general or as focused as the situation requires. The teacher may wish to comment on the child's overall behavior during the course of the day, or focus on one specific behavior. It is important to remember that examining one or two behaviors at a time will result in a higher rate of success for the child.

A planning session to begin the passport notebook should include:

1. *Discussion of goals for the child.*   Keep goals short and attainable. Set short-term goals that move toward the desired result. Make sure that parents and the teacher are in agreement about the goals that are set (Shea & Bauer, 1991).

2. *A description of the incentive and point systems being employed.*   In order to gain the child's cooperation in delivering the passport, many teachers find that a point system tied to incentives ensures an acceptable level of compliance. During the planning conference, teachers and parents can collaborate on the number of points, as well as the frequency of rewards that seem appropriate for the age of the child (Shea & Bauer, 1991).

3. *Discussion of the nature of feedback.*   The teacher should model the type and length of the entries so that parents know what to expect and understand the kinds of comments that are most helpful to the teacher. Assurances to parents that it is their input that is valued rather than their spelling or handwriting will go a long way toward gaining full cooperation. Teachers need to be sensitive to the concerns some parents may experience when writing to the school, especially if their literacy level is low. Use informal language to make the entries as clear and as jargon-free as possible (Berger, 1995).

4. *Periodic conferences to discuss student progress in greater depth.*   Plan to meet periodically for an in-depth discussion of the child's progress. Agree on a tentative schedule and then keep the appointments, even when things are going well. This will reinforce the concept that not all conferences are about problems.

Since the goal of the notebook is ongoing communication, it is important to bear in mind that positive references are more easily received by parents than are daily doses of negative comments or criticism. Emphasis on positive behaviors can be modeled for parents through use of the passport system. As an example, consider Mark, who is 5 years old and in kindergarten. He is generally disruptive during group and center time by using a very loud voice, talking out repeatedly when others are speaking, and teasing other students with silly names. His parents and his teacher have agreed to focus on Mark's disruptive speech first.

POSITIVE EXAMPLE:

Mark exercised self-control during show-and-tell today and responded to the first reminder given to let others have their turns. He is still working on quiet behavior in the library during storytelling time.

NEGATIVE EXAMPLE:

Mark had to be reminded three times during show-and-tell to stop yelling out. The librarian had to remove him from the group because of his loud talking.

As a teacher, try to imagine being on the receiving end of your comments from time to time to ensure that lapses into purely "bad news" entries have not become the focus of the passport. It can be very discouraging for a parent, as well as a student, to be unsuccessful for long stretches of time. If there is little or no progress, it may be necessary to consider shorter intervals for reporting success or a modification of the reward system.

METHODS OF ASSESSMENT/REPORTING PROGRESS TO PARENTS

There is probably no single communication between home and school that is as emotionally charged and misunderstood as the report card. Parents expect to find a single grade that summarizes their child's progress and achievement in each content area. The traditional three letter (E = excellent, S = satisfactory, and U = unsatisfactory) or five letter (A, B, C, D, F) systems are often complicated by the use of pluses and minuses, which do little to clarify the status of the child's achievement in any given subject. Interpretation of the grading system and how individual grades are computed is further confused by the fact that grading scales and criteria for assigning grades vary not only from school to school, and grade to grade, but between individual teachers. Report cards often include the assignment of an effort grade, which is usually translated into a conduct grade by both parents and teachers. It is little wonder that many parents feel anxiety and tension when confronted with the report card four times each year (Routman, 1991).

One of the greatest drawbacks to the traditional report card is that it conveys very little specific information about grade level expectations relative to the child's performance and developmental level (Routman, 1988). Parents of even "A" students would find it difficult to compose a list of the skills and behaviors that comprise a reading, writing, or math grade. They should not be expected to do so. However, it *is* the responsibility of the educational system to provide parents with an accurate picture of the myriad of skills and behaviors that contribute to becoming an accomplished reader, writer, and problem solver. In order to be involved in their child's education, it is necessary to inform parents of their child's specific strengths and weaknesses as well as the particular expectations for academic achievement at each grade level.

PORTFOLIOS

Recent research concerning ways to improve reporting methods to parents has yielded several promising practices that present to the parent a more complete and detailed assessment of their child as a learner and a thinker (NAEYC position paper, 1988). Educators in early childhood and primary classrooms have included the *portfolio approach* as a method of charting student progress. A portfolio is a folder or file with individual work samples of both the child's and teacher's choosing that can be examined to assess growth and maturation in the learning process (Fisher, 1991; Wolf, 1989). Teachers select samples, date them, and often write an anecdote on the back to describe the focus of the lesson at the time. Parents and teachers can then observe strengths, weaknesses, and areas of interest that reveal specific information about the child and his or her development level (Chittenden & Courtney, 1989). A teacher may add notes on writing and reading conferences held throughout the quarter. Portfolios also may include inventories, checklists, and rubrics that organize skills and information about particular content areas in addition to collected work samples.

Bobbi Fisher, a whole language kindergarten teacher and author of *Joyful Learning* (1991), has devised a system of child assessment folders, class assessment profiles, and anecdotal class grids for the maintenance of progress report records to be sent to parents or filed in portfolios. Charting individual behaviors involves a system of six symbols and numbers to be used in a flexible manner to record observations as accurately as possible:

NUMBER SYSTEM	SYMBOL SYSTEM
1 = Most of the time	* = Has full command
2 = Some of the time	. = In control
3 = Not noticed yet	0 = Needs time

These are transcribed from the class assessment profile observations in three content areas: math, reading, and writing.

Individual assessment profiles then become the basis for reporting to parents on a child's progress. In addition, the parent is becoming educated about the specific behaviors and skills that correlate with the expectations at each grade level.

Raines and Canady (1990) also advocate the use of multiple observations, tape-recorded interviews of children's reading, and examples of students' writing, all of which may become a part of a portfolio. Teachers collect, date, and record notes on the selected samples to be filed in the portfolio. Teachers record observations of the child's interest in books and listening behaviors, as well as make notations on story retellings and shared reading experiences. These logs may also be kept for use at parent-teacher conferences (Sharp, 1989).

One advantage of the portfolio method is that it can be adapted for use with any age or grade (Whitman & Baskwill, 1988). On the early childhood level (birth through third grade), the portfolio approach can become a valuable aid in documenting the maturation through the developmental stages of writing, emergent literacy behaviors, and a variety of social skills (Lee, 1992). When a narrative is written for the report card or progress report, the teacher focuses on the "whole child" as a listener, speaker, beginning reader, writer, and thinker. Comments include the level of social-emotional development and fine and gross motor coordination. The use of multiple assessments allows a teacher to record more than just "paper and pencil" scores from standardized tests and screenings (Leavitt & Eheart, 1991; Paulson, Paulson, & Meyer, 1991). A parent and teacher can more easily assess the impact each facet of development has on the whole child as a learner when all domains of development are fully examined. In this way, parents are also learning about the process of reading and writing, the expectations for the individual grade level, and the rate at which maturation and important developmental milestones can be expected to occur.

REPORT CARDS

For teachers in many districts, the traditional report card is a required format for reporting progress to parents. Improvements on the singular letter or number grade can be found by schools experimenting with report card terminology. Modification of the standard reporting instruments include revision of descriptors and categories to allow greater accuracy and depth in conveying information to parents.

Many school districts are revising the descriptors used on the traditional report card in order to more accurately reflect the child's developmental level. Routman (1991) indicates the importance of utilizing descriptors that indicate developmental readiness, instead of failure or mediocrity as conveyed by letter grade assignments. Her research has shown that the specific words used to convey meaning to parents are critical, and for that reason words and phrases need to be chosen carefully. For example, instead of a high-medium-low rating system, Routman advocates the use of less evaluative words. The terms "proficient," "consistently," "usually," and "effectively demonstrated" are less judgmental and more informative than "high" to indicate an accomplished reader and writer. To indicate an average level of proficiency, the words "demonstrated some of the time," "developing," and "generally" can be employed. Levels that have not yet been mastered are more accurately described by "not noticed yet," "working on," or "infrequently," rather than by "unsatisfactory" or "cannot." The goal of a concerned educator is not only that parents obtain a fair assessment of their child's progress but that they begin to understand the skills that build upon each other in the process of learning.

In support of more effective communication, many school districts are revising reporting methods to parents and replacing the traditional grading system with a more flexible, informative assessment. Routman (1991) describes a checklist and narrative format used in the K-3 grades in her district; letter grades begin in the fourth grade. Checklists comment on observable behaviors that correlate with those used by Fisher's Individual Assessment Profile. The system of "O" (outstanding), "S" (satisfactory), "I" (improving), and "N" (needs improvement) did not match their school's philosophy about language learning and fostered competition among parents. The terms were replaced with descriptors such as "consistently," "occasionally," "seldom," and "not evaluated at this time."

The descriptors and behaviors observed should be individualized to fit a program and age level. A Head Start or prekindergarten class may focus on social-emotional skills and preemergent literacy behaviors and share that information with parents at conference time. Kindergarten teachers should develop an assessment tool to fit the curriculum used in their school or district. In lieu of formal report cards, kindergarten parents often attend parent-teacher conferences and receive a midyear progress report. The report is used to help the teacher and parents stay current with the child's progress and is reevaluated at the end of kindergarten. Parents benefit from the detailed listing of anticipated skills to be covered in kindergarten. When discussing behavior, emerging literacy skills, and social development, parents and teachers can communicate more effectively and efficiently when both understand the curriculum and expectations.

SUMMARY OF NEW APPROACHES

The task of improving communication between parents and teachers regarding student achievement and progress is addressed by Routman in *Transitions*

(1988). While many school districts continue to require standardized testing and the inclusion of scores in a student's file, Routman has developed a comprehensive list of evaluative methods to be used in conjunction with test scores to create an accurate profile:

> running records
>
> tape-recorded oral reading
>
> oral responses
>
> oral reading records, folders, and notebooks
>
> reading response logs
>
> writing journals
>
> writing folders
>
> conference notes and interviews
>
> written tests
>
> written responses for real purposes
>
> extension activities
>
> self-evaluation

Any of these systems used in combination with the portfolio and anecdotal records will show development on more than one level (see Figures 5.8, 5.9, and 5.10). Empowering parents to become their child's partner in the development of reading and writing skills results in many benefits for the parent, child, and teacher. Since collaboration between home and school is the primary goal of communication, it is imperative that teachers assist parents in becoming able participants in this process.

GROUP/SCHOOLWIDE COMMUNICATIONS

NEWSLETTERS

Newsletters are an extremely important channel of communication between parents and schools, community resources, hospitals, doctors' offices, and many other institutions (Becker & Epstein, 1982). Newsletters are as diverse as the organizations that produce them. Newsletters from public libraries inform parents about upcoming children's events; newsletters from hospitals describe scheduled classes and support groups; and newsletters from community resources such as museums, zoos, and the YMCA keep parents in touch with programs for children and families. Schools and day-care centers often will publish a newsletter about their programs in order to keep parents up-to-date on the latest events, policy and personnel changes, and general news pertaining to the

FIGURE 5.8
Language Arts Observation Form

Child's Work and Behavior in Language Arts
(cite specific indications of skills or knowledge)

Settings and Activities	Examples of Child's Activities
Story Time: Teacher reads to class (responses to story line, child's comments, questions, elaborations)	
Independent Reading: Book time (nature of books child chooses or brings in, process of selecting, quiet or social reading)	
Writing: (journal stories, alphabet, dictation)	
Reading, Group/Individual: (oral reading strategies, discussion of text, responses to instruction)	
Reading Related Activities, Tasks: (responses to assignments or discussion focusing on word letter properties, word games/experience charts)	
Informal Settings: (use of language in play, jokes, story–telling, conversation)	
Books and Print as Resource: (use of books for projects; attention to signs, labels, names; locating information)	
Other:	

FIGURE 5.9
Reading Record from a Child's Folder

TA = Teacher Assistance   Child's Name ____M____

‖ = Pause   Teacher___M.J.___Grade _1_

                             Date ___5/11/95___

                                      1st Reading

FLY WITH ME Teacher Read Title

        w   TA
Fly <u>with</u> me. isolated w

                      TA
Fly with me‖ <u>up</u>‖ <u>and</u> up.   —— Looked back to page 2
                                        Re-read sentence on page 2
Fly with me down‖ <u>and</u> down. ←   several times then read "and"

Fly with me into the‖ clouds Looked at picture

 TA   TA   TA
<u>and</u> <u>around</u> and <u>around</u>. Looked back to page 2 but this time
        Let's go fly over   couldn't remember "and"
Long ‖ <u>Look out for</u> the hill. added "over"
Pause   ∧
        let's go fly over a river
     <u>Look out for</u> the <u>bridge</u>. "added over"
                   ∧
 Let's not Fly   omit again
     <u>Look out for</u> the ground.
                ∧

                    (40 words)

text	substitution		text	substitution
with	" w "		the	a
and	———		bridge	river
around	———		ground	again
look	let's			
out	go			
for	fly			

FIGURE 5.10
Language Arts Checklist

Kindergarten and First-Grade Language Arts Outcomes

Name_____ Date_____ Grade_____

Attitudes   The student:
1. Is comfortable speaking in front of others.
2. Values and respects what others have to say.

Concepts   The student:
1. Understands when it is important to listen.
2. Knows language is used to share ideas and feelings.

LISTENING/SPEAKING LEARNING INDICATORS The student:	Usually	Occasionally	Working On	Comments
1. begins to develop active listening skills (looks at speaker, responds appropriately)				
2. follows simple oral directions				
3. listens attentively while others read				
4. remembers ideas, characters, and events from stories				
5. expresses complete thoughts				
6. uses age-appropriate vocabulary				
7. participates in class discussions				
8. participates in chants, poetry, dramatizations, etc.				
9. retells familiar stories				
10. speaks audibly with accurate pronunciation and standard English				

class or center. Researchers publish newsletters to reach an audience interested in current studies, trends, and legislation concerning children and families. As a source of information, newsletters are invaluable for keeping parents abreast of the things they need to know for and about their children (Swick, 1991; Davies, 1991).

FACTORS TO CONSIDER

There are several factors to consider before undertaking the publication of a newsletter; reviewing these may help a school or center determine whether a newsletter is the best method available. First, decide if the information to be delivered is already being presented to the target audience in another form: workshops, conferences, magazines, or other school publications (Neugebauer, 1981). To be useful to the proposed audience, a newsletter must contain articles that will be timely and relevant. Avoid duplication of the efforts of another source, such as the school office, which may be doing an adequate job of conveying specific types of news for parents. The staff may decide that parent meetings or "make it and take it workshops" accomplish the stated purpose more effectively if curriculum information is the goal. When it is decided that a newsletter is the best vehicle for dispensing information, consideration of several factors can help create a focus for the publication.

In order to write a successful newsletter an audience must be determined. In a school setting, for example, will the news be strictly for the parents, or is it also for other teachers in the school or center? Will the news be about a specific class, or will all classes be included in one general effort? The audience needs to be clearly defined so that the material will be relevant to the readers. It is also wise to consider the literacy level of the primary audience, ensuring that the publication is useful to those for whom it is intended (Neugebauer, 1992).

The next task is to determine the overall purpose of the newsletter. Examine the partial listing of purposes a school newsletter may adopt. Several may be worked into one publication; again, it is crucial to state the purpose in order to judge what is appropriate to print for a particular audience. An editor of a school paper, for example, could consider the following purposes:

- to keep parents informed about classroom activities (Harms & Cryer, 1978).
- to educate parents with information on child development.
- to provide insight into the educational purposes of classroom activities (Harms & Cryer, 1978).
- to keep teachers informed about events in other classrooms.
- to act as a "clearinghouse" for parenting books, videos, parent education classes, and events in the community designed to appeal to families (Shea & Bauer, 1991).
- to assist in the recruitment of volunteer help (Shea & Bauer, 1991).
- to acknowledge donations of time, materials, and money (Neugebauer, 1981).

A school or center may choose a single purpose as a primary focus or use a combination of these to achieve the correct balance of information. Another factor to be considered is the choice of an editor/writer for the newsletter (Baskwill, 1992). Some publications come from a director's office and are totally under his or her control, while others have submissions from classroom teachers, parents, and students. Another type of newsletter is one that is published by the individual teacher for and about his or her students. If the objective is to be the source of a variety of information, it may be wise to include many people on the staff and appoint one person as the editor. Special care should be taken to choose someone who has excellent writing and grammar skills and who is conscientious about details and deadlines. If the purpose is solely to educate parents, it may be wise to leave all editorial choices to the newsletter originator, who will be responsible for the entire content.

Time must be allocated to research, write, edit, and produce a good newsletter. If there is the possibility of release time for handling the duties of writing and editing, be certain it will be of an ongoing nature. If it is to be the sole responsibility of a classroom teacher (to be added to an already long list of tasks), then careful consideration will need to be given to the length and frequency of publication.

CONTENT AREAS

There are a variety of content ideas that can be included in the publication of a newsletter. Some are regular features, appearing in every issue, while others appear when appropriate. It is important to have regular features that parents can anticipate reading; if specific types of information are routinely included, the newsletter will develop a good readership.

For example, the Frank Porter Graham Child Development Center in Chapel Hill, NC, devised a "talk-about page" to encourage discussion between a parent and child about the past week's activities and to provide "language starters" to facilitate meaningful discussion. It is a regular feature that parents look forward to in each issue, and it provides an extension of the center's emphasis on language activities.

General classroom news is especially effective when specific children's names are included (as long as each child can be mentioned during the year). Be certain to include special projects or productions that students may be involved in; parents are always interested in reading about the wide range of activities that take place in a busy classroom. See Figure 5.11.

Description of upcoming units will explain to parents the educational goals of planned activities. This can be helpful in reviewing classroom routines or in understanding changes to be made in the regular scheduling. It can also be a method of soliciting the donation of particular items needed for a unit, or of receiving volunteer help from parents who may have a talent or skill in the topic area being covered (Wenig & Brown, 1975).

A section covering *parenting ideas* is another content area often covered in a newsletter (Gestwicki, 1987). A particular area of interest can be featured in

FIGURE 5.11
Teacher's Newsletter

SEPTEMBER
BAKER'S BULLETIN

Please check your school calendar for important dates. If you need to talk to me, you may call me at school. I am here from 7:45 until 3:45. Other arrangements can be made if those times aren't convenient.

Also, I would like to offer the class a snack, in the morning, just for the first couple of weeks. I'd appreciate your help if you would send a box of cereal or crackers to school to share with the class. Thanks!

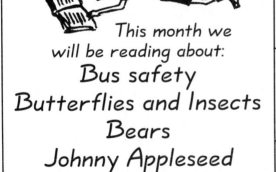

This month we will be reading about:
Bus safety
Butterflies and Insects
Bears
Johnny Appleseed

REMINDER

UPCOMING DATES
No school Labor Day, September 7.

Sept. 10, State Park permission slips due.

Sept. 16, 1/2 day. Dismissal at 2:00 p.m.

Sept. 23-28, Life Education Van at East.

Sept. 26, Johnny Appleseed's Birthday. (more information later)

Sept. 29 East individual school pictures.

BOOK SUGGESTIONS
Hungry Hungry Caterpillar
Brown Bear Brown Bear
Johnny Appleseed

If you have any books or materials that will help us, please send them to school.

BONUS BORDER!!!
Have your child name the pattern at the bottom of the page and color it!

Thanks for the prompt return of the student emergency cards and child release forms.

each issue, perhaps at the suggestion of parents. This type of content can enable the director/editor to describe examples of developmentally sound activities that parents and children can share. It can also be an excellent chance for the editor to elaborate on elements of child development and how they relate to classroom incidents. A teacher may find that an article on separation anxiety in young children, for example, will give a more detailed explanation of behavior occurring in the classroom. Similarly, the sharing of information will aid parents and teachers in choosing a consistent method of handling the numerous incidents that require tact and understanding, both in the classroom and at home. The editor can research (and credit) parenting information from the many available resources or write material of her own.

A popular content area is the *clearinghouse* for reviews of many types of information for parents: magazines, books, videos, speakers, parent education programs, or local library story hours (Neugebauer, R., 1981). A well-organized and accurate listing of events is a great service for busy families and will encourage attendance at quality programs for children.

Children's art and stories also are featured in many newsletters as a way to highlight ongoing activities. Even the simplest newsletter can employ this technique, using a copier to reduce drawings. The newsletter will be eagerly anticipated if a parent sees his child's efforts being publicly recognized (Fisher, 1991; Hagerty, 1988). Again, it is important to include examples from all the classes and/or students on a rotating basis. A simple checklist can be maintained to ensure that all children are included during the year.

A *calendar of events* from a school is an efficient way for parents to know what to expect in the coming weeks and may reduce the need for a steady stream of notes and reminders (see Figure 5.12). For a broader-based newsletter, a calendar can chart upcoming community events of interest to parents and children, important deadlines about screenings, immunization dates, and registrations of class dates and times. For a classroom, the calendar is an easy method of preparing parents for all upcoming activities, deadlines, messy art or playground days, snack contributions, or volunteer obligations. Encouraging parents to use and refer to the calendar will increase the chances that the newsletter will be regularly read.

Want ads are a popular feature, especially for baby equipment, winter clothing, and babysitter needs. Parents can begin to network with other parents for exchange of goods and services within a similar group of families. A simple request for ads to be included in each issue could be posted on the parent bulletin board.

Publicity and public relations needs of the school or center can be handled through the newsletter. Highlighting an exceptional teacher, student, special event, or achievement can be a way of creating local interest in the school or center. This feature can also be a place to thank parents for donations of time, money, or materials. It is important to remember that volunteers need recognition, and this is an excellent way to show appreciation to those who contribute.

FIGURE 5.12
Activity Calendar

January

S	M	T	W	T	F	S
1 WELCOME TO 1996!	**2**	**3**	**4** SNACKS: HOLLY	**5** DRESS FOR OUTSIDE PLAY!	**6**	**7** PAINTING DAY— DRESS IN OLD CLOTHES
8	**9**	**10**	**11** SNACKS: BOBBY	**12**	**13** COOKING: SNOW ICE CREAM	**14**
15 NO SCHOOL TEACHER INSTITUTE	**16**	**17**	**18** CHILI SUPPER 6:00–8:00 PM	**19**	**20**	**21** PROGRESS REPORTS
22 SNACKS: LINDSAY	**23**	**24**	**25** SNACKS: JIMMY	**26** REMINDER: PERMISSION SLIPS DUE TUESDAY!	**27**	**28** 1:00 PM FIELD TRIP TO LIBRARY
29	**30**	**31**				

A year-long theme, such as family literacy, family math, or cooking with children, can also be a regular feature in the newsletter. An editor could choose useful information from a book or magazine and share it with parents in an effort to promote parent-child interaction at home. Copyrighted material should be credited each time it appears.

Staff biographies are another way to familiarize parents with teachers, administrators, and other support employees (Galinsky, 1980). Short descriptions of interests, goals, or talents help parents see staff members as interesting people.

A section of the newsletter devoted to *parent opinions* may help parents "sound off" about issues related to children both in school and around the community. An open forum in the style of "Letters to the Editor" could welcome parent input.

Any parent-teacher or home-school organization operating in the school or agency may desire space for reporting recent activity and *membership news*. A regular feature ensures greater exposure, which could result in increased participation in fundraisers or at meetings.

A *children's page* of simple activities helps ensure that children will deliver the newsletter to their parents. A first-grade teacher solved the problem of newsletters "missing in transit" by including a clip-art pattern of shapes along the bottom of the first page. After their parents were finished with the newsletter, students were to color a pattern similar to patterns being explored in math class. Readership improved dramatically when students had a chance to demonstrate their newly acquired skills.

Community-based organizations can use newsletters to their advantage. They can be a useful tool for fundraising and publicity efforts when distributed in places where members of the desired audience are likely to be: doctors' offices, churches, children's clothing stores, and other places frequented by parents of young children. In this way, news of special programs, classes, and services can reach those who would benefit the most.

Newsletters can also be a vehicle for publicizing past successes and accomplishments, using that forum to gain new members or donors. The St. Louis Ronald McDonald House, for example, uses its newsletter to explain new services, post wish lists for needed supplies, thank fundraisers for their efforts, and publish names of new donors. Some newsletters are devoted to a particular area of interest to parents. For example, *Pediatrics for Parents* deals primarily with topics concerning the health, nutritional, and medical needs of children. In Waban, MA, the Center for Parent Education Newsletter, by Dr. Burton L. White, focuses on programs and information across the United States for children through age 3 and contains updates on pending legislation affecting children's programs. In contrast, *Leaves from the Family Tree* newsletter (Lafayette, LA) and *Pacesetter* (The Parent and Child Education Society, Western Springs, IL) have local coverage of parenting information including articles on family communication, program schedules, membership information, recipes, and regional news.

NEWSLETTER FORMATS

A format can be created through the use of lines, boxes, blank spaces, graphics, and type size. Consider the overall appearance desired when deciding on a format. A newsletter with columns unbroken by lines and boxes creates a scholarly, academic appearance. Boxes and clip art used strategically will evoke a more informal appearance and is easy on the eyes and simple to read and absorb (Neugebauer, R., 1981).

Use of identifying logos is a good way to add graphic interest to each page. Decide on a logo and use related art work to denote article beginnings and endings, important "blurbs" of information, etc. For example, a school district parent education program that features a baby tiger (the district sports mascot) as a key part of its logo uses small pawprints as lead-in graphics for each article. These methods help guide the reader's eyes to specific blocks of information, as well as provide relief from columns of print. The use of logos also helps the reader "connect" the newsletter to the school or agency.

To increase readability, experiment with page layouts, blank space, graphics, and print to find a combination pleasing to the eye. Time spent organizing and arranging in the beginning stages of production is time well spent. When an easy-to-write, appealing-to-read newsletter has been designed, the staff will be proud to share it with administrators, parents, and prospective families. See Figures 5.13 and 5.14.

TYPES OF NEWSLETTERS

There are primarily three types of newsletters a school or center may wish to consider: teacher-generated, prepublished, and professionally printed. There are also combinations of the three that may be adapted to suit individual needs.

The easiest and most personal type is the teacher-generated newsletter that is often handwritten and photocopied in school. The teacher has complete control over the content and total responsibility for distribution to the parents. This type of newsletter is always well received because individual children are named and specific activities described. A simple page with seasonal graphics and a few rules or boxes can be an easy method of organizing information. Newsletters of this type can be mimeographed or photocopied at school on colorful paper. There are numerous school-related clip-art books available at teacher supply stores and libraries that cover every imaginable content area, fundraiser, theme, or holiday. Uncomplicated letterhead forms can be found in many clip-art books, and computer software packages are published for virtually all levels of computer expertise (Krause, 1990). Both methods can create an interesting format that will save time and be simple to use. See Figure 5.15. For minimal investment, this type of newsletter can be within reach of the tightest budgets.

A middle-of-the-road approach could be to purchase a newsletter from a publishing company and personalize it with a school address and logo. This is

FIGURE 5.13
Shape Format Newsletter

FIGURE 5.14
School Newsletter

an easy way to dispense parenting information and articles related to child development without placing undue strain on any single teacher or the director. There are newsletters directed to every age, covering topics relevant to those families. This is a costlier method than the teacher-generated publication, but it requires far less investment of time, research, materials, and labor. Preschools and day-care centers often use a prepublished, purchased newsletter with a handwritten note from individual teachers attached. See Figure 5.16.

A professionally printed newsletter will undoubtedly be too costly for most classrooms or groups, although a center or elementary school could ask a staff member with desktop publishing experience for a comparable effect. There are numerous software programs available that produce newsletters with extremely professional results. A professionally printed newsletter has an almost unlimited range of color combinations, photographs, graphics, and paper quality. Design and layout services generally are included in the cost of printing in order to assure a superior product. See Figure 5.17.

FIGURE 5.15
Library Newsletter

ThePage

Activities of the Edwardsville Public Library
112 South Kansas • 692-7556 • FAX 692-9566 • Edwardsville, Illinois

Fall/Winter 1992

STORY TIMES

Saturdays, 10:30 - 11:15 a.m.
in the Community Room

Taleypo, The Storyteller
and Shel Silverstein send you this.....

INVITATION
If you are a dreamer, come in,
If you are a dreamer, a wisher, a liar
A hope-er, a pray-er, a magic beanbuyer..
If you are a pretender, come sit by my fire
For we have some flax-golden tales to spin.

Come in!   Come in!   Come in!

Sept. 5	I Cannot Go To School Today
19	Boa Constrictor
Oct. 3	The Edge of the World
17	Me and My Giant
31	The Googies Are Coming*
Nov. 14	I Must Remember*
28	What's in the Sack?
Dec. 12	Santa and the Reindeer*
26	If I Had a Brontosaurus

Titles from *Where the Sidewalk Ends*
*Puppet Plays

Land 'O Goshen Storytelling Festival
Sunday, Sept. 27   1 - 5 p.m.

Bring a blanket and a basket of goodies, then settle in
for some good old-fashioned stories with the
**Riverwind Storytellers featuring Kathy Schottel and
Mike Hall.**

Pre-school and Parents Story time
Ages 2½ to 5   10:30 - 11:15 a.m.

Session 1:   Wednesday, September 23 - October 14
Session 2:   Thursday, September 24 - October 15

Registration Required Call the Library - 692-7556

BABY LAP-SIT STORY TIME
Ages 0 to 2   10:30 - 11:50 a.m.

Tuesdays: September 22
                    October 6 and 20
                    November 3 and 17

Registration required by Sept. 18
Call the library at 692-7556

WITCH'S BREW
with the Riverwind Storytellers.

Sponsored by the
Edwardsville Library Friends

Friday, October 23 - 7:00 p.m.
City Park Bandshell

TIME FOR BOOKS

Fall Reading Program

Sign up now until Sept. 13 for your back-to-school
reading.

Pledge to read a certain amount of minutes per week
for 4 weeks - Sept. 13-Oct. 17.

Receive a McDonald food certificate.

**THE NOVEMBER BALLOT WILL INCLUDE THE PROPOSAL FOR THE EDWARDSVILLE
REGIONAL LIBRARY DISTRICT. BE SURE TO VOTE NOVEMBER 3, 1992**

FIGURE 5.16
Early Childhood Program Newsletter

Region 1
Venice - Madison - Granite City
Early Childhood Program

September, 1994   Vol. 10, No. 9

Growing Together
Newsletter for parents of preschool children

Parenting

Parents can be cranky, too!

Even the best parents have days when they're ready to give up.

But instead of trying to be perfect, allow yourself to step off the pedestal once in a while.

Sensitivity, warmth, and enthusiasm are all admirable, desirable qualities for parents.

But parents are also human beings, and human beings are subject to fatigue, illness, and emotional stress.

While it is never acceptable to become abusive with your child, it is okay to be cranky or maybe just worn out. Parenting is a demanding job. And just like any other job, you'll have good days ... and not-so-good days.

So, don't be so hard on yourself when your child gets on your nerves. Give yourself a break. Be cranky if that's what works today.

Tomorrow is another day. ❑

Developmental

Children love to pretend

An important form of play in early childhood is sometimes called fantasy or pretend play.

This type of play usually involves imaginary roles for the child as well as imaginary companions.

By 3 years of age, children want to try out many different roles experienced in the real world: father, mother, doctor, nurse, police officer, or fire fighter.

A child may use pretend play to assume the role of some superhero that he has seen on television. Or maybe he makes up his own character.

Sometimes a child may reenact a previous experience, positive or negative, that he changes to suit his own purpose.

For example, if he was frightened by some monster on television, he might later change the part to a kind monster for the story to have a happy ending.

Preschool children frequently create imaginary companions in their play. At this age, it is perfectly normal to have make-believe friends.

Usually by the time a child goes to school, his interests will shift from imaginary to realistic activities.

Imaginary companions are useful for several reasons. They provide comfort and support for the young child when needed

since they always behave as the child wants.

For example, when a young child has to deal with the conflict between the need for being cared for and the need to be independent, it's possible for him to be both a baby and a baby doll's caregiver.

Imaginary companions can also serve as useful scapegoats that can be blamed and corrected as needed (for having soiled pants, for example).

It doesn't help to tell a preschooler that his imaginary companions don't exist. They enable him to experience his own developing sense of self. And he does this in the safe environment of imaginary friends over whom he can exercise control.

In this safe pretend world, a young child will often display strong expressions of emotion. This provides both a release of tension and a means to explore a whole new world of feelings. ❑

FIGURE 5.17
Parent Education Newsletter

BENEFITS

Central to parent involvement, whether at a school, day-care center, or community organization, is the communication between that organization and its parents. Planned communication reassures parents that they will be routinely informed about events, upcoming news, and important policies that may affect them or their children. It is an important instrument that can be used to inform, introduce, educate, and relate ideas about children, parents, and their families. Regular communication brings all parents together and connects them with a common thread: their desire to actively learn, grow, and share as parents.

PARENT HANDBOOKS

Parent handbooks are an efficient way to convey the basic policies and requirements of a school or center (Berger, 1995). Pertinent information is readily available when questions arise, eliminating the common misunderstandings that often result from poorly communicated policies (Swap, 1993). Parents are more likely to keep a handbook for future reference than a stack of individual handouts on topics ranging from illness to holiday schedules. An effective handbook will communicate to both prospective parents and those currently enrolled in a program. The information presented in a handbook can be divided into four categories: school philosophy, basic operating information, school policies, and general information.

SCHOOL PHILOSOPHY

Central to a parent handbook is the school philosophy. The parent handbook serves as an excellent vehicle for stating the basic philosophy guiding the school and its curriculum. Attitudes about children's learning, classroom environment, and discipline should be outlined in a concise, jargon-free statement. This working philosophy should be reviewed periodically to ensure that it accurately reflects the curriculum and instructional methods.

BASIC OPERATING INFORMATION

Basic operating information consists of information unique to a specific school or center, such as:

name of school
address and map
phone numbers
employees' names and titles
hours of operation
calendar of school days
list of holidays when the school or center is closed

pick-up and drop-off locations and routines

bad weather and emergency procedures

tuition amount, date due, method of payment, consequences of late payment

absence notification procedures

immunization requirements for school entrance

This information also is important as a quick reference for relatives and babysitters in need of phone numbers or emergency information.

GENERAL SCHOOL POLICIES

General school policies are formulated by the director or principal with input from their staff. Policies should be modified periodically to reflect the changing needs of the families served. For example, some schools concerned about the increased interest in action cartoons have banned certain toys brought from home for "show and tell," or have limited the children's free time because of aggressive, disruptive play. Diversity in the school population also may necessitate modification of holiday celebrations to eliminate some traditional festivities, such as Halloween and Christmas, and include new observances, such as Fall Festival, Harvest Time, and Friends and Family (Spodek, 1985). These policies should be responsive to the needs of the participating families, and policies should respect the backgrounds of the families represented in the school (Neugebauer, 1992).

One policy often described in the handbook are health guidelines. Timetables for returning to school after illnesses such as the chicken pox, flu, fever, and common colds are crucial to the well-being of the staff and students. Educating parents about basic health rules at school is a function of the staff. For many parents this is their first introduction to practical methods of dealing with childhood illnesses and their transmission. It is also important to specify under what conditions a student must immediately be picked up from school (i.e., injury, acute illness) and how emergency numbers will be utilized. Medication policies should be outlined in this section so that parents have clear-cut answers about which medications are permitted to be given by staff and which are not. Keep in mind that it is far easier to enforce stated health practices when parents have been informed prior to school or program entry.

Discipline is a major concern of parents, teachers, principals, and directors of facilities that provide care for young children. It is essential that the staff explore various methods of discipline and develop a philosophy about classroom management. Each staff member should be able to articulate the specific steps that will be taken to maintain an environment that encourages respect for all participants (Wallach, 1993). All teachers and aides need to have a thorough understanding of how to handle the many day-to-day situations that arise in the classroom in order to ensure consistent, fair treatment of all children. This is especially important in full-day programs where staff changes may occur two or more times during the day. Behavior modification, reward systems, token economies, and assertive discipline are just a few of the classroom management techniques available to teachers. Educators at a well-run school or center will have spent considerable time researching and exploring various options, as well as sharing input with one another, before choosing a workable method. The discipline philosophy should then be described in clear, understandable terms so that parents know what the expectations are for their child's behavior at school.

Parent involvement policies are necessary to educate and inform parents about their rights and responsibilities concerning participation in their child's education (Elkind, 1988). A comprehensive list of ways to involve parents, both in and out of school, may encourage even reluctant parents to participate. Tasks or responsibilities should cover a broad range of levels of commitment and complexity to appeal to a variety of talents, interests, and schedules (Greenberg, 1989). (See Chapter 10, Parents and Community Volunteers). A school or center may wish to include a list of the types of volunteer help needed and the staff members to be contacted for more information. This section also should include any requirements of parents who want to participate in the classroom or in a special program. For example, some districts require TB tests and background checks for all volunteers. Emphasis should be not only on required hours of time spent, but also on the numerous benefits for parents when they are involved in a program (Gestwicki, 1987).

School policies concerning the methods of reporting student progress can also be addressed in the handbook. Schools and centers vary greatly in the type and frequency of progress reports and parent-teacher conferences each academic year. Early childhood classrooms, including kindergarten, rely on the parent-teacher conference (Raines & Canady, 1990). This is an opportunity for parents and teachers to have an uninterrupted, face-to-face conversation about the emotional, social, and academic progress of the individual child. Conference frequencies can vary from one to four or more times per year (see Chapter 9, Parent-Teacher Conferences). The progress report is a written summary of work habits, academic skills, and social behaviors described in narrative, symbol, or checklist form. Placing a blank copy of this report in the handbook gives parents a clear picture of the evaluation methods used and the topics to be discussed. This allows parents time to formulate questions and comments (App, 1991).

Financial assistance criteria for free breakfast or lunch programs can be described in this section to help parents determine whether or not they qualify for services. If scholarships or tuition assistance programs are available, a contact person and phone numbers could be listed, along with a confidentiality statement regarding inquiries or referrals.

Other policies that may be included are:

- registration procedures
- school facilities
- supplemental programs available to students
- birthday parties and invitation procedures
- preschool screening locations and dates

GENERAL INFORMATION

The fourth section of a parent handbook serves as a overview of miscellaneous information of interest to families. Included may be a listing of ongoing fundraising projects, their goal for the school or center, and to what degree each family is expected to participate. If a school relies heavily upon the fundraising efforts of its member families for revenue, it is wise to list the projects, their approximate duration, and the timing of commitments to ensure good participation. This section could spotlight previous moneymaking projects and describe how they benefited the children. Programs in existence (i.e., water safety lessons, computers and software, cultural events, foreign language programs) funded by these projects should be mentioned so that prospective and incoming parents understand the need for cooperation and support.

Descriptions of school facilities such as outdoor play areas, computer labs, gymnasiums, and the cafeteria help parents become better acquainted with the entire campus. A clearly labeled map of the school and grounds with areas of interest to parents—the office, main entrances, visitors' parking spaces, conference rooms, auditoriums, and gyms—will be helpful when a parent visits the school to volunteer in the classroom or attend a school function.

Supplemental programs available to students can be listed in this section. Preschools and day-care centers often provide transportation to local facilities offering swimming or gymnastic lessons and will supervise children who may wish to enroll. An elementary school may offer a before- and after-school care program for the supervision of children during nonschool hours. Programs open to families, such as parent education classes, parent-child activity classes, and other meetings, may have short program descriptions and enrollment information listed.

Staff biographies are an excellent way to help parents become acquainted with the many teachers, administrators, and support staff in a school or center. Parents appreciate reading about the people who interact daily with their children.

Parent-teacher organizations and parent advisory boards that exist in a school or program are often described in the handbook. Membership information, a list of contact people and current board members, and schedules of regular meetings may increase interest in these groups and attendance at their functions. Information can be updated from year to year as the handbook is revised (Swap, 1987, 1993: Henderson et al., 1993).

PUBLISHING THE PARENT HANDBOOK

A parent handbook is generally published for distribution at the school or at the center. Many schools and centers rely on the school logo and assorted reproductions of children's art work to illustrate the handbook. Each grade level may include a page that gives specific information relevant to it, such as immunization requirements, special fees, extra supplies, etc.

The simplest, most economical method of publication is through the use of a word processor, copier, and assorted clip art. Information stored on a disk can be quickly retrieved and modified when updates are necessary. It is fairly easy to produce a readable, personalized handbook that can be collated and assembled by parent volunteers before the start of school.

There are several inexpensive methods of binding the handbook. Depending on its length and the tools available, the handbook can be stapled with a colorful cover and distributed in a large envelope with other paperwork during registration. A spiral binding machine that uses plastic combs creates a workbook-like appearance that can be produced assembly-line style with volunteers and a relatively small investment in materials. Some programs put the handbook in a folder that can also be used to store other school forms and notices sent home during the year.

Budget restrictions generally determine the type of handbook that is to be produced. Experimentation with format will result in a product that suits the needs of the individual program or school. Do not overlook fundraising revenues or the resources of a parent-teacher organization as a source of dollars to cover the cost of the handbook. Many organizations are interested in specific ways to contribute and may have volunteers willing to assist in the assembly of the handbook as well.

YEARBOOKS

A lasting way to establish a school or classroom identity is through a yearbook. Yearbooks may be as simple or as elaborate as the teacher or staff desires; it is the message—"We had a great year; we learned about each other and grew as a group"—that counts. A yearbook is a valuable keepsake for students and parents alike; it allows teachers to highlight special events and student milestones. Prospective and newly enrolled families can readily see the day-to-day workings of a classroom by skimming through this collection of photographs, drawings, quotes, and awards.

PUBLISHING A YEARBOOK

A yearbook may be a published schoolwide effort that is made available to families for a fee. Occasionally a portion of the cost is underwritten by a parent-teacher organization or a booster club. When a yearbook is to be professionally printed and bound, a committee should oversee its production. Tasks include collecting news from all classrooms, arranging for photographs to be taken, contacting companies for printing prices, and gathering content information. The selection of graphics, proofreading, and order tabulation are additional tasks that can be handled by parent volunteers. Some schools offer a stipend to the teacher who agrees to lend expertise and leadership to such an endeavor.

Frequently a classroom will create a single album to document the year's events. When new topics need to be chronicled, working on the album can be a choice at the writing center. As an ongoing project in an early childhood classroom, the yearbook is often handled by a parent volunteer working at school or at home. Events covered include classroom parties, field trips, special visitors, events, musical programs, unusual centers, new students, student teachers, and new siblings or families. As a class project, older students can exercise almost total control over the editorial content of their yearbook. This project can be an excellent vehicle for allowing students to experience the entire writing-editing-rewriting-publishing process associated with current language arts curricula. One elementary school was fortunate enough to have a former newspaper reporter among its parents, and he was willing to supervise the entire project. The parent volunteered one hour per week assisting children as they selected material, cut and pasted photographs, and illustrated written accounts of classroom events.

As a tool for communication, yearbooks from previous years can be circulated during registration and orientation meetings to help new parents envision the myriad of activities that will take place in the coming year. Pictures convey significant amounts of information about the children, the classroom environment, the staff involvement, and kinds of experiences the children enjoy.

PARENT BULLETIN BOARD AND POSTED ANNOUNCEMENTS

In addition to the newsletters, handouts, and notes that go home with students on a regular basis, many teachers find that a parent bulletin board is an efficient way of dispensing information to families and caregivers (Bundy, 1991). Located near pickup and drop-off areas or in the classroom, the parent bulletin board serves several useful purposes. Many teachers routinely post the snack schedule, school calendar, lunch and breakfast menus, volunteer schedules, recent newsletters, book orders, and other distributed material in order to inform noncustodial parents or those who may have misplaced the information. Last minute reminders about deadlines for book orders, fundraiser money, or permission slips are apt to be read and acted upon, especially while the parent is in the building. Unclaimed articles of clothing can also be posted for parent identification. A bulletin board can instantly communicate an outbreak of chicken pox, for example, hours before individual notes can be sent home.

Parent bulletin boards can also be a vehicle for parents who want to share information with each other about parent-teacher news, room-parent responsibilities, parent advisory group minutes or decisions, and community events. Another purpose served by the parent bulletin board is program information for incoming parents. Raines and Canady (1990) suggest that photographs of children involved in whole language activities be accompanied by a short, explanatory caption to help parents visualize the centers and activities in use. This can be of special interest at orientation meetings or registration times.

Creation of a special place where parents can share and receive information is a way of indicating respect for families and their value to the school. The parent bulletin board should be easy to spot and be updated regularly to attract an audience.

PARENT SUGGESTION BOX

Communication between parents, teachers, and administrators is often encouraged through personal meetings and conferences. However, due to time restrictions or fear of confrontation, a parent may prefer to voice an opinion in writing. A parent suggestion box placed in a well-marked, centrally located spot in the school can provide a way for parents to share comments or make suggestions (Bundy, 1991). Care should be taken to respond to all suggestions so that participants feel that their opinions were received and acknowledged. It is usually school policy to request a parent's name and phone number on any suggestion so that further comments or information can be obtained, if necessary. Suggestions that may have wide appeal to other families, such as the addition of a new fundraiser, a social event for the school, or ways to improve an existing extracurricular program, could be added to the school newsletter to begin an open discussion.

The suggestion box also can serve as the receptacle for parent evaluation forms following parent/teacher conferences, workshops, or parent meeting.

INFORMATIONAL PACKETS

When a school or program has numerous applications, brochures, fact sheets, and handbooks about a variety of services, it is useful to package them together in an informational packet (Arizona Department of Education, 1989). Creating a packet simplifies enrollment when a new student arrives midyear or when a family requests information about eligibility for a supplemental program such as prekindergarten, Parents as Teachers, or Title I. Volunteers can assemble necessary literature to make distribution more efficient and complete. Outreach programs often will package materials in this manner because they rely on professionals outside the district to make parent contacts. Churches, preschools, day-care centers, hospitals, greeter services, physicians' offices, and visiting nurses may provide this service because they deal with a wide spectrum of families. Tapping these resources for outreach, as well as using in-district channels, increases the service visibility in the community.

BROCHURES

Computer software has made the process of creating a unique and personalized brochure quick and easy to do. A brochure can describe the features of a program or a service (Ball, 1985). Using colorful paper and computer or clip-art graphics, a simple brochure can be an inexpensive way to publicize important resources for parents. Programs or services that can be advertised include:

- toy lending library
- parent resource library
- parent room

FIGURE 5.18
Parent Education Brochure

home visiting services
early childhood screenings
parent education series
prekindergarten classes
speech and languages services
psychological testing services
tuition scholarships
before- and after-school child-care programs
local social service agencies
special education services and parents' rights

Brochures are a tool for communicating with parents who may be difficult to reach or reluctant to consider a particular program suggested during a conference or staffing. Brochures may "open the door to dialogue" by giving parents "food for thought" (Baskwill, 1989). They also provide a measure of outreach for parents to share with other parents who may have limited contact with the school. See Figure 5.18.

SUMMARY

Communication is the key to initiating and maintaining positive relationships between parents, teachers, administrators, and the community. This chapter has described a number of methods of written communications, including notes, letters, happy-grams, invitations, parent handbooks, bulletin boards, newsletters, and brochures—all of which convey important information from schools to the students' families. Other methods of one-way communication, such as report cards, often initiate further contact and are critical in laying the groundwork for positive relationships in future meetings. Passport systems, dialogue journals, and daily logs represent "written conversations" that encourage parents' broader level of ongoing participation and input in their child's day-to-day school experiences.

Implementation of new techniques, followed with evaluation by both schools and families, ensures meaningful communication that will create a climate for increased levels of parent involvement. Educators and administrators need to be aware of the changing communication needs of the broad spectrum of families that schools serve today.

ACTIVITIES FOR DISCUSSION, EXPANSION, AND APPLICATION

1. Discuss strategies available to the individual teacher for increasing the level of communication between the classroom and students' families.

2. Discuss strategies that could be implemented collaboratively among a group of teachers or an entire school to facilitate improved home-school communication.

3. Develop a comprehensive, one-way communication plan for a specific type of program: Head Start, prekindergarten, or a primary grade. Describe how the methods chosen will serve the parents' need for information and encourage participation in their child's education.

4. Develop a typical school newsletter that would incorporate goals, purposes, and content areas appropriate for a specific population of parents (i.e., Head Start, day-care center, kindergarten class, etc.).

5. Initiate a passport book with a student (or hypothetical student), and model responses appropriate to a specific situation (i.e., aggressive behavior in the classroom, difficulty getting assignments completed, lack of respect for classroom materials).

6. Design a report card for a specific age or grade level that effectively communicates to parents the components of the curriculum. In a developmentally appropriate manner, use terminology that expresses the child's progress to date.

7. Write an example of a welcome letter, a difficult letter about a behavioral problem, a note requesting a parent conference, and a happy-gram.

REFERENCES

Association for Childhood Education International. (1988). J. Isenberg & N. Quisenbery. Position paper. Play: A necessity for all children. *Childhood Education, 64*, 138–145.

App, M. (1991). *Families and education: An educator's resource for family involvement.* Madison, WI: Wisconsin State Department of Public Instruction.

Arizona Department of Education.(1989). *Parent-teacher communication: A handbook for teachers and parents.* Arizona Department of Education. ERIC Source: ED 321 896.

Autrey, R. (1989). In *Parent-teacher communication: A handbook for teachers and parents.* Arizona Department of Education. ERIC Source: ED 321 896.

Ball, R. (1985). Ideas: Parent-school involvement. *Dimensions, 14*(1), 15–18.

Baskwill, J. (1989). *Parents and teachers: Partners in learning.* Toronto: Scholastic.

Baskwill, J. (1992). "Ask me about": A newsletter with a difference. *Teaching K-8,* 44–46.

Bauch, J. (1988). *Parent involvement using high tech for maximum impact.* Research paper presented at annual conference of Southern Association for Children Under Six. Birmingham, AL.

Berger, E. (1995). *Parents as partners in education: Families and schools working together* (4th ed.). Englewood Cliffs, NJ: Merrill.

Biagini, J. (1991). *Guidelines for serving students with limited English proficiency.* St. Paul, MN: Minnesota Department of Education.

Bundy, B. R. (1991). Fostering communication between parents and preschools. *Young Children, 46* (12), 12–17.

Carney, T. (1989). *Parent-teacher communication: A handbook for teachers and parents.* Arizona Department of Education. ERIC Source: ED 321 896.

Cataldo, C. Z. (1987). *Parent education for early childhood.* New York: Teachers College Press.

Chittenden, E., & Courtney, R. (1989). Assessment of young children's reading: Documentation as an alternative to testing. In D.S. Strickland & L.M. Morrow (Eds.), *Emerging literacy: Young children learn to read and write* (pp. 107–120). Newark, DE: International Reading Association.

Corbett, S. (1993). A complicated bias. *Young Children, 48*(3), 29–31.

Davies, D. (1991). Schools reaching out: Family, school, and community partnership for school success. *Phi Delta Kappan, 22*, 383–388.

DeVincentis, S. (April 1984). *Lekotek: Swedish play intervention for handicapped children.* Paper presented at the annual convention of the Council for Exceptional Children, Washington, DC.

Elkind, D. (1988). Parent involvement. *Young Children, 43*(2), 2.

Epstein, J. (1991). Paths to partnership. What we can learn from federal, state, district, and school initiatives. *Phi Delta Kappan, 1*, 344–349.

Fisher, B. (1991). *Joyful learning.* Portsmouth, NH: Heinemann.

Galinsky, E. (1980). Newsletters for and about parents. *Child Care Information Exchange, 6*, 33–34.

Gestwicki, C. (1987). *Home, School, and community relations: A guide to working with parents.* New York: Delmar.

Greenberg, P. (1989). Parents as partners in young children's development and education: A new American fad? Why does it matter? *Young Children, 44*(4), 61–75.

Goetaski, J. (1983). *The implementation of a P.E.T. training program to develop effective parenting skills.* Ft. Lauderdale, FL: Nova University.

Guy, G. (1988). Let the presses roll. *Instructor,* 70–72.

Harms, T. O., & Cryer, D. (1978). Parent newsletter: A new format. *Young Children, 7,* 28–32.

Henderson, A., Marburger, C., & Ooms, T. (1993). *Beyond the bake sale: An educator's guide to working with parents.* Washington, DC: National Committee for Citizens in Education.

Honig, A. (1979). *Parent involvement in early childhood education.* Washington, DC: National Association for the Education of Young Children.

Hunter, M. (1989). Join the "par-aide" in education. *Educational Leadership, 10,* 30–41.

Hunter, M. (1991). *Parent-teacher communication: A handbook for teachers and parents.* Arizona Department of Education. ERIC Source: ED 321 896.

Jackson, S., Robey, L., Watkus, M., & Chadwick, E. (1991). Play for all children: The toy library solution. *Childhood Education, 68*(1), 27–31.

Johnson, V. (1990). Schools reaching out: Changing the message to good news. *Equity and Choice, 6*(3), 20–24.

Juul, K. (April 1984). Toy libraries for the handicapped: An international survey. Paper presented at the annual convention of the Council for Exceptional Children, Washington, DC.

Katz, L., and Chard, S. (1989). *Engaging children's minds: The project approach.* Norwood, NJ: Ablex.

Krause, L. (1990). Roll out the computer, then the presses! *Day Care and Early Education,* 16–17.

Leavitt, R., & Eheart, B. (1991). Assessment in early childhood programs. *Young Children, 46*(5), 4–10.

Lee, F. Y. (1992). Alternative assessments. *Childhood Education, 69*(2), 72–74.

Morris, B. (September 1991). The child's right to play. Paper presented at the Early Childhood Convention, Dunedin, New Zealand.

National Association for the Education of Young Children. (1988). Position statement on standardized testing of young children 3 through 8 years of age. *Young Children, 43*(3), 42–47.

Neugebauer, B. (1981). Publishing your center newsletter: A practical guide to layout and design. *Child Care Information Exchange, 12,* 6–10.

Neugebauer, B. (1992). *Alike and different.* Washington, DC: National Association for the Education of Young Children.

Neugebauer, R. (1981). Tips on publishing a center newsletter. *Child Care Information Exchange, 11,* 26–32.

Nimnicht, G., & Brown, E. (1972). The toy library: Parents and children learning with toys. *Young Children, 28*(2), 110–116.

Patterson, C.J. (1992). Children of lesbian and gay parents. *Child Development, 63,* 1025–1042.

Paulson, E.L., Paulson, P.R., & Meyer, C.A. (1991). What makes a portfolio a portfolio? *Educational Leadership, 48*(5), 60–63.

Popkin, M. (1987). *Active parenting.* New York: Harper & Row.

Raines, C., & Canady, R. (1990). *The whole language kindergarten.* New York: Teachers College Press.

Rich, D. (1985). *The forgotten factor in school success: The family.* Washington, DC: Home and School Institute.

Rich, D. (1987). Schools and families: Issues and actions. Washington, DC: National Education Association.

Rich, D. (1987). *Teachers and parents: An adult to adult approach.* Washington, DC: National Education Association.

Routman, R. (1988). *Transitions.* Portsmouth, NH: Heinemann.

Routman, R. (1991). *Invitations: Changing as teachers and learners K-12.* Portsmouth, NH: Heinemann.

Runge, A., & Shea, T. (1975). A passport to positive parent-teacher communication. *Teaching Exceptional Children* 7(3), 91–92.

Sharp, Q.Q. (1989). *Evaluation: Whole language checklists for evaluating your children.* New York: Scholastic.

Shea, T., & Bauer, A. (1991). *Parents and teachers of children with exceptionalities.* Boston: Allyn & Bacon.

Spodek, B. (1985). *Understanding the multicultural experience in early childhood education.* Washington, DC: National Association for the Education of Young Children.

Stone, M. (1983). Toy libraries. *Day Care and Early Education,* 19–22.

Swap, S.M. (1987). *Enhancing parent involvement in schools.* New York: Teachers College Press.

Swap S.M. (1993). *Developing home-school partnerships.* New York: Teachers College Press.

Swick, K.J. (1984). *Inviting parents into the young child's world.* Champaign, IL: Stipes.

Swick, K.J. (1991). *Teacher-parent partnerships to enhance success in early childhood education.* Washington, DC: NEA/SACUS.

Wallach, L. (1993). Helping children cope with violence. *Young Children, 48*(4), 4–11.

Wardle, F. (1990). Endorsing children's differences: Meeting the needs of adopted minority children. *Young Children, 45*(5), 44–46.

Wenig, M., & Brown, M. (1975). School efforts + parent/teacher communications = happy young children. *Young Children, 7,* 373–376.

Whitman, P., & Baskwill, J. (1988). *Evaluation: Whole language, whole child.* Ontario, Canada: Scholastic.

Wickens, E. (1993). Penny's question: I will have a child in my class with two moms—what do you know about this? *Young Children, 48*(3), 25–28.

Wolf, D.P. (1989). Portfolio assessment: Sampling student work. *Educational Leadership, 46*(7) 35–39.

Chapter 6

VERBAL COMMUNICATIONS

READERS WILL BE ABLE TO:

- Identify important factors to consider in choosing a published parent education program.
- Identify qualities necessary for an effective parenting group leader.
- Describe the role of incidental contacts, social events, audio- and videotape, and the mass media in involving parents.
- Describe the purposes and key factors involved in open houses and orientation meetings.
- Identify types of toy-lending libraries and guidelines for their operation.
- Discuss the importance of telephone calls in maintaining home-school relationships and the use of advanced technology to increase the effectiveness of this strategy.
- Describe strategies and techniques for encouraging parent attendance at various school events.

Two-way verbal communication strategies involve a wide range of contacts that occur between parents, administrators, and teachers. These contacts can range from incidental meetings in the school or community to shared participation in a parent education series lasting six or more weeks. Each type of contact adds to the collection of impressions that families have about the school and staff; together, they form the basis of a relationship. When positive contacts outweigh negative ones, either in number or depth, the teacher's chances of building a partnership with a child's family is increased—which is to the child's ultimate advantage.

Central to open communication is the belief that interaction between home and school is valued. An open-door policy is usually interpreted as teachers and administrators welcoming parent involvement, parents as decision makers, and parents as advocates for their child's education.

This chapter describes the concept of parent education in published programs, discusses the characteristics of effective group leaders, lists strategies for encouraging parent attendance at groups, and offers alternative formats for presenting parenting programs. Orientation meetings, open houses, social events, telephone calls, parent spaces, the use of audio- and videotape, and support groups also are examined.

👤 PARENT EDUCATION

Parent education is not a single concept that comes in one easy-to-identify package. Rather, it is a group of strategies that can assume a number of directions and formats. Parent education is the parent meeting that a teacher holds to demonstrate math and math manipulatives used in her first-grade classroom. It is also the guest speaker hired to address an auditorium full of parents. Parent education is the home-based teacher who models the use of developmentally appropriate books and fine motor activities for the parent of a 3-year-old. It is the information shared on a "warm line" that links a neonatal nurse to the distraught parent of a newborn (Elder & Maloni, 1986; Butts, Brooten, & Brown, 1988). Parent education is instruction that focuses on the parent's role in supporting the child's development and personal growth, and on understanding the learning process and how children's educational programs function (Cataldo, 1983). A significant portion of this learning process should engage parents in forming new images of how their new status as parents influences the need for new roles, new resources, and new skills (Swick, 1991).

This section will examine published parent education programs, describe the characteristics of an effective group leader, present strategies that encourage parent attendance, and suggest alternative formats of program design.

PUBLISHED PARENT-EDUCATION PROGRAMS

Parent education often takes the form of a series of group meetings that focus on the development of specific techniques for managing and understanding behavior and discipline. A variety of parent education programs developed by psychologists and educators are readily available through training workshops or in prepackaged curricula.

Three successful published parent education programs—Parent Effectiveness Training (PET), the Early Childhood Systematic Training for Effective Parenting (STEP), and Active Parenting—share several common theories about discipline and parent-child communication. Key concepts include: "I" messages, "you" messages, no-lose methods of conflict resolution, natural and logical consequences, and active and reflective listening techniques. Based largely on the works of renowned psychologists Rudolph Dreikurs and Adolph Adler, these programs draw heavily on the strength of parent participation and the benefits of group discussion. Both STEP and Active Parenting, which are video-based and discussion-based, use a group facilitator; PET requires its leaders to participate in a one-week training workshop.

Another highly successful program, Megaskills™, addresses parent education through increased parent involvement in their children's education. The program incorporates activities that parents can do at home to reinforce the skills children are learning in school, such as responsibility, effort, confidence, initiative, caring, common sense, teamwork, motivation, and problem-solving. Dorothy Rich, founder of the Home and School Institute and author of Megaskills™, draws frequent comparisons between skills that enable students to be successful in school and those that indicate career success as adults. A goal of the program is to help children develop these skills at the same time they are developing their academic talents.

Megaskills™ leader training consists of a two-day workshop. The book is available in bookstores.

FACTORS TO CONSIDER

When considering a particular parent education series, it is important to research the authors and their programs to determine what style of discipline is advocated and which psychological theorists' ideas they support. Scan the materials to determine if the content and advice correspond to program goals and beliefs. Each program differs in its methodology and philosophy; it will be necessary to match the needs of your parent population, the philosophy of the school, and the published curriculum to find a compatible match. Other factors to be considered include the cost of the program, availability of specialized leader training, cost of additional materials necessary to facilitate a group, and the feasibility of reusing the materials.

Programs that require leader training may pose a problem in schools or centers with high staff turnover. Materials-based curricula make it easier to share leader responsibility, but may require a TV or VCR equipment in order to present the program. Determine whether purchasing parent manuals would be a financial burden for parents; also compare the reading level of the text to the literacy level of the parents being served. Does the book resemble a textbook, and is it likely to be read only by better educated and highly motivated parents? Is it an easy-to-read manual that, when given a quick glance by a busy mother, will convey some substance? Is the information presented in such a manner that parents who have difficulty reading will be able to understand it? Have parent advisory boards or parent councils review the material to ensure acceptance from participating parents. A careful examination of these factors will maximize the dollars spent on parent education programs.

CHOOSING A LEADER FOR A PARENTING GROUP

It is often assumed that teachers are best suited to lead parenting groups. Unfortunately, many teachers, even early childhood educators, have had little, if any, training in working with parents (Greenberg, 1989). Many parenting programs draw group leaders from the "helping" professions: nursing, education, social work, counseling, and the clergy. The following qualities are instrumental to the success of a parenting group.

The group leader should have a solid *background in child development* in order to credibly and accurately educate parents about the growth and development of children. While experiences with children and families may take many forms, there is no substitute for a working knowledge of child development. A parent educator's expertise will be called upon when questions arise about discipline, parent expectations, and developmental timetables (Cataldo, 1983). An effective leader needs to be able to relate anecdotal experiences to accepted practice.

Consider the abilities of the potential leader for *building rapport* with many kinds of people. An effective leader is not only sensitive to cultural diversity among families but is able to deal with parents from a wide range of socioeconomic backgrounds, often blending the two within a single group. This may require research about a variety of cultural norms and customs in order to provide a meaningful experience for all parents. Differences in socioeconomic levels can be minimized by promoting casual attire for meetings and placing minimal emphasis on career or job titles during mixers and introductions. All parents have the right to feel welcomed and respected, regardless of their profession or level of education.

Parenting experience is not required but can certainly be a factor in gaining credibility with a group of parents. Curran (1989) suggests that educators who are not themselves parents should emphasize their experience with children on the job and in volunteer work.

Select a professional with good *organizational skills* because there are numerous details that ensure the success of the group's progress: mailings, up-to-date social service information, the ability to make referrals to local agencies, and follow-ups on requests for additional information, to name a few. It is also critical to have someone who is well prepared for each session and has done the necessary background work so that each session will flow smoothly. This includes such details as a comfortable room arrangement, availability of proper equipment (such as overhead projectors, VCRs, tape recorders), and appropriate handouts for each session, as well as adequate preparation for the subject matter of each session.

An effective leader will have *good communication and public speaking skills* and the ability to create a relaxed, nonthreatening atmosphere for all participants. A leader should become familiar with a variety of strategies and techniques in group dynamics in order to more effectively lead and focus discussions.

First-time leaders uncertain of their skills may find the *dual-leader* format an excellent way to ease into the role of parent educator while gaining valuable experience working with groups. There are advantages to having members of complementary professions work together, for they bring to the group a wider range of expertise. Consider these pairings:

- for an infant development class: an obstetric nurse and an early childhood educator.
- for a group of parents whose children experience developmental delays and are a part of a kindergarten class through inclusion: an early childhood special educator and an early childhood teacher.

Include parents when choosing meeting topics.

Most parenting programs either train parents in a group or offer training manuals for self-study. Fees for training and materials vary widely; if there is a limited budget, sponsoring agencies might decide to invest in personnel training or reusable materials.

The overall success of any parent education program usually rests on the personality and professionalism of the group leader (Curran, 1989). Consideration of these factors will ensure that parents who attend an introductory session will complete the entire series.

Strategies and Techniques to Encourage Parent Attendance

1. *Find out what topics interest parents.*

A significant factor in the success of any program is to determine what parents want to know. It is difficult, if not impossible, to maintain attendance at meetings that do not address relevant concerns of the parents involved (Rasinski & Fredericks, 1990; Swick, 1991).

There are several ways to find out what parents want. One way is to form a committee to canvass all parents with either a written or a phone survey (Swap, 1987). In this way, each parent has the opportunity to voice an opinion or make a suggestion about the focus of upcoming meetings. While the survey method can be time-consuming, it does allow a realistic profile of all parents involved and may lead to other valuable information about needed events or services.

Another method for obtaining information is to request that an existing advisory board or council review suitable programs and decide what is in the best interests of the group (Curran, 1989; Swap, 1987). There is a strong relationship between the anticipated outcomes of the parent education program, the location, and the nature of the population it serves. Rural vs. urban, married vs. single, adult vs. adolescent mothers are all factors that will test the effectiveness of a particular program. Advisory boards and parent councils should develop a clear picture of the population they hope to serve and match the program to the needs of the group (Stevens, 1978).

2. *Be sensitive about wording when choosing a title.*

The title chosen for the series may have a great effect on the level of interest. Use positive words or concepts—"Those Terrific Two's" instead of "Surviving Toddlerhood," for example. Few parents will wish to attend sessions with a negative title or about topics that imply a deficiency in their parenting skills. Humor can relay the message of the program without making the topic seem overbearing or heavy (Curran, 1989). The term "parent education" itself might offend parents who are less than confident about their skills. Consider wording that conveys the content but does not lable attendees in a negative manner. Educators have found that labels, which can be devastating for children, have an equally negative effect on parents.

3. *Explore many avenues for advertising.*

In order to reach a wide group of parents, it is helpful to look at a number of options for advertising. If the budget allows it, consider ads on local radio and community access television. If your group is a not-for-profit organization, you may qualify for free public service announcements. Often, local newspapers publish a calendar of community events as a public service. Teachers may request space in their school or district newsletter. Flyers, bulletin board signs, and report card enclosures also provide wide coverage for a minimal investment of paper and time.

4. *Choose a site that is centrally located.*

The choice of the site may determine how many people attend the program. If evening sessions are planned, consider the neighborhood; the safety of the building; the amount of adequate, lighted parking; and accessibility to public transportation. Try to arrange for a quiet room whose dimensions suit the anticipated number of parents. A large cafeteria for a group of 10 will not be conducive to a warm, sharing environment, just as a preschool room with child-sized furniture won't be adequate for 30 adults.

5. *Determine whether or not to offer child care and transportation.*

The makeup of the school population can help determine what services to offer. If lack of reliable child care would be a major impediment to parent attendance, then it might be worth the expense to arrange for this service (Curran, 1989). On-site child care could be provided by a paid babysitter or by volunteers, such as other parents, high school students, Girl Scouts, church youth groups, etc. Other options include purchasing child-care slots from a family day-care home or local center for use during meetings, or reimbursing parents for an in-home sitter.

Transportation costs often cover public transportation or taxi service, as well as the expenses of volunteer drivers from the school or an outside program. These costs may add significantly to the overhead of the classes; however, the participation of many parents may depend on their availability. The parent survey can give an idea of whether transportation is needed and its probable cost.

6. *Arrange the room to promote comfort and a willingness to share.*

When a room has been selected for the parent education classes, allow ample time to inspect it for several important features. Check the number and condition of chairs and tables to ensure the comfort of adults. Be certain that the room can be arranged in such a manner that conversation and group sharing can be facilitated easily and that each member of the group can see each other with ease. A semicircle, large square, or large circle are effective at bringing in all seated adults with equal visibility (Berger, 1987). If tables are needed for notetaking, check that there is enough space between tables and chairs to accommodate all sizes of adults. Role-playing activities may require extra chairs or space in front of the group and should be arranged before the start of the meeting.

Locate and examine the temperature controls; keep the room comfortable and well ventilated, especially if it is closed during the day or on weekends. Determine whether there is adequate lighting, rest room facilities, and kitchen or sink space for serving refreshments.

Place projectors and screens so that they don't block anyone's view, yet are near electrical outlets. A group leader who suddenly finds that there is no outlet for a planned video will suffer needless embarrassment over an unchecked detail and may hold up the meeting.

7. *Be flexible about scheduling.*

Depending on the group leader's availability, sessions should be offered at a variety of times to allow maximum participation from all interested parents. If the school is hiring an outside leader, there may not be much control over the times and dates the classes can be offered; if a teacher or other school employee is the group leader, there may be more flexibility. Information can be gathered through a written or phone survey to determine the most convenient times for the majority of parents.

Be aware of local "customs" when scheduling a series of ongoing classes. For example, in many communities Wednesday evenings are unofficially reserved for choir, religious classes, or services. In other towns or neighborhoods there may be a long-standing tradition for sports leagues or school functions on a particular evening. Be alert to school holiday schedules and try not to compete with fundraisers, parent-teacher conferences, or three-day weekends. Attendance at the classes is bound to suffer if parents have too many responsibilities in one night.

ALTERNATIVE FORMATS

In addition to traditional parenting class formats, there exists parenting information that is tailored to fit today's tightly scheduled lifestyles. For many mothers and fathers, attendance at an evening series would be difficult to sustain over a period of 6-8 weeks. To accommodate families with two working parents, single parents, and parents with complicated home situations, educators have experimented with alternative formats that make parenting classes more accessible.

1. *Consider a flexible time and format.*

Parents may prefer to attend a lunch-hour seminar instead of an evening class. Some employers offer brown-bag seminars for employees who wish to participate in parenting skills classes but lack the time outside of the office. A once-a-week or once-a-month format could be arranged to cover topics chosen by the employees (Leuthy, 1991).

After-school classes might appeal to teachers, shift workers, and stay-at-home mothers who want to be at home in the evenings with their families. A latchkey program at the school could provide child care at a nominal cost. For parents with behavioral or academic questions about their child, consider a "warm line" staffed by teachers, social workers, nurses, or school psychologists.

2. *Tie parent education material to a social function.*

Some programs have found increased attendance for special speakers or topics if a social event is offered at the same time. For example, a potluck supper could be preceded with a 30 minute talk by a guest speaker or could occur while children are being entertained by a storyteller or busy with a hands-on art activity. A coffee or lunch at school could serve as the starting point for the distribution of materials related to a parenting topic; a more formal series of classes could come later.

3. *Tie the classes to necessary resources.*

One day-care center chose the dinner hour for parent education classes, promising extended, no-cost child care for parents who participated. Directors also offered the opportunity to newer staff members, who also benefited from the material presented. Discussion between staff and parents proved valuable in helping each group understand the other's point of view in handling children.

Another school district took advantage of a new park to provide supervised outdoor play while parents took part in informal classes. Parents whose children were enrolled in a morning preschool program decided to take part in parent education classes that were offered simultaneously in the same facility.

⬛ TYPES OF PARENT CONTACT

DAILY AND INCIDENTAL CONTACTS

Daily contacts are generally limited to those parents who drop off and pick up their children from a school or center. It is a time when parents like to share information about the child's mood or behavior, state of health, or concerns that may surface during the day. Teachers who develop a good rapport with their parents through short, frequent conversations find that they are better able to cope with the child's needs, both academically and socially. These contacts provide the opportunity to deal with questions or problems immediately rather than through letters or journals and may lead to faster resolution of problems.

Incidental contacts occur frequently when teachers and students reside in the same community. It is not unusual for students and their parents to have chance meetings with teachers in the supermarket, mall, church, or restaurants. It can sometimes be difficult to keep conversation to nonschool issues, and it will not always be possible to avoid discussing why Susie is having trouble sitting still during group time. Most experienced teachers have developed some ready phrases to ward off serious discussions that would be better off held in private. Explanations such as "I'd like to discuss this with you when I have Susie's portfolio in front of us; why don't you call me on Monday and set up a conference?" usually let a parent know that the interest expressed is genuine.

SOCIAL EVENTS

The strategies of involving parents in school through social events is limited only by the imagination and interest of the staff. There are numerous types of get-togethers that can enhance the home-school relationship. Listed below are ideas of social events that encourage participation.

- *Breakfasts for parents.* Invite parents to share a light breakfast together to discuss common concerns, interests, school improvements, etc.
- *Volunteer teas or luncheons.* Teachers can prepare lunch or snacks and serve them to their parent volunteers in recognition of their efforts during the school year.
- *Potluck suppers.* A school, grade level, or class can set aside regular times throughout the year for potluck suppers. Parents can enjoy a ready-made meal with their families and relax with teachers and other staff members.
- *Picnics.* A picnic held at the beginning or end of the school year can help staff members and students' families become acquainted and renew old friendships.
- *Lunch with the principal.* Parents invited to share lunch at school is a proven way to maintain open lines of communication.
- *Grade-level sessions.* Similar to the open house format, a grade-level session can familiarize parents with the typical schedule and materials that their child experiences each day.

The key to conducting successful social events is to gain the cooperation and commitment of the teachers and administrators involved. Genuine interest in spending time with families is an absolute necessity. A less than enthusiastic staff will convey a poor attitude to parents and reinforce negative biases that some parents have toward educators and schools. The effort to plan such gatherings must be a joint commitment on the part of parents and teachers. When successful, families and staff begin to view each other as real people, with common interests and concerns. Trust and meaningful relationships can build on this type of foundation. The benefit to the child is realized when parents and teachers work in a partnership for the child's best interests.

OPEN HOUSE

Open houses or back-to-school nights are important strategies for the creation of a welcoming atmosphere for parents and families in the school. Parents feel more "connected" to their child's school experience when they can see the room, examine books and materials, and meet staff members face-to-face. Open houses are most successful when scheduled at the beginning of the school year because they allow parents and teachers to meet on a positive note before any problems appear (Carney, 1984).

Students of all ages can become involved in the preparation for an open house. Even young children enjoy the anticipation of creating writing and artwork displays and welcome signs, and preparing the room for their families. Children will also be a strong influence on their parents to attend the open house. It is an important element in building children's self-esteem and attitudes toward school when they are able to share their environment with their families and receive positive feedback.

TIPS FOR A SUCCESSFUL OPEN HOUSE

- Display the papers or artwork of all children if you prepare such a display.
- Send invitations or flyers well in advance of the scheduled date so that parents with varied work, school, or custody schedules can plan to attend.
- Inform parents on the invitation that one-to-one conferencing will not be held at the open house, but can be arranged for another time.
- Provide name tags for parents—perhaps with their child's picture on it—to facilitate conversation among parents and to assist the teacher in connecting children with their families.
- Hang a poster or chart outlining the schedule of a typical school day.
- Have extra copies of school handbooks, forms, and paperwork on hand for new parents who may not have received them.
- Consider staggering families' arrival times, perhaps alphabetically by last name, so that not all families are present at one time. This method frees the teacher to talk with more parents and avoids overcrowding.

Families enjoy getting acquainted.

Generally, open houses are meant to be relaxed and informal meetings between teachers and families. It is difficult, then, when a parent seizes the opportunity for a detailed, personal conversation with the teacher about one child's progress. This not only places the teacher in an awkward position but is unfair to the parents. Privacy and access to the child's records are important components of a conference, and the open house provides neither. Experienced teachers are prepared with suggestions for scheduling a conference at another time, and they know how to close off discussions about personal matters.

Another popular style of open house structures the parents' visit so that they experience a miniversion of their child's schedule. In this format, teachers explain curriculum, materials, methods, and evaluation systems in place in the classroom. Parents follow the class schedule in an abbreviated form that would omit specialist times (PE, music, art) and lunch time. Parents gain valuable information about classroom expectations for behavior and academics, as well as become familiar with the materials appropriate for the age or grade level of their child. They also gain a sense of the rhythm of their child's day and the variety of adults with whom the children have daily contact.

ORIENTATION MEETINGS

The transition to a new grade is often accompanied by an orientation meeting for both parents and students. Preschool, kindergarten, junior high, and high school are typical new beginnings that are marked by a formal orientation meeting. The purpose of the orientation meeting is to provide parents and children the opportunity to visit the new building, meet the staff, and learn about the policies and schedules of the upcoming year. Orientation meetings are an efficient way to relay new information and answer questions.

Information that is helpful to have at a meeting includes parent handbooks, volunteer information, medical forms, supply lists, permission slips, parent surveys or questionnaires, emergency information cards, and any other district requirements for that grade or classroom. Parents also appreciate hearing a description of the curriculum and materials their children will be using, specific information about discipline policies, and the teacher's general philosophy of education (Henderson, Marburger, & Ooms, 1986).

Tips to running a successful orientation meeting include:

- Consider limiting the number of parents attending any one session (if more than one can be arranged) so that individual questions can be answered and time can be spent getting to know parents.
- Print tags with both the parents' and the child's names to help the teacher begin to associate names and faces.
- Keep the meeting flowing and stick to the predetermined time schedule. If individual parents need more time to discuss special situations, suggest a conference, when information can be shared in private. Don't allow one or two parents to dominate the meeting.
- Have quiet activities planned for children (if invited) that will occupy them during the adult portion of the meeting.
- Have extra materials available for newly registered students or for noncustodial parents who may wish separate sets of school packets. Prepare several packets to have on hand for students who enroll midyear.

FIELD TRIPS/ROOM PARTIES

Field trips and room parties are time-honored ways for parents to participate in schools. Parents feel comfortable with these familiar roles and may become interested in pursuing greater levels of involvement after establishing relationships with teachers and other parents. Field trips and room parties may, therefore, serve as a springboard to involvement for many families.

In order to make the experience with these strategies a positive one, teachers should provide parents with specific information in advance of the event. Details about school policies and procedures, methods of handling discipline/behavior problems, beginning and ending times of the event, and clear descriptions of the schedule and all activities expected of the parent should be shared in advance of the trip or party. This information may be covered at an orientation meeting, in a handout, or in the parent handbook.

Planning will ensure a safe and pleasant experience for all involved. Future volunteer commitments may be gleaned from parents who feel that their help was needed and appreciated, and that they made a difference.

TOY-LENDING LIBRARIES

Another type of parent contact occurs through the use of toy-lending libraries. Many programs that serve young children use the toy library as a method of extending developmentally appropriate activities and books from the classroom to the home.

Play is a central theme to most early childhood programs (Jackson et al., 1991). Long recognized by educators and child development specialists as critical to healthy growth, play "is part of an interactive process in the child's development of social, cognitive, and physical abilities" (Dempsey & Frost, 1993). Toys are the tools through which children learn and practice social skills, develop critical thinking processes, use their imagination, and increase visual, gross, and fine motor abilities (Morris, 1991). Lack of access to a wide range of developmentally appropriate toys can hamper these critical elements of development for many children. The first toy library was created to fill this need and provide resources for parents to supply necessary toys for their children.

A BRIEF HISTORY OF THE TOY-LENDING LIBRARY MOVEMENT

Toy libraries originated in England more than 50 years ago and spread to include most European countries. In 1935 the first toy lending library was established in California (Jackson, 1991). Currently there are two basic models of toy libraries in operation throughout the United States and Europe. The first, termed the British model, is usually located in a public institution such as a school, hospital, church, or library and is staffed by paraprofessional volunteers. Often privately funded, these libraries serve low-income, at-risk families as well as the general population (Jackson et al., 1991). Under the guidance of a volunteer, parents visit the library to choose a toy that will suit the age and development level of their child. In some programs, the parents have access to training sessions that demonstrate the many ways a toy can be used to facilitate language, fine and gross motor skills, and show how to match toys to the child's individual needs (Nimnicht, 1972).

Variations on the British model enable the toy library to reach a wide range of parents. The *early education stationary library* is usually housed at a preschool, church, or other facility for use through that building. The *early education mobile unit* is taken to families, often through a home visiting program on a rotating basis. The *therapeutic toy library* may be limited to the families enrolled in a special education program and designed to promote learning at a particular stage or for a specific disability.

The second model is the Lekotek toy library, which was developed in Scandinavia and specifically designed for youngsters with disabilities (Juul, 1984). The primary components of Lekotek are family support, sharing of play techniques, monthly family visits, and parent support groups. Lekoteks were created because children with special needs, during the 1960s, were without services until the age of 4. Karen Stenland Junker and Evy Blid, themselves parents of children with special needs, desired intervention that would reduce the loneliness and isolation felt by these families. They also wished to promote information and intervention during the first year of life, a critical determiner of future development. Today, Lekoteks serve all children with special needs, mental as well as physical, and "are an important part of the team of professionals that provide service to the child and family" (deVincentis, 1984). Lekoteks provide assistance to preschools in promoting the successful integration of children with special needs into mainstream classrooms. The Lekotek provides a resource teacher who oversees the children while in school, plus provides inservice programs, technical assistance, and loans of materials to the nursery school. Funding is obtained through corporation grants, foundations, private donations, user fees, fundraisers, and the United Way.

SETTING UP A TOY-LENDING LIBRARY

Community-based organizations interested in setting up a toy-lending library can do so by following some basic guidelines. Adaptations and modifications can enable a large facility (such as a hospital or church) or an individual teacher to create a similar service for parents and children (Stone, 1983).

1. *Locate appropriate storage space for toys and materials.*
2. *Develop a catalog system for labeling and classifying toys.* Label toys by their age appropriateness, such as infant, toddler, preschooler, etc., or by their functional use, such as promotes fine motor development, provides practice in specific concept learning, etc.
3. *Develop an inventory system.* Keep records on the place and date of purchase, price paid, availability of replacement parts, address of manufacturer, and directions.
4. *Establish a circulation process.* Develop policies about checkout, renewal, overdue materials, replacement of broken toys, eligibility, and family registration.
5. *Set aside a play area for demonstrating toys.* In a school setting, this may not be necessary. A place for volunteers to sort, store, and check out materials may be the only requirements for space. In a facility where parents may want to be shown how to use a toy or have a child examine it, space may need to be allocated.
6. *Establish an intake file to record family registrations.* Information such as name, address, phone number, work number, ages and names of children, children's developmental ability if a disability is involved, and any other relevant facts could be filed on an index card or registration sheet.
7. *Survey parents periodically to evaluate the library services.* Surveys and questionnaires can be helpful when making decisions about additional purchases, expansion of hours and services, etc.

8. *Develop ways to publicize the toy library.* Brochures, pamphlets, flyers, and newsletter articles can inform local parents about the library and its services. Provide a list of the policies, procedures, and responsibilities of the library.

EXAMPLES OF SCHOOL-BASED TOY-LENDING LIBRARIES

Educators Teresa Harris, a kindergarten teacher in O'Fallon, Illinois, and Kathy Gary, a parent educator in Belleville, Illinois, have taken the concept of the toy-lending library and adapted it to suit their individual parent populations. Their programs have been designed and modified as a result of experience, use, and parent input. The results are unique programs that fulfill the specific objectives that each teacher has for her families.

"Loveable Bags" and "Fun with Boxes"   Teresa Harris developed her bags and boxes to enrich her students and extend kindergarten learning activities to their homes. Over several years, Teresa has developed 60 take-home activity bags that allow families to work with materials, games, and books that are developmentally appropriate. Each activity consists of:

- one or two books
- a laminated sheet of instructions for parents
- various manipulatives to facilitate a game or a learning experience
- a parent evaluation sheet
- a list of the ways the activity supplements learning and which skills are being enhanced

Activity bag and box checkout is handled by parent volunteers each morning and afternoon. They record the child's name and bag number on a clipboard, as well as any items that need to be replaced or repaired in any of the bags or boxes. Bag and box distribution is initiated at a parent meeting where the concept is shared and parents are allowed to preview the contents. One bag is circulated among all students first (one per school night) until all students have experienced the activity and returned it to class on time. Gradually, Teresa adds to the number of bags traveling to students' homes each week.

Activity bags can be filled with yard sale toys, discount store party favors, wholesale club merchandise, and items from teacher supply stores. Student book clubs can be a source of inexpensive, easy to replace books, keeping the cost of each unit to a minimum. See Figures 6.1, 6.2, and 6.3 for examples of an activity and the checkout grid.

Parent-Infant Activity Bags   Kathy Gary, looking for a way to provide home activities for her parents and infants, adapted the toy-lending library concepts for her Parents as Partners home visiting program. Her interest was in sharing developmentally appropriate, inexpensive toys, books, and games with parents of infants. Kathy found that when parents engaged in one-to-one activities with

FIGURE 6.1
Activities for Children to Check Out and Take Home

Loveable Bags
&
Fun with
Boxes

Presented by Teresa
Kindergarten Te
Estelle Kampmey
O'Fallon,

TIPS IN CREATING LOVEABLE BAGS

1. Choose your favorite book or one the children really like.
2. Read through the story and jot down questions that will help develop comprehension, prediction, thinking, and reasoning skills.
3. Brainstorm activities that center around the theme of the book (i.e., <u>If You Give a Mouse a Cookie</u> – one activity definitely would be to make cookies).
4. Write or type the format out–be sure to list the contents of the bag. This will help to keep track of the items as the bags are returned.
5. Collect materials needed for the activities.
6. Organize in folder or just by placing the items in the bag.
7. Enclose a Parents Response Sheet.
8. Place a tag on the bag and number the bag.
9. List the number and title on checkout sheet.
10. You're ready to share the bag and observe the excitement of the children!

TIPS IN CREATING FUN BOXES

1. Think of skills that your children enjoy doing or that need to be developed.
2. On an index card, write out the title and instructions on how to use the materials in the box.
3. Place the card and materials in the box. My goal and hope is that parents will be inspired to create the same "fun." Therefore, I try to use materials that parents could easily find right in their homes.
4. Number the box, list number and title on the checkout list.
5. Have fun.

A super resource is <u>I Can Do It! I Can Do It!</u> by LaBritta Gilbert, Gryphon House, Inc.

FIGURE 6.2
Take-Home Activity Explanation Sheet

BOOK: If You Give a Mouse a Cookie
by Laura Joffe Numeroff

Contents: small paperplates, crayons, pipe cleaners, scissors, holepunch, yarn, construction paper.

Activities

1. After reading the story, share a paperplate and the ear pattern with your child.

2. Together create a mouse mask by helping your child trace the ear patterns onto their choice of paper.

3. Allow your child to glue their ears, add whiskers or other features on their mask.

4. Help your child punch a hole on each side of the plate. Place a piece of yarn through the holes and tie to fit around their head.

5. Encourage your child to act out the parts of the mouse as you re-read the story.

6. Review the order of the story by asking your child what happened first, next, next and last?

Bag Activity Page 1

—filled together times...

...yons and a piece of paper with your ...when finished, be sure they sign ...ke the mouse. Then display their ...gerator.

...take part in making chocolate ...r child use the mouse shape cookie ...n to the cookies. Be sure to top ...lass of milk!

...to make playdough with your child creating with the playdough.

Skills that will meet specific developmental areas: sequencing, fine motor, gluing skills, tying skills, eye-hand coordination.

Bag Activity Page 2

FIGURE 6.3
Take-Home Activity Checklist

Fun in a Box
Loveable Bag

	1	2	3	4	5	6	7	8	9	10	11	
Amanda		X										
Brian			X									
Joshua	X											
Dimitri				X								
Keneesha					X							
Ling								X				
Miguel						X						

Parents need space to meet informally.

their infants they were helping them develop important language and motor skills. Parents can check out materials during the home visit and exchange bags at subsequent meetings. Each activity is created to suit a particular age and stage of growth and development.

PARENT SPACES, ROOMS, AND RESOURCE LIBRARIES

A common barrier to parent involvement is that schools are obviously designed for their traditional residents: students and teachers (Swap, 1987; Berger, 1987; Baskwill, 1989). One way to overcome this barrier is to create a parent room for visitors and volunteers. A parent room is a visible indication of the importance the school places on the parents' presence in the school or program. The function of the parent space is twofold: It acknowledges the needs of parents for a place to meet informally with other parents and volunteers, and it serves as a central location for resource information.

Consider the following scenarios with School A and School B. Picture yourself as parent in each facility and visualize the difference a parent room can make to the atmosphere in the school.

Imagine entering School A, perhaps to volunteer or to speak to a class, and discovering that there is nowhere to hang your coat or make a phone call to your sitter. You are early for your volunteer shift so you wait, standing, in the hall. How welcome do you feel?

Now picture yourself in School B, where you've come to volunteer in the media center. You arrive 30 minutes early to enjoy coffee with fellow PTO members and make phone calls to recruit extra help for the school book fair. You examine several new articles on helping children improve peer and sibling relationships; you consider checking them out. How welcome do you feel in this school?

SETTING UP A PARENT ROOM

The physical requirements of a parent room or space are relatively simple; many items can be obtained by donation from families and businesses. A comfortable sofa, several chairs, small tables, a telephone, a coffeepot, bookshelves, magazines, audio- and videotapes, and a bulletin board for posted announcements would adequately serve the purpose. If school space does not permit an entire room, consider making a portion of a workroom or a lounge into a parent space (Davies, 1991).

The key point is that a specific place is designated for parents who spend time in the school to set up a "home base" and communications center (Swap, 1993). The presence of this area sends a positive message to parents and other adults who volunteer their time: The teachers and administrators welcome them as partners in education and value their efforts, by making them feel a part of the school (Becker & Epstein, 1982).

SETTING UP A PARENT-RESOURCE LIBRARY

The parent-resource library, often located within the parent room, contains materials to assist families in their many roles. Topics are almost limitless, provided they serve the needs of the families of the school population. Examples are:

child health and wellness	stress management
pregnancy and childbirth	sibling rivalry
birthday party ideas	breastfeeding
positive discipline	family finances
choosing and making toys	infant care
family vacation information	general parenting
finding child care	toilet training
children's games	

In addition to books and parenting magazines, audio- and videotapes on related topics also are a significant part of the library. These enable parents

FIGURE 6.4
Parent Resource Registration Form

**FAMILY MATTERS!
PARENT RESOURCE
LIBRARY REGISTRATION**

Name:_____

Address: _____

Phone: _____

Names of Child(ren) at this School:_____

_____

THANK YOU!

who are visually or hearing impaired or who have poor reading skills to have access to parenting information. Depending on its size and the availability of volunteers, the resource library could be staffed during specific hours of the day or evening by a parent or other community volunteer. A simple file card system to organize checkout procedures is quick and inexpensive. Parents using the library could fill out a registration form similar to the one in Figure 6.4.

Once registered, the adult family members receive a list of all material available for checkout, the library's operating hours, and guidelines for using the facility. See also the discussion on toy-lending libraries beginning on Page 162.

FUNDING SOURCES

Sources of funding are as varied as the materials housed in the library. Sources to be investigated include:

- business or private donations of money or materials.
- minigrants from local businesses or foundations.
- fundraising proceeds from the PTO/PTA.
- community college family literacy programs or grants.

- local adult education/literacy programs.
- collaboration with other district services such as Title I programs, prekindergarten, at-risk programs, special education cooperatives or districts, Even Start programs, parenting programs (Parents as Teachers, etc.), local PTA/PTO organizations, and district media/library services.

Contacts Through Technology

Telephone Calls

Telephone calls from the school have earned a dubious reputation. Generally a phone call is connected with discipline problems, illness, accidents, incomplete work, tardiness, or requests for help (App, 1991). It is no wonder that parents steel themselves for unpleasantness when a teacher or principal phones them at home or at work. This situation is unfortunate because the telephone also can be used to relay positive information to parents. Consider the reaction of a parent to a congratulatory phone call by a child's teacher on a recent accomplishment:

> Elizabeth was able to participate in a playground game for the entire PE session today.

> Kevin made the longest unifix cube chain the class had ever seen, and his group counted each block.

In less time than it takes to write a note, the phone call lends a warm, personal touch to communication between home and school.

Scheduling phone time can be troublesome if the only access is located in a busy school office. The following suggestions may help facilitate teacher phone time in a practical way:

1. Try to locate a phone in a private area so that background noise and other people are not part of the conversation (Swap, 1993).
2. Request additional phone lines if access to an open line is a chronic problem. This may require a commitment of money to install; however, it is a feature that benefits all teachers in the school (App, 1991).
3. Be realistic about time allotments for phone use. If scheduling daily or weekly phone calls to parents cannot be accommodated within the regular teaching day, consider phoning just one family per week. At the end of the typical school year, this method would reach 36 families (App, 1991).

ADVANCED TECHNOLOGY

Some districts have successfully utilized the advanced technology afforded by computers working with the telephone in order to improve access to teachers.

One district in Tennessee pioneered the use of voice mail to promote better communication between teachers and parents. Each teacher was given an electronic voice mailbox and 1 to 3 minutes of message time. Possibilities include homework information or general tips supporting literacy at home. Parents simply call a designated number to play the message from a specific teacher (Bauch, 1989). Phone calls from parents at schools implementing this system increased by more than 500% without significantly increasing personnel time (Bauch, 1989).

Other schools have employed a computer calling system that forwards phone calls to specific parents or groups of parents with information supplied by the administrators or teachers. Content varies from attendance information to school schedule changes.

While administrative support is critical to the success of any new parent-teacher effort, the planning must be a joint effort to ensure commitment (App, 1991). One way to realize the effectiveness of the program is to maintain a record of positive phone calls made. Parents and teachers will be encouraged to continue the program when the log of positive contacts grows and teachers begin to reap the rewards of improved relationships with their students' families.

AUDIO- AND VIDEOTAPES

In order to effectively reach all parents, educators need to devise innovative ways to communicate (Rich, 1992; Bauch, 1989). Advanced technology has made it possible for a meeting to come to a parent's home if that parent is unable to attend it at school. Consider the wide variety of uses that audio- and videotapes provide as a means of relaying information to parents with special needs, parents who are homebound because of restrictive family situations, and parents who have work schedules that do not permit attendance at traditionally scheduled times. Some ideas include:

- Have a volunteer record the parent handbook onto an audiocassette for use at home or in the car. Visually impaired adults, those who are nonliterate, or parents who simply spend a lot of time in their cars might appreciate this method of reviewing school policies.
- Have a volunteer videotape a parent meeting or speaker so that families unable to attend can still benefit.
- Videotape everyday classroom routines to create, for example, a composite tape of "A Day in First Grade," which could be rotated among students to share at home with family members unable to visit the classroom.
- Focus on a subject area—language arts, for example—to portray how the class functions during this time. The tape could be shared at parent or orientation meetings to give parents a visual record of a whole language classroom or developmentally appropriate center time.
- Use cassette tape to record individual students reading aloud. When done periodically throughout the year, this can be a wonderful tool to track the growth and progress of beginning readers. It is also a valuable assessment method for teachers to share with parents at conferences.

- Videotape or tape-record children's concerts and plays to share with incoming students, as a teaching tool and for enjoyment. Many parents appreciate the opportunity to copy these tapes for their own home libraries.
- Have a parent volunteer videotape the class orientation meeting to share with students entering midyear who would not otherwise have the opportunity to attend such a session. This is an excellent way to make a new family feel welcome.

MASS MEDIA

Using the mass media as a source of communication to parents and families is often overlooked by educators. They assume it is too costly and difficult to arrange. There are, however, a number of strategies that make the use of radio, TV, and newspapers a powerful tool and often a free source of publicity for a school or program.

RADIO AND TELEVISION

Local radio and television programming often is geared to discussions of interesting events in and around the community. Interview and phone-in program formats offer the opportunity for a teacher or administrator to publicize upcoming events that would be of interest to local families. Free radio and television time can often be arranged by requesting public service announcement time. A parent education series, homework hotline, or upcoming speaker could be advertised to reach parents not affiliated with the schools or who have difficulty reading printed materials sent home with students.

Local cable community access stations are able to air longer video segments to promote parent programs or display an interesting presentation by students. Request information in advance to determine specific time and tape requirements. In some instances, a staff member from the station may record a class performance for future airing. This is an effective way to include all families in the enjoyment of a play, concert, or holiday presentation by students.

NEWSPAPERS

Newspapers can serve a dual role in bringing students and programs to the attention of the general public. Most newspapers have a community calendar section that heralds upcoming area events. Activities such as parent education series, open houses, workshops, and informational meetings can be included free of charge and will reach a wide audience.

Newspapers also are interested in publishing human interest stories and pictures of children participating in interesting activities. Notify the local paper of special events the class is planning and arrange for a visit by the photographer. It is exciting for students to gain recognition for their efforts in this manner and allows the community to see the positive things occurring in schools.

SUMMARY

There are a number of levels of verbal communication that can occur between parents and teachers. Some, such as telephone calls and incidental contacts, are relatively short and infrequent. Others, such as field trips, open houses, and orientation meetings, provide greater opportunities for parents and teachers to interact and begin to develop a relationship based on mutual trust. The parent education strategy provides parents with meaningful dialogue and the chance to relate as parents and adults who share common struggles and successes.

Some parents feel comfortable enough to quickly build a relationship with their child's teachers; others move slowly as confidence and trust replace fear and suspicion. It is well worth the effort on everyone's part to attempt to reach all families and extend the opportunity to work together.

ACTIVITIES FOR DISCUSSION, EXPANSION, AND APPLICATION

1. Create an outline for a kindergarten orientation meeting. Include a short description of all information presented to parents and written materials distributed.

2. Imagine you are the director of a child-care/preschool facility serving 80 families. Parents and staff have expressed a strong interest in parenting classes that could be offered at the center. Create a schedule of parent education offerings in combination with other strategies presented in this chapter that would represent the overall plan for one school year.

3. An early childhood center, housing grades prekindergarten through second, would like to request funding for a toy-lending library. Write a rationale for this request including information about the population to be served, staffing, and benefits to families.

4. As an early childhood professional, you have decided to increase the verbal communication between your families and the school/center. Describe strategies that might be employed to address the needs of all parents involved. Specify the age and grade and location of school or center (rural, urban, private, suburban, public, etc.).

5. A school or center located in a culturally diverse neighborhood is evaluating the strengths and weaknesses of the verbal communication strategies currently in use. Discuss the implications such a population might have on new techniques to be added and on modifications to those already in place.

REFERENCES

App, M. (1991). *Families and education: An educator's resource for family involvement.* Madison, WI: Wisconsin Department of Public Instruction.

Arizona Department of Education. (1989). Parent-teacher communication: A handbook for teachers and parents. ERIC Source: ED 321 896.

Baskwell, J. (1989). Parents and teachers: Partners in learning. Canada: Scholastic.

Bauch, J. (1989). The transparent school model: New technology for parent involvement. *Educational Leadership, 10,* 32–34.

Becker, H.J., & Epstein, J.L. (1982). Parent involvement: A study of teacher practices. *Elementary School Journal, 83,* 85–102.

Berger, E.H. (1995). *Parents as partners in education: Families and schools working together.* Englewood Cliffs, NJ: Merrill.

Butts, P., Brooten, D., & Brown, L. (1988). Concerns of parents of low birth weight infants following hospital discharge: A report of parent-initiated telephone calls. *Neonatal Network, 7*(2), 37–42.

Canter, L. (1991). *Parents on your side.* Santa Monica, CA: Lee Canter and Associates.

Carney, M. (1984). *Parent-teacher communication: A handbook for teachers and parents.* Arizona Department of Education.

Cataldo, C. (1983). *Infants and toddlers programs.* Reading, MA: Addison-Wesley.

Cataldo, C. (1987). *Parent education for early childhood.* New York: Teachers College Press.

Curran, D. (1989). *Working with parents.* Circle Pines, MN: American Guidance Service.

Davis, D. (January 1991). Schools reaching out: Family, school, and community partnerships for student success. *Phi Delta Kappan,* 378–380.

Dempsey, J., and Frost, J. (1993). Play environments for early childhood education. In B. Spode (Ed.), *Handbook of research on the education of young children* (pp. 306–320). New York: Macmillan.

Dinkmeyer, D., McKay, G., Dinkmeyer, J. (1989). *Parenting young children.* Circle Pines, MN: American Guidance Services.

Doss, R. (1985). *Parent-teacher communication: A handbook for teachers and parents.* Arizona Department of Education.

Elmer, E., & Maloni, J. (1986). Parent support through telephone consultation. *Maternal-Child Nursing Journal, 13,* 13–23.

Gordon, T. (1970). *Parent effectiveness training.* New York: Penguin.

Greenberg, P. (1989). Parents as partners in young children's development and education: A new American fad? Why does it matter? *Young Children, 44*(4), 61–74.

Henderson, A., Marburger, C., & Ooms, T. (1986). *Beyond the bake sale: An educator's guide to working with parents.* Washington, DC: National Committee for Citizens in Education.

Jackson S., Robey, L., Watjus, M., & Chadwick, E. (Fall 1991). Play for all children. *Childhood Education, 68*(1), 27–30.

Juul, K. (April 1984). Toy libraries for the handicapped: An international survey. Paper presented at the Annual Convention of the Council for Exceptional Children. Washington, DC.

Leuthy, G. (1991). An example of parent education at the work site. *Young Children, 46*(4), 62–63.

Morris, B. (September 1991). *The child's right to play.* Paper presented at early childhood convention, Dunedine, New Zealand.

Nimnicht, G., & Brown, E. (1972). The toy library: Parents and children learning with toys. *Young Children, 28*(2), 110–116.

Popkins, M. (1987). *Active parenting.* San Francisco: Harper & Row.

Powell, D.R. (1989). *Families and early childhood programs.* Washington, DC: National Association for the Education of Young Children.

Purnell, D. (1985). *Parent-teacher communication: A handbook for teachers and parents.* Arizona Department of Education.

Rasinski, T., & Fredericks, A. (September 1990). Working with parents. *The Reading Teacher, 44*(1), 76–77.

Rich, D. (1992). *Megaskills®.* Boston: Houghton Mifflin.

Schaefer, E. (1991). Goals for parent and future-parent education: Research on parental beliefs and behavior. *The Elementary School Journal, 91*(3), 239–247.

Shea, T., & Bauer, A. (1991). *Parents and teachers of children with exceptionalities.* Boston: Allyn & Bacon.

Stevens, J. (1978). Parent education programs: What determines effectiveness? *Young Children, 5,* 59–65.

Stone, M. (1983). *Enhancing parent involvement in schools.* New York: Teachers College Press.

Swap, S.M. (1993). Developing home-school partnerships. New York: Teachers College Press.

Swick, K. (1991). *Teacher-parent partnerships to enhance school success in early childhood education.* Washington, DC: National Education Association.

Vincents, S. de. (April 1984). *Play intervention for handicapped children.* Paper presented at the Council for Exceptional Children, Washington, DC.

Waxman, P.L. (1991). Children in the world of adults—onsite child care. *Young Children, 46*(5), 16–21.

Chapter 7

HOME VISITS

READERS WILL BE ABLE TO:

- Identify model programs that have home visits as a major component.
- Elaborate on the necessity of having a purpose when making a home visit.
- Describe the key components of a successful home visit.
- Describe the criteria that can be used to select a home visitor.
- Identify behaviors that should be avoided by home visitors.

Home visits by early childhood, elementary, and secondary school teachers are becoming increasingly common. More and more, boards of education and school administrators are supporting school personnel in this effective strategy, which enhances family-school relationships. In this chapter we examine how home visits have been utilized since the turn of the century as a means of involving families in the education of their children. The advantages and disadvantages of this strategy are presented. Procedures to follow when making home visits as well as practices to avoid are covered. Model programs that have home visits as a major component are described and referenced. Both traditional school-based visits and home-based visit programs are addressed.

HISTORICAL PERSPECTIVES

Home visiting has been practiced for years in Europe and in this country as a method of working with needy families. At the turn of the century, it was common to see doctors, nurses, and teachers making home visits. Home visiting was one way to meet medical needs, teach parenting skills, and provide support for high-risk families (Miller, 1987). Seefeldt (1980) reported that even before the time of Margaret McMillan, the founder of nursery education early in this

Home visits are becoming increasingly common.

century, teachers of young children visited homes as a means of involving parents in the educational progress of their children.

Hendrick (1988) suggests that as the home visitor interacts with the child,
the goal is to also draw in the parents so that they can gradually add to their
own repertoire of ideas and activities that will enhance their child's growth. As
the parents begin to understand how important it is to develop language competence in young children, and learn in simple and practical ways how they can
foster this ability, a positive, continuing influence has been built into their children's lives.

During the 1960s and 1970s, numerous intervention programs incorporated home visits in response to the needs of children who were developmentally delayed, economically disadvantaged, socially constrained, or in some way
disabled as learners. These programs placed a heavy emphasis on involving parents in the enhancement of their children's health, social/emotional, and cognitive development.

In more recent years, home visiting has moved from primarily being an intervention to that of being a strategy of reaching people before problems develop. This emerging discipline is called prevention. Prevention efforts strive
to promote positive qualities and strengths in people and families to empower
them to function in healthy ways.

The following are models of programs currently operating; they offer
training and/or materials that can assist programs that wish to initiate home
visiting. A list of telephone numbers and addresses is included in the Appendix.

MODEL HOME VISITING INTERVENTION PROGRAMS

HIGH/SCOPE

The High/Scope Perry Preschool Program began in 1962 as an intervention program that consisted of 2-1/2 hours of preschool five days a week for 7-1/2 months each year for two years. In addition, teachers made weekly, 90-minute home visits to the families of all the children enrolled in the program. This program has been duplicated in this country and overseas. The longitudinal effects on the children initially enrolled have been most favorable throughout their childhood and into their adult years.

HEAD START

Head Start is a federally funded, comprehensive child development program that has mandated home visiting since its inception in 1965. One of the major components of the program is parent involvement, in such areas as parent education, program planning, and facility operation. Many parents serve on policy advisory councils and committees to provide input on administrative and managerial situations. The program requires that every family in center-based programs receive at least two home visits a year. In addition to teacher visits, the program also employs social service staff members to make home visits and provide services that include community social service referrals, family needs assessments, information on available services, recruitment and enrollment of children, and emergency assistance and/or crisis intervention.

MOTHER-CHILD HOME PROGRAM

The Mother-Child Home Program (MCHP), developed by Levenstein's Verbal Interaction Project in 1965 under the direction of Phyllis Levenstein, is an example of a home-based intervention model in which home visitors, called toy demonstrators, visit homes twice a week over two years to families with children aged 2 to 4 years. Following the school calendar, a total of 92 visits are made. During the visits, parents are given instruction on how to introduce toys and books to their children as well as how to model positive language interaction in play situations. By 1993, 29 replications of this program served an estimated 4,000 mother-child pairs throughout the United States (Honig, 1975; Cataldo, 1983; Berger, 1991; Behrman, 1993).

PORTAGE PROJECT

The Portage Project, established in 1969 in Portage, WI, serves children between the ages of birth and 6 years who have diagnosed disabilities, or who are developmentally delayed or economically disadvantaged. Visitors make weekly, 90-minute home visits during which time they work with parents to plan and implement strategies for addressing the needs of the child, as identified through an initial assessment process. These strategies are incorporated into the family's daily routine to help family members become involved in the child's developmental program. The home visitor also works with parents to develop or strengthen their support network, develop action plans for addressing broader family concerns, and access community resources. The materials needed for the program include a developmental checklist of 580 developmentally sequenced behaviors divided into six areas: infant stimulation, self-help, language, cognition, motor skills, and socialization. A set of 580 cards describes activities for the parents to use to help their children develop specific behaviors in the six areas. A manual of instruction provides detailed directions on how to implement the Portage Project. This home visiting model has been replicated in private schools, public schools, and Head Start programs throughout the United States. Several countries, including the United Kingdom and Japan, also have incorporated the program. The materials are available in 30 languages (Cataldo, 1983, Berger, 1991; Behrman, 1993).

HOME INSTRUCTION PROGRAM FOR PRESCHOOL YOUNGSTERS

The Home Instruction Program for Preschool Youngsters (HIPPY) began in Israel in 1969 and was introduced to the United States in 1984 with the assistance of the National Council for Jewish Women. This model targets parents with limited formal education and their children aged 4 and 5. Paraprofessionals make biweekly home visits to provide parents with books and activity sheets. They teach parents how to use the materials with their children; parents and children then work together for 15 to 20 minutes each day. During each of two years, the program provides 30 weeks of activities for parents, scheduled to generally coincide with the school year. The activities include basic reading skills, such as tactile, auditory, visual, and conceptual discrimination; language development; verbal expression; eye-hand coordination; premath concepts; logical thinking; self-concept; and creativity. On alternate weeks, the parents, the home visitors, and the program coordinator meet to role-play the week's assigned activities and discuss parenting issues of concern. The paraprofessional home visitors are members of the participating communities and often are recruited from the same pool of families that initially enroll in the program. Eighty-one programs now operate in 23 states, and some 10,000 children and their families participate each year. Funding includes public sources and private foundations (HIPPY USA, 1994; Behrman, 1993).

FAMILY, INFANT, AND PRESCHOOL PROGRAM

The Family, Infant, and Preschool Program began in 1972 in North Carolina. It serves families of young children who have been diagnosed as having developmental disabilities or who are thought to be at risk of developing such disabilities. Home visits can begin immediately following birth and may continue until a child is 5 years old. Home visitors assess child and family needs, explore options for meeting needs, develop strategies for implementing interventions, and revise and update individualized family support plans as needs are met or new needs arise. The assessment and intervention model includes four primary components: specification of family needs, mobilization of intrafamily resources and capabilities, mobilization of extrafamily sources of support and resources to meet needs, and utilization of a variety of staff roles in helping families access resources from their social support networks. Other services are available as needed, including case management, parent-child community groups, center-based programs for children, parent support groups, pediatric services, physical therapy, respite care services, equipment for special needs children, and an adult learning center. Approximately 27 programs throughout the country are based on this model (Behrman, 1993).

MODEL HOME VISITING PREVENTION PROGRAMS

NEW PARENTS AS TEACHERS

The New Parents as Teachers (NPAT) program, which focuses on first-time parents, is a model prevention effort. The program began in 1981 as an adaptation of the parent education model developed by Burton White. In this program, there are two forms of contact with the parents: home visits and group meetings. During the home visits, curriculum materials relevant to the child's current age, as well as upcoming stages of development, are distributed and discussed. Home visits are scheduled once every six weeks and last one hour. Along with home visits are group meetings in which seven to eight couples come together to discuss child development topics. These meetings are held once a month and serve the dual function of social support and to increase the parents' knowledge base. In 1993 there were 1,600 NPAT programs in 42 states serving approximately 90,000 families a year. The program is offered statewide in Missouri and is funded by the Missouri Department of Education, with additional money provided by local school districts (Behrman, 1993).

HAWAII HEALTHY START

The Hawaii Healthy Start program is another model prevention approach. It was started in 1985 by the Hawaii Family Stress Center as a federal demonstration project to prevent child abuse and neglect. The program has evolved into a statewide program funded by the Maternal and Child Health division of the Hawaii State Department of Health. There currently are 13 sites in Hawaii. During fiscal 1993, 74% of the $7 million provided by the state was earmarked for home visiting services. During 1993, 54% of Hawaii's newborns were screened.

Home visits are a widely used strategy for family involvement.

The goals of the program are:

1. Assure that all families have a primary health-care provider.
2. Assure that there is proper use of community resources.
3. Promote positive parenting.
4. Enhance parent-child interaction.
5. Enhance child health and development.
6. Prevent child abuse and neglect.

Home visits are conducted by paraprofessionals. Services begin at the birth of a child and continue until age 5. If a hospital recorded review suggests the possible need for service, the family is interviewed in the hospital shortly after the birth of the child. Home visits are offered to families who exhibit the need for such assistance based on their scores on a family stress inventory administered during the hospital visit. At first, visits are conducted weekly, with their frequency reduced as families resolve specific needs. The program receives funding from both public and private agencies.

RESOURCE MOTHERS PROGRAM

The Resource Mothers Program is a prevention model that began in 1980 in South Carolina. Approximately 300 now operate across the nation. The program employs paraprofessionals from participating communities to visit pregnant women and their children. The goals of the program are to improve birth outcomes, decrease injuries to children, and lower child abuse rates by providing information about maternal and child health and development. There is also an effort to empower mothers to utilize health and other community services. The home visitors serve as mentors to the expectant mother throughout her pregnancy, delivery, and the first year of her child's life (Behrman, 1993).

THE PURPOSE OF THE HOME VISIT

The appeal of the home visit as a strategy for parent involvement is based on the opportunity that it provides for the school to work with individuals within the context of the family. The home visit provides an avenue for the teacher to get to know the child's family, environment, and culture in order to serve both child and parents more effectively (Shea & Bauer, 1991).

A home visitor should never make a visit without having a specific, planned purpose. Watson (1990) cites the following purposes:

- To get parents involved with their child's learning.
- To use parents' skills and knowledge, family interests, and resources to teach children.
- To teach parents developmentally appropriate ways to reach specific objectives.
- To get families involved with the program, the school, and the community.
- To determine and address needs of children and their families.
- To provide information about community resources.
- To provide guidance for families in getting the help they need. (As well, to strengthen parents by encouraging them to meet their own needs.)
- To broaden the experiences of children.
- To increase the self-esteem of children and parents.

Bundy (1991), on the other hand, concludes that the express purpose of the home visit is to introduce the children to their teachers and other staff members in familiar surroundings.

THE EFFECTIVENESS OF HOME VISITS

The home visit as a strategy for involving parents as partners is becoming more prevalent as schools and agencies that receive state and federal funds are mandated to visit the homes of the children enrolled in their programs. A wide diversity of programs utilize home visiting. Their structure, goals, and the families they serve limit to some extent the lessons we can draw from research about their effectiveness. Weiss (1993) reports that home visiting in and of itself has never been an effective cure-all in addressing the complicated needs of families. Still, research suggests that the most effective programs are comprehensive, continuous, and family focused. The evaluation of effectiveness is further complicated because home visiting programs offer different curricula and different frequency of visits, and employ staff members with different backgrounds and skills—all of which can be strong variables in program effectiveness. Despite these problems, some programs have demonstrated positive health and/or developmental outcomes for children. Many also have found positive effects on the mothers' personal development measured in terms of higher self-esteem, continuing education, and a movement toward self-sufficiency.

Cataldo (1987) suggests that home visits offer a sense of support in knowing that somebody cares, and such caring helps socially isolated families feel more important. Powell (1990) reports that early studies of home visiting uncovered positive effects of home-based early intervention of the children's cognitive and social development, as well as on adult development. He further indicates that recent studies have shown positive effects on improving child and maternal health. Wasik (1993) notes that the home visit offers benefits that increase the ability of the program staff to help the families they serve. These benefits include: (1) gaining access to information about the conditions in which the family lives, (2) learning about family interaction patterns, (3) discovering family values and beliefs, and (4) finding out about the social and material resources that are available to support the family. The information collected can serve to prompt intervention efforts that are more family centered and sensitive to the families' environment.

Gestwicki (1992) indicates that home visits provide a setting that fosters increased trust on the part of the parents, child, and teacher. The visit also affords the teacher with insight into how the parents and the child interact in their home environment. The teacher uses this information to match the child's needs and to utilize the parents' resources, which were learned about during the visit. Shea and Bauer (1991) suggest the home visit helps the teacher get to know the child's family environment and culture better, a help in serving the child and parents more effectively. The visit is an occasion for the teacher to meet the other members of the child's family and become acquainted with the child's learning context. Home visits provide an opportunity to get to know the family, to give an explanation of the representative program, to gather information, to report the child's school progress, to problem solve, and to get parental input for additional parent involvement strategies.

SUCCESSES

At a home visitor training conference, trainees whose home visiting experience ranged from 2 to 22 years were asked to list the successes of this strategy (Rockwell, 1993). Their responses were as follows:

- Changes in family attitudes.
- Improves ability of family to work with child.
- Increases utilization of outside resources.

- Getting to know the family.
- Bridges gap between home and school.
- Improves collaboration skills.
- Creates positive relationships.
- Builds self-esteem in parents and child.
- Develops an understanding of the child's environment.
- Positive child behavior changes.
- Parents become involved in school activities.
- Parents become resource to teacher.
- Fathers become involved.
- Empowerment: parents setting up their own support group, returning to school to obtain GED, finding employment.
- Positive results (feedback) from what we have done or suggested.
- Sharing success stories.
- Parents see children in a positive light (learn how to enjoy them).
- Increases teamwork.
- Creates friendships and respect.
- Changes attitudes (positive from negative).
- Parents view school and staff as partners rather than foes.
- Parents support child's attendance in program.
- Parents view themselves as the child's first teachers.
- Positive overall change in families' lives.
- Seeing real change or progress.
- Wanting home/visitors to return.
- Increases notes and phone calls.

DISADVANTAGES

Home visits do have some disadvantages. The time required to plan, schedule, and conduct the visit is the most frequently mentioned disadvantage. Presuppositions that both the parents and the home visitor bring to the setting also can be a problem. Negative past experiences often pose a barrier that clouds all efforts of involving the parents. It is critical that the initial home visit be used to eradicate any negative experiences that might serve to derail the future involvement of the family.

Home visits to high-crime neighborhoods or to isolated rural areas can be dangerous. Some programs use teams of two or more visitors. Visitors in problem areas often carry cellular phones in case of emergencies.

DIVERSITY IN HOME VISITING PROGRAMS

Home visiting programs can be quite different in content and methods. The practice itself is a generic label representing a service delivery system. Programs vary considerably as to whether the substance of the home visit is focused primarily on the child (single focus) or includes attention to the parent and family function (multiple focus). Regardless of the type of program—school-based, home-based, single-focused, multiple-focused, intervention, or prevention—the home visitor will be working with the entire family. When issues arise that are out of the parameter of services offered by a specific program, the home visitor will respond by assisting the parent in making contact with an appropriate community resource.

CULTURAL SENSITIVITY

Cultural background lays a foundation of values and perspectives of the world that help family members define who they are. A family's values and practices often will differ from those of the home visitor. This implies that the home visitor must cultivate rapport and trust with families that may view the world very differently. If the home visitor is to develop a sensitivity and respect for the cultural backgrounds of the families with whom they work, they must be given training that focuses on the fundamental values, beliefs, customs, practices, and traditions of those families. The understanding that will be gained through such training will enrich the home visit and promote a more supportive partnership between the home and the school. (See Chapter 3 for additional information.)

QUALIFICATIONS FOR HOME VISITORS

Unless a staff member has had some training in social work, it is doubtful that he or she will have had any experience or background in how to plan or conduct a home visit. Training will help avoid problems that could jeopardize all future parent involvement strategies. A study by Wasik and Roberts (1993) involved a national survey of home visitor characteristics, training, and supervision. The respondents represented public or private health, education, social service, and Head Start programs. The findings revealed that the percentage of home visiting programs that offered training ranged from 40% for private education to more than 70% for Head Start programs. The programs using a written curriculum for training ranged from 12% to 30%. The wide diversity of programs within given communities offers an excellent opportunity for the various programs to work collaboratively not only in developing home visiting training materials, but also in offering joint training opportunities.

Coordination of training efforts also can provide those who are new to this strategy an opportunity to learn from those who have had more experience. An example of a home visitor training program that brings both experienced and novice trainees together is shown in the box titled Home Visitor Training Program.

HOME VISITOR TRAINING PROGRAM

1. As an introduction, list three things that describe how you felt when you made your first home visit. Participant gives his/her name and agency, then shares feelings. (Mixer)

2. Give an overview of and the history of home visiting. (Minilecture)

3. Break into small groups and write down the problems that individuals in the group have had in making home visits. (Brainstorming and small-group discussion)

4. Write the success experiences that individuals in the same small groups have had in making home visits. (Brainstorming and small-group discussion)

5. Post the problems and the success experiences on the wall. Choose one of the problems and prepare a 2 to 3 minute role play that demonstrates the problem. The small group also should be prepared to offer its collaborative decision as to how this problem might be resolved. (Small-group discussion and role-playing preparation)

6. Have each group role-play its problem and solicit audience reaction and feedback as to how audience members might resolve or have resolved the problem. The group also can share its solution. The experience of group members should be capitalized on here. (Role playing large-group discussion)

7. Allow each group to shares its success experiences. (Large group)

8. Break for 10 to 15 minutes.

9. Give the rationale and philosophy for home visiting. Programs represented can share their rationale and philosophy. (Large group)

10. Discuss the personal traits required of the home visitor. (Brainstorming, large group)

11. Describe how to conduct a home visit. Share the step-by-step components that are a part of all home visits. (Transparencies and overhead projector, minilecture, and large-group discussion)

12. Ask small groups to compile a list of do's and don'ts for home visitors. (Small-group discussion)

13. Post lists of do's and don'ts. Compare and develop a master list as a collaborative effort by the entire audience. Record the list and share it by mail with all participants. (Large and small groups)

14. Stress the importance of communication skills. Classify listening skills and do active-listening exercises. (Large and small groups)

15. Close.

PERSONAL TRAITS

The U.S. Department of Health, Education, and Welfare (1974), through its Office of Child Development, discusses several personality traits that will serve home visitors well as they attempt to get parents to open the doors not only to their homes but to their lives.

Home visitors should be warm, outgoing, energetic, enthusiastic, and dignified. They should be able to adapt their personality to meet varying needs. Home visitors must relate well with both adults and children and be able to listen well and communicate effectively. Home visitors have learned that there is no single right or wrong way to approach all the situations they will face. They must be sensitive to the actions and reactions of others and be able to change strategies easily when subtle signals indicate resistance or nonacceptance. Home visitors must be able to see the other person's point of view and want to work out solutions that are not only "right," but also acceptable for each family. Home visitors should have an eager interest in the job and the motivation to work long and hard hours.

Whatever the culture or background of the families to be served, home visitors must be able to win their confidence quickly so as to be accepted and trusted. Trust does not come automatically—it must be earned. Home visitors should have the ability to converse with families using the families' native language. If necessary, an interpreter should accompany the home visitor. Home visitors should be able to respond to families' needs as they arise. Some visits may need to be made on weekends or during the evening. Such visitation should have the family's approval. Home visitors also must keep privileged information confidential and must respect each family's privacy.

MAKING THE HOME VISIT

Regardless of how much training a person has received, making the first home visit is never easy. The first-time visitor is usually nervous, fearful, unsure of what to expect, uncertain of what to say or do, and afraid that something might be said that will offend the family. The best antidote for these emotions is to realize that they are very common and that after making a few visits, they begin to disappear.

Here are some important points to consider arranged in order:

1. *Plan the visit.*

   Why are you making the visit? What will you try to accomplish? Gather information regarding the child in question. If presenting a lesson or an activity, collect your materials and organize them.

2. *Schedule the visit.*

   Inform the parents that you are coming. This can be accomplished by telephoning or sending a note or letter to the home indicating the purpose, date, time, and length of your visit. That allows the parents to let you know whether the time is convenient and to suggest an alternative time or place. Some families would rather meet in a neutral site such as a restaurant or a church; this request should be honored.

3. *Go to the home.*

   Be sure to arrive on time.

4. *Establish rapport.*

   When you ask for the person or persons being visited, use full names. Introduce yourself and explain the purpose of your visit. Open the conversation by briefly telling something about yourself, your background, and your relationship to the school. Be open to discussing problems that might be foremost on the parents' mind. Attempt to deal with problems if possible. Be positive, pleasant, sincere, and caring.

5. *Convey a genuine interest.*

Interest is the key word, particularly an interest in the child or children. Review the last contact, whether at school or at a previous home visit. What were the recommendations at that time? Gather and record information about the accomplishments that pertain to previous recommendations. Identify strengths and weaknesses. Reinforce accomplishments and efforts. If dealing with a lesson or a specific activity that was left during the previous visit, be prepared to reteach if necessary.

6. *Conduct the planned activities.*

Follow your objectives, yet be prepared to adjust and modify them to fit the circumstances. No matter how well prepared you are, there will be an untold list of situations that will distract you and the parents. Always try to focus on the parent, child, or both, according to your program plan.

7. *Review the activities that were presented.*

Allow time for and encourage parents to ask clarification questions. Have the parents demonstrate any new activities.

8. *Make announcements regarding future parent-child activities at school and in the community.*

Distribute the materials you plan to leave. Gather the materials you plan to take with you. Make an appointment for the next visit.

9. *Conclude the visit.*

Remind the parents of important things to do. Say good-bye to everyone.

10. *Evaluate yourself after the visit.*

Ask these questions:

- Was I prepared?
- Was I successful in establishing rapport?
- Did I engage in a two-way dialogue?
- Did I utilize active-listening skills?
- Did I respond to parent concerns?
- Were the materials adequate?
- Did I explain the activities in an understandable manner?
- How did the child react?
- How did the parents react?
- What was the highlight of the visit?
- What problems were there?
- How could I improve?
- What changes were observed in the child? In the parents?
- What can I do to expand on today's learning?

SPECIFIC BEHAVIORS TO AVOID WHEN WORKING WITH FAMILIES

1. *Don't push your values on the families.*

   We all have our own values and must appreciate and allow others the right to have theirs.

2. *Never do for the family what its members are capable of doing for themselves.*

   Help empower them to become competent in meeting their specific child and family needs.

3. *Avoid diagnosing and prescribing for families and telling them what to do.*

   You can assist as they assess their own needs and interject your own observations if necessary.

4. *Do not stereotype families.*

   Each family is unique, with its own strengths and weaknesses.

5. *Do not assume the role of Mr. or Ms. Fix-it.*

   You cannot resolve all the world's problems with some instantaneous cure-all. It is critical that home visitors be knowledgeable of community agencies where families can go to obtain needed services. Networking with agencies within your community will increase your effectiveness when needs occur.

6. *Be consistent.*

   It is imperative that you keep appointments and follow through with all commitments. The family must be able to trust that you are being honest and acting in the best interest of the child and family.

7. *Do not expect too much too soon.*

   Habits and ways of relating to people and situations have been formed over years and do not change overnight. It is perfectly OK to expect change, but expecting it too quickly can be frustrating and self-defeating for everyone involved.

8. *Avoid letting the family become dependent upon you.*

   Do be a professional helper. Do not offer to lend money or provide transportation for personal activities. The home-visitor relationship must be a friendly one. Keeping it on a professional level will assist you in preventing it from becoming counterproductive.

9. *Do not violate confidentiality.*

   What families tell you is to be held in confidence. Never discuss these families with your own family or friends. Families should be told that the information and data you collect while in their home will be held in strict confidence.

SUMMARY

Home visiting is a parent involvement strategy that, if employed successfully, can be the foundation for all future involvement of the family in the education of the child. It is a strategy that provides unique access to families and extensive information about their home situation. The primary aim is to encourage parents to take an active interest in the education of their children and to work as partners with school personnel in meeting goals that will be beneficial to all.

ACTIVITIES FOR DISCUSSION, EXPANSION, AND APPLICATION

1. Divide the class into two groups. Have one group discuss and list what it believes are the advantages of home visits. The second group will list disadvantages. Post the two lists and discuss the pros and cons of home visits.

2. Divide the class into groups. Have each group select a problem from one of the following hypothetical situations that one might encounter when making a home visit. Follow these steps:

- Choose a group recorder.
- Read the problem situation.
- Discuss the strategies that the group might use to resolve the problem.
- Prepare a dramatization to demonstrate the problem or situation.
- Role-play the problem or situation.
- Solicit class reaction and feedback on how to resolve the problem.
- Share the group's consensus on how the problem was resolved.

SITUATION 1

The family is never home when you visit.

SITUATION 2

What should you say or do when the home is infested with roaches and rats?

SITUATION 3

You are to visit and work with one child, yet there are three other children in the family and they are always there when you arrive.

SITUATION 4

The parent spanks the child or children in your presence.

SITUATION 5

You arrive for the visit and the only one home is the mother's boyfriend.

SITUATION 6

While visiting the home, there is constant interruption from telephone calls and from people you do not know who are coming and going in and out of the house.

SITUATION 7

The family speaks a language that you are unable to understand. Further, the family cannot read or understand English.

SITUATION 8

There is a power struggle between the parents as to how best raise the child.

SITUATION 9

The child (5 years old) is being raised by grandparents, and they are at their wits' end as to how to handle his quite-normal restlessness. "He just can't sit still for more than 5 minutes!" they complain.

SITUATION 10

You can never find the homes of the children. You seem to always get lost and end up driving in circles.

SITUATION 11

Every time you visit, the mother watches the television soaps while you work with the child.

SITUATION 12

You are confronted by those friendly and not-so-friendly pets.

SITUATION 13

While interviewing the mother, you see evidence that she has been abused.

SITUATION 14

While visiting, you see evidence of child abuse.

SITUATION 15

You have made numerous visits, and the family never follows through with suggestions you have made for working with the child.

SITUATION 16

You arrive at the door for a home visit just as the mother is leaving. She asks you to stay with the child until she gets back. "It's only for a minute. I'll be right back," she says.

SITUATION 17

During the home visit, the parents dominate the conversation with issues that are not related to the child.

SITUATION 18

You fear for your physical safety in this neighborhood.

SITUATION 19

The parents have a negative attitude toward the school.

SITUATION 20

The parents provide food and a drink when you really don't want them.

SITUATION 21

You arrive at the home and find the child or children home alone.

SITUATION 22

A parent answers the door unclothed.

SITUATION 23

The parents are sleeping when you arrive.

SITUATION 24

During the visit, you observe weapons under the sofa.

SITUATION 25

The parents refuse to let you enter the home.

SITUATION 26

A parent asks you to sit on the sofa, and as you do, you discover that it's wet.

SITUATION 27

The parent tells you that she is considering suicide, because she is so fed up and stressed with her life.

3. Discuss the problems your personal values could present as you make a home visit. How might this issue be resolved?

4. Discuss the basic guidelines for making a home visit.

5. Would you feel comfortable making a home visit? Explain your answer.

6. You are the director of a prekindergarten program that serves 200 families. Staff members have never made home visits, nor have they received training. Outline what you believe should be included in a home visitor training program for your staff.

7. Should teachers make home visits, or should they only be made by people specifically hired to do them? Explain your position.

8. Contact one of the home visitor models mentioned in this chapter. Prepare a detailed report of the model, and share it with the class.

9. How would you react to a home visit made to your home? Share with class members both positive and negative reactions.

REFERENCES

Barnett, M.F., & Meyer, T. (1992). The teacher's playing at my house this week. *Young Children, 47*(5), 45–50.

Behrman, R.E. (Ed.). (1993). *Home visiting: The future of children.* Center for the Future of Young Children, The David and Lucile Packard Foundation, *3*(3), 208.

Berger, E.H. (1991). *Parents as partners in education: The school and home working together* (3rd ed.). Columbus, OH: Merrill.

Bundy B. F. (1991). Fostering communication between parent and schools. *Young Children, 46*(2), 12–17.

Cataldo, C.Z. (1983). *Infant and toddler programs.* Reading, MA: Addison-Wesley.

Cataldo, C.Z. (1987). *Parent education for early childhood.* New York: Teachers College Press.

Gestwicki, C. (1992). Home, school and community relations: A guide to working with parents. New York: Delmar.

Hendrick, J. (1988). *The whole child.* Columbus, OH: Merrill.

HIPPY USA. (September 15, 1994). [Telephone interview with Home Instruction Program for Preschool Youngsters]. HIPPY USA, 53 West 23rd St., 5th floor, New York, NY 10010; 212-678-3500.

Honig, A. (1975). *Parent involvement in early childhood education.* Washington, DC: National Association for the Education of Young Children.

McConkey, R. (1985). *Working with parents: A practical guide for teachers and therapists.* Cambridge, MA: Brookline Books.

Miller, A.C. (1987). *Maternal health and infant survival.* Washington, DC: National Center for Clinical Infant Programs.

Powell, D. R. (1990). Research in review: Home visiting in the early years: Policy and program design decisions. *Young Children, 46*(2), 66–73.

Rockwell, R.E. (April 30, 1993). Home visits workshop. Moline, IL: Project Apples, Western Illinois University.

Seefeldt, C. (1980). *A curriculum for preschool.* Columbus, OH: Merrill.

Shea, T.M., & Bauer, A.M. (1991). *Parents and teachers of children with exceptionalities.* Boston: Allyn & Bacon.

U.S. Department of Health, Education, and Welfare, Office of Child Development. (1974). *A guide for planning and operating home-based child development programs.* Washington, DC: U.S. Government Printing Office, 33-37.

Wasik, H.B. (1993). Staffing issues for home visiting programs. In R.E. Berhman (Ed.), *Home visiting: The future of young children,* 3(3), 140–157. Center for the Future of Young Children, The David and Lucile Packard Foundation.

Wasik, H.B., & Roberts, R.N. (1993). Home visitor characteristics, training, and supervision: Results of a national survey. In R.E. Berhman (Ed.), *Home visiting: The future of young children.* Center for the Future of Young Children, The David and Lucile Packard Foundation, 3(3), 150.

Watson, S.D. (1991). *Handbook for home visits.* Greenville, IL: Bond County Community Unit No. 2.

Weiss, H.B. (1993). Home visits: Necessary but not sufficient. In R.E. Berhman (Ed.), *Home visiting: The future of young children,* 3(3), 113–128. Center for the Future of Young Children, The David and Lucile Packard Foundation.

Chapter 8

PARENT GROUP MEETINGS

READERS WILL BE ABLE TO:

- Discuss a variety of parent group meeting formats.
- Identify the most common problems that parents give for not attending group meetings.
- Discuss how to plan, prepare, conduct, and evaluate a parent group meeting.

The parent group meeting as a parent involvement strategy can be a beneficial and productive form of parent-teacher collaboration. In this chapter we examine formats of parent group meetings, from small to large. A common complaint that school personnel give for not utilizing this strategy is that parents never come. We have interviewed parents throughout the country and will present their side of the story. Ways to overcome the barriers that parents have to this form of parent involvement are addressed. General issues in planning and conducting large and small parent group meetings are discussed. A detailed model for planning, conducting, and evaluating parent group meetings is given. A sample meeting is also provided.

RATIONALE FOR THE PARENT GROUP MEETING APPROACH

Meeting with parents in a group setting offers the teacher yet another strategy to work with parents as partners. People feel more comfortable and relaxed in group settings. Group settings provide a supportive and friendly environment in which learning activities can be optimally presented. There may be an initial hesitation to discuss feelings and unspoken thoughts, but after getting acquainted in an informal setting, participants often can overcome social anxiety

Schools are good settings for parent meetings.

and speak openly. As the group develops a history of positive interaction, the interest and excitement of the participants will build and be reflected in greater initiative and a feeling of *esprit de corps*.

Shea and Bauer (1991) indicate that parents and teachers meet in groups for three major purposes: to transfer information, to teach and learn behavior management or interpersonal communication techniques, and to give and receive social and emotional support. Whatever the primary purpose, every group will to some extent include all three elements.

McConkey (1985) suggests there are six potential advantages to parents working with teachers in group meetings.

1. Parents learn from other parents.
2. Parents have a chance to acquire a broader understanding of how children learn and why their behavior can be atypical.
3. Parents can facilitate change through good discussion.
4. Parents can develop new friendships.
5. Fathers can get involved.
6. Working mothers and single parents can get involved.

WHY PARENTS FAIL TO ATTEND GROUP MEETINGS

In many schools, parent involvement is synonymous with group meetings. If parents are invited to attend group meetings, then the school considers its obligation to parent involvement fulfilled (Cook, Tessier, & Klein, 1992).

When parents don't attend they often are labeled as not caring about the school or their children. Little or no attention is given to whether the planned meetings address the needs of those invited. These meetings usually are large in size and are designed to give educational information in a lecture format. The speakers often use vocabulary that is not totally understood by the parents or is patronizing to them. Many parents avoid asking clarifying questions at such meetings because they feel intimidated and don't want to risk looking foolish. As a result, they may attend one meeting but do not return.

In an attempt to identify the factors that cause parents to avoid this involvement strategy, we have made extensive inquiries over the past 30 years with parents in 29 states. The following factors that discourage parents from attending group meetings have been reported. Some suggested ways these problems can be ameliorated also are provided.

1. *Parents receive late notification.*   Send home an invitation to the meeting at least two weeks in advance. Send home one or more reminder notes the week of the meeting.

2. *Meetings are not held at convenient times.*   Do not schedule all meetings in the same time slot. Try a variety of meeting times: morning, before school, during school, after school, and weekends. Do this in consideration of parents who have work schedules that prohibit them from attending afternoon or evening meetings.

3. *No child care is provided.*   Child care should always be provided by competent caregivers in a safe environment. Care providers should be more than just a few years older than the children they are caring for. The room where care is provided should be well equipped with cribs and toys that are appropriate for a wide range of ages.

4. *Parents are not included in planning topics of interest to them.*   Parents should be given numerous opportunities to say what meeting topics and presenters they're interested in. Do not ask for this input until the parents are acquainted with each other and the staff members. Usually by the second or third meeting, trust has been established and the parents feel their input does matter.

5. *Meetings often do not start or finish on time.*   It is critical that all meetings begin and end as scheduled. This is appreciated by both parents and teachers.

6. *Meetings are usually too long*   A good time frame for a parent group meeting is 1 to 1½ hours in length.

7. *Teachers complain when the parent attendance is small.*   It's normal to be disappointed when only a few parents show up for a meeting. Do not complain; present the meeting as planned with the same enthusiasm you would have had if 50 parents had come. The word will spread about the great meeting that so many missed. The next meeting should show an increase in attendance. This may take more than one meeting to achieve, as parents have good recall of past, unproductive meetings.

8. *Meetings are often too formal.*   Informal or casual is the most popular dress for meetings. However, it is important to let parents know. Notification can be accomplished via the meeting invitation and the reminder notice.

9. *No refreshments are served.*   Refreshments are a critical component of a meeting. They do not have to be expensive or elaborate. Cookies, coffee, and soft drinks can contribute to a relaxed atmosphere that is more conducive to sharing and working together as partners.

10. *No transportation is provided.*   Many parents have no way to get to the meeting. This is a problem that should not be ignored. Some programs offer bus service, while others offer rides with other parents and teachers who have cars.

11. *There is often a small clique of parents that dominates sessions.*   This is a problem that cannot be tolerated. We need to be assertive in conducting meetings and allow all present to participate.

12. *Parents are not given an opportunity to evaluate meetings.*   All meetings should be evaluated by parents and staff members. The results should be used to plan future meeting topics and speakers of interest to the families served by the program.

To maximize the value of the parent group meeting strategy, staff members need to keep in mind the potential problems just listed as they plan and conduct meetings.

TYPES OF PARENT GROUP MEETINGS

Parent group meetings occur in a variety of sizes, and range from formal lectures to informal workshops. Numerous formats are used in programs serving children from birth through high school.

Berger (1995) describes these meeting formats:

1. *Roundtable discussion:* All participants sit in a circle or around a table. A topic is chosen when the meeting is scheduled. A parent, teacher, or a guest serves as the moderator. A good moderator can prevent a few parents from dominating the discussion. The discussion is limited to the preselected topic or topics.

2. *Concentric circle:* This approach is similar to the round table. There are two circles, one inside the other, with all participants facing the center. The group in the smaller, inside circle discusses the chosen topic for a given period of time, usually 10 to 15 minutes. The larger group, in the outside circle, listens and prepares questions and reactions. When the time runs out, the entire group is free to interact and further discuss the topic.

3. *Buzz sessions:* Participants are divided into groups of from two to eight people. The ideal size is four, as this allows everyone to have input. The buzz session allows participants to share their feelings on an issue that is to be discussed later in the meeting by the entire audience. Each group chooses a leader and a recorder. The groups are placed around the room as far away from each other as possible to avoid distraction. After a given time period (20 to 30 minutes) the large group reassembles and everyone discusses the topic at hand.

4. *Brainstorming:* When using this form of participation, it is critical to accept all of the audience's contributions. Everyone is encouraged to speak up; there are no wrong suggestions. Participants may add to, combine, or modify ideas. Encouraging and accepting all ideas from the group stimulates an abundance of diversified thought.

5. *Workshops:* This strategy has proven most effective for the authors of this book. When parents are asked, "How do you learn best?" the response usually given is, "By doing." The workshop format enables the participants to capitalize on this learning style. The major component of a workshop is the active involvement of the participants.

6. *Role playing:* Role playing is a dramatization of a hypothetical yet realistic situation where participants place themselves in a designated role. This strategy is often received reluctantly by participants. However, after practicing, their hesitancy and reluctance to participate begins to disappear.

7. *Panel discussion:* Information on a topic or issue of concern is given by four presenters. A panel moderator introduces the speakers and the topic. Each presenter is allowed 10 minute to share his or her thoughts. Following the presentations, the panel moderator asks for questions from the audience. All panel members respond, if appropriate. The moderator summarizes the major points discussed and the conclusions reached, then ends the meeting.

8. *Colloquy:* This is a form of panel discussion that allows the audience to interject questions or make comments throughout the presentation, rather than waiting until the speakers have finished.

9. *Debate:* A controversial issue is chosen as a topic, and two teams of five to six members each are formed to present both sides of the issue. The audience listens as each speaker is allowed 2 to 4 minutes to present a point of view. The teams alternate with pro and con views. A moderator times the presentations and keeps the debate moving. After all team members have spoken, the moderator asks for questions from the audience to be directed to the debate team members.

10. *Symposium:* Several speakers give a formal presentation on various aspects of a topic chosen in advance. Each speaker is allowed 5 to 15 minutes. After the presentations, a moderator directs questions from the audience to each speaker. The moderator summarizes and closes the meeting.

11. *Lecture:* A speaker is chosen to lecture on a given subject for 30 to 45 minutes. The speaker should be chosen not only for his or her knowledge of the subject, but also for the ability to relate to the parent audience.

Parents should have input in choosing meeting topics.

12. *Video presentations:* There is an abundance of good videos that deal with a wide range of parent and child issues. Local and state film libraries often will provide films at no cost. You might also make a video of class activities to share with parents.

Shea and Bauer (1991) report that parent-teacher collaboration groups can choose specific models that are appropriate in fulfilling the group's specific purposes. They can consider informational meetings, orientation meetings, open houses, commercial programs such as Parent Effectiveness Training (PET) and Systematic Training for Effective Parenting (STEP), problem-solving groups, discussion groups, and training groups.

McConkey (1985) suggests the following as popular formats: school meetings, classroom meetings, courses for parents, mother and baby groups, and self-help groups.

This list is not intended to be exhaustive, but it does capture the great diversity of approaches available to parent-teacher groups. It is important to remember that no single approach will meet all the group's needs. Therefore, the teacher must use professional judgment in matching group processes to parents' stated needs, strengths, personal characteristics, and cultures.

GUIDELINES FOR PLANNING PARENT GROUP MEETINGS

Regardless of the type of meeting format, the teacher should follow a guideline when planning the meeting, if only to avoid some of the pitfalls that have kept parents away.

DEVELOPING A PURPOSE

All meetings should have a purpose. We need to ask ourselves—and the parents—what we wish to accomplish by conducting this meeting. Whether the purpose is to introduce parents to the program, to get acquainted, or to recruit parent volunteers, we should never proceed without collaborating with parents on why the meeting is being held.

CHOOSING A TOPIC OR TITLE

The definition of a group is a collection of people with a common denominator. What is the common denominator for the parents with whom you are working? The most effective way to get an answer is to ask. When making home visits, doing intake interviews, sending home questionnaires, or conversing informally with parents, ask what they'd like to have information about and what would interest them if a parent group was formed. Once the group is started and a trusting relationship has been established between parents and the teacher, real personal and family needs will begin to surface. Be alert to these needs as they are shared, and plan future meeting topics accordingly (Foster, 1994).

The title of the meeting is important. It should be catchy and upbeat rather than negative if you want parents to come. For example, the title "Healthful Snacks" can be upgraded to "Dealing With Snack Attacks—Some Tasty and Healthful Alternatives." The title "Dealing With Stress" might be more attractive as "How to Make Stress Work for You."

DELIVERING ADVANCE INFORMATION TO PARENTS

It is important to inform parents about the meeting well ahead of time. This can be accomplished by sending a flyer home. The flyer should describe the meeting and include such information as who, what, where, when, why, dress (informal or formal), babysitting availability, refreshments, and a number to call to RSVP or to obtain further information. The flyer should be sent home with the children at least two weeks before the meeting. It can be sent again 1 to 3 days before the meeting as a reminder.

Additional strategies to publicize meetings are a formal letter mailed to the home and word of mouth (Curran, 1989). Word of mouth is the most effective approach, but it requires people who can share information about the meeting

Reminders can be sent home with the children.

and the importance of attending. Some programs have computer-based calling from the school and use electronic mailboxes so that parents can call and hear a message from the teacher every day (Bauch, 1990). The messages provide parents with homework pointers, information, and reminders of upcoming events. A telephone committee can make reminder calls. The children are excellent source of publicity as well. Tell them about the flyer they are taking home. They can deliver the written message, plus encourage their parents to attend. This strategy is obviously most effective when the children are going to be part of the meeting. Obviously, do not exploit the children into pressuring their parents to attend.

DEVELOPING A PLANNING SCHEDULE

An important component of a parent meeting is a planning schedule that will assist the teacher in planning and conducting the sessions. When meetings are not planned, problems can occur that result in chaos and wasted time. Table 8.1 on page 207 is an example of a planning schedule for a parent group meeting.

DEVELOPING A MEETING AGENDA

A meeting agenda will assist the teacher in starting the meeting on time and in conducting it as planned.

- *Registration*: Greet parents as they arrive. Make them feel welcome. Distribute name tags.
- *Mixer*: Develop an activity that will help parents and staff members get acquainted. The activity should set a fun, relaxing tone for the meeting. An example is given in the box titled Mixer Example.
- *Opening*: Give a general welcome. Introduce yourself and staff members.
- *Purpose*: Explain the purpose of the meeting and any special procedures that are to be followed.
- *Content*: Conduct the meeting.
- *Closing*: Briefly summarize the session and state what was accomplished.
- *Evaluation*: Distribute evaluation forms and explain where to leave them when completed.
- *Refreshments*: Serve refreshments.
- *Closing*: Say goodbye to parents and clean up.

This sample agenda for planning, conducting, and evaluating a parent meeting can be followed regardless of the meeting theme. See Figure 8.1 to see how these steps were applied to a Discovery Science Family Night.

MIXER EXAMPLE

Yarn Web

Purpose: To break the ice and help parents and teachers get acquainted

Materials: Ball of yarn

Procedures: All participants stand in a circle.

The person holding the yarn states his/her name and one activity he/she enjoys doing with his/her child at home. That person holds on to the end of the yarn and tosses the ball to another person. The person who catches the ball states his/her name and what he/she enjoys doing with his/her child, then tosses it to another person. The game continues until everyone has had a turn. At the end, a web will have been created. This web is symbolic of how we work together to create a cooperative learning environment for our children.

FIGURE 8.1

Program Materials for Discovery Science Family Night

Discovery Science Family Night

Dear Family,

This year we will be using a program designed to introduce your child to the exciting world of science. The program is called Discovery Science, and it is just that. It enables children to learn science through discovery—through interactions with materials in their everyday environment at home, at school, and in the world. They will be learning science the way we all learn best: by doing, exploring, asking questions, and finding answers.

This is your invitation to come and learn what Discovery Science is all about and how we plan to include it in our curriculum. The meeting will last for about two hours. You will have the opportunity to try many of the activities the children will be doing over the next year. By the close of the meeting, you will have an understanding of the philosophy, goals, and activities of Discovery Science. You will also know your three- or four-year-old will be learning science in a developmentally appropriate way.

We want you to be comfortable, so please dress casually. The meeting will start and finish on time. We will have refreshments. Because this is an "adults only" meeting, child care will be provided. We will supply transportation if needed.

The meeting will be held at _____ on _____ from _____ to _____. If you are able to attend, please return the bottom portion of this letter. Let us know how many adults will be coming and whether you will need child care.

We look forward to doing Discovery Science with you.

Sincerely,

- -

Please Detach and Return by _____

_____ adults will attend the Discovery Science meeting.

_____ children, ages _____ will need child care.

Transportation needed?   Yes   No

We can provide transportation for another family.   Yes   No

Name _____

Phone _____

Reminder Flyer

DON'T FORGET!

YOU ARE INVITED TO A DISCOVERY SCIENCE FAMILY MEETING

REFRESHMENTS WILL BE SERVED

CHILD CARE WILL BE PROVIDED

DATE: _____

TIME: _____

PLACE: _____

Please reserve two hours. This will be an excellent chance for you to discover Discovery Science, the exciting new science curriculum we are introducing this year. You will be able to take part in activities that will enable your children to develop their natural science abilities as they interact with materials in the environment of our center.

Sample Agenda for Planning the First Family Night

Purpose: To introduce families to the Discovery Science curriculum, philosophy, goals, and activities.

Three Weeks Before Meeting

1. Clear meeting date with the center director.
2. Secure authorization for building and room use.
3. Secure a room for child care.
4. Make arrangements for several child-care providers to be on standby. Need will depend on the number of children that will be brought.
5. Select a transportation committee chairperson to make arrangements for families who need rides.
6. Select a refreshment committee chairperson. Post a sign-up sheet where families have access to it as they drop off and pick up their children.
7. Ask for volunteers or staff members to assist at the interest centers. They will explain procedures to families.

Two Weeks Before Meeting

1. Prepare and send invitations.
2. Lay out the physical arrangement of the meeting room on paper.
3. Decide which Discovery Science activities will be used in each of the interest centers.
4. Choose one or two activities for each center.

One Week Before Meeting

1. Prepare name tags.
2. Prepare Discovery Science Scavenger Hunt bags and checklists.
3. Prepare evaluation form and make copies.
4. Check with refreshment committee chairperson. Remind families of foods they have signed up to bring.
5. Send home a reminder flyer with each child.
6. Check with transportation committee chairperson to see if all who need rides are accommodated.

One Day Before Meeting

1. Send home final reminder.
2. Check progress of the refreshment committee. Get a final head count.
3. Verify that you have enough child-care providers for the age and number of children coming, and remind child-care providers of the time of the meeting.
4. Check with the transportation committee chairperson to verify rides for families needing them.
5. Check with the refreshment committee chairperson to touch base on arrangements.
6. Locate a bell, small alarm, or timer to use to tell people when to move to the next activity.

Day of Meeting

1. Set up interest centers with one or two Discovery Science activities for each of the centers. Mark the centers 1–4.
2. Put up signs directing families to the meeting location.
3. Place name tags, pins, pens or pencils, and Scavenger Hunt bags and checklists on a table near the entrance to the room. Have evaluation forms handy.

Name Tag and Mixer

MIXER PROCEDURE

Trace the name tag pattern on construction paper and cut out the magnifying glasses. Write a number from 1 to 4 on the back of each name tag. This number will be used to assign each family member to one of the four interest centers: How Objects Are Alike and Different, How Objects Move, How Objects Change, and How Objects Are Made and Used. Set up these centers in open areas that will accommodate the materials and numbers of people attending. Gather the items for the scavenger hunt (listed below). Put several items in a bag, one bag for each guest.

As people arrive, hand each a name tag, a pin, and the bag of a collection of science items. Ask that they write their name on the tag, pin it on, and be seated.

After all the people have arrived, distribute the Discovery Science Scavenger Hunt Checklist. (Change the items if you can't locate some of these; use duplicate items if many people are expected.) Explain that you want them to stand, move around the room, and interact with one another while trying to find people who have objects on the checklist. Tell them that they should try to collect a different person's signature for each discovery item.

Sample Discovery Science Meeting Plan

Time	Activity	Technique	Resources/Materials
7:00 – 7:10	Greeting	Greet families as they arrive. Hand out name tags, pins, and Scavenger Hunt bags.	Name tags, pins, pencils or pens, and bags containing science collections.
7:10 – 7:20	Mixer	Introduce and begin Scavenger Hunt.	See page titled "Name Tag and Mixer" for mixer procedure.
7:20 – 7:30	Welcome participants. Introduce Discovery Science curriculum and explain centers.	Mini-lecture. Welcome families. Introduce Discovery Science curriculum and interest centers. Explain that people will go to the center matching the number on the name tag. When the bell rings, they will rotate clockwise to the next center. There will be one or two Discovery Science activities at each of the four stations.	Introduction to Discovery Science.*
7:30 – 8:30	Family members go to four centers.	Family members interact with materials at each center. A staff member or volunteer at each center can explain procedures and assist with the activities.	Four interest centers: How Objects Are Alike and Different, How Objects Move, How Objects Change, and How Objects Are Made and Used.
8:30 – 8:45	Reassemble into large group.	Wrap up. Hand out copies of "What Is Discovery Science?"	Handout: "What Is Discovery Science?"**
8:45 – 9:00	Closing Evaluation Refreshments	Hand out evaluation forms; serve refreshments; invite families to the next meeting	Evaluation forms, pencils, or pens.

*From *Discovery Science: Explorations for the Early Years, Pre-Kindergarten* by D.A. Winnett, R.E. Rockwell, E.A. Sherwood, and R.A. Williams, 1996, Menlo Park, CA: Addison-Wesley.

Discovery Science Family Meeting Evaluation Form

We are interested in knowing whether you enjoyed the meeting this evening. Please circle the magnifying glass that best describes your understanding about the theory behind Discovery Science. The space at the bottom of this page is for questions or suggestions you have. We value your feedback, so please feel free to comment.

NOT FOCUSED   IT'S STARTING TO GET CLEARER   IT'S PERFECTLY CLEAR

WHAT DID YOU LEARN TONIGHT?

_____

WHAT HOPES DO YOU HAVE FOR YOUR CHILD IN DISCOVERY SCIENCE?

_____

WHAT INTERESTS OR SPECIAL SKILLS DO YOU HAVE THAT MIGHT RELATE TO SOMETHING WE WILL BE DOING IN DISCOVERY SCIENCE?

_____

COMMENTS _____

NAME _____

Table 8.1

Planning Schedule

One month before the meeting:

1. Decide on a topic that fits stated parent needs.
2. Clear, then set a date and time.
3. Reserve a room.
4. Contact the personnel involved (volunteers, speaker, co-workers, etc.)

Two weeks before the meeting:

1. Send out flyers and invitations.
2. Arrange for transportation and babysitting.
3. List supplies needed and begin to collect them.
4. Reaffirm the date, time, and place.

One week before the meeting:

1. Duplicate handout materials.
2. Make name tags.
3. Organize supplies.

Day before the meeting:

1. Send out a reminder of the meeting.
2. Check with the janitor to arrange for extra chairs, tables, a key, etc.
3. Buy refreshments.

Day of meeting:

1. Remind children to remind their parents about the meeting.
2. Arrange the room.
3. Make sure you have all of the necessary materials.
4. Prepare the refreshments.
5. Arrive early.

Summary

The parent group meeting is an involvement strategy that has been used for decades. A meeting at the school is often difficult to fit into the parents' already crowded schedule. For that reason, we should not be upset with parents who cannot attend every meeting. Meetings should cover topics that address the stated needs of families. They should be carefully planned and utilize meeting formats that vary according to topic and group size. They should be held at a variety of times in order to reach all parents. The length of the meetings should rarely exceed 1-1/2 hours. Child care should be provided by competent care providers, and parents should be asked to evaluate and give feedback about each meeting.

ACTIVITIES FOR DISCUSSION, EXPANSION, AND APPLICATION

1. Develop a rationale for incorporating a parent involvement program into an elementary school, grades K–5.

2. Prepare and present in class a simulated parent group meeting.

3. List and share class members' reasons for not attending meetings.

4. Invite a group of parents to the class to discuss the problems—and successes—they have had with meetings held at school.

5. Discuss the meeting formats that class members would feel most comfortable with as they initiate parent group meetings in their respective programs.

6. Generate some group mixers that might be used at meetings as icebreakers to make parents feel welcome.

7. Attend a parent group meeting in your community. Critique the meeting and share your findings with the class.

REFERENCES

Bauch, J.P. (1990). The transparent school: A partnership for parent involvement. *Educational Horizons, 58*(1) , 187–189.

Berger, E.H. (1995). *Parents as partners in education: Families and schools working together* (4th ed.). Englewood Cliffs, NJ: Prentice Hall Inc.

Charner, K. (Ed.). (1989). *The preschool letters and notes to parents book.* Mount Rainier, MD: Gryphon House.

Cook, R.E., Tessier, A., & Klein, M. (1992). *Adapting early childhood curricula for children with special needs.* New York: Macmillan.

Curran, D. (1989). *Working with parents.* Circle Pines, MN: American Guidance Service.

Diamondstone, J.M. (1980). *Designing, leading, and evaluating workshops for trainers and leadership personnel in early childhood education.* Ypsilanti, MI: High/Scope Educational Research Foundation.

Endres, J.B., & Rockwell, R.E. (1993). *Food, nutrition, and the young child* (4th ed.). New York: Macmillan.

Foster, S.M. (1994). Successful parent meetings. *Young Children, 50*(1), 78–80.

Gestwicki, C. (1992). *Home, school and community relations: A guide to working with parents.* Albany, NY: Delmar.

McConkey, R. (1985). *Working with parents: A practical guidebook for teachers and therapists.* Cambridge, MA: Brookline Books.

Rockwell, R.E. (1993). Parent involvement. In K. Henderson & B.J. Howery (Eds.), *Early childhood education handbook.* Springfield, IL: Illinois State Board of Education.

Shea, T.M., & Bauer, A.M. (1991). *Parents and teachers of children with exceptionalities.* Boston, MA: Allyn & Bacon.

Stile, S.W., Cole, J.T., & Garner, A.W. (1979). Maximizing parent involvement in programs for exceptional children. *Journal of the Division of Early Childhood Education, 1*(1), 68–92.

Chapter 9

PARENT–TEACHER CONFERENCES

READERS WILL BE ABLE TO:

- State a rationale for the parent-teacher conference.
- Describe a procedure to follow in planning and conducting an effective parent-teacher conference.
- Explain parent-teacher conference follow-up strategies.
- List the benefits of parent-teacher conferences for all involved.

The process of communicating with parents is an essential component of being an effective teacher. Research in the area of teacher education has revealed that an effective teacher must exhibit competence in human relations and planning skills (Alper, Schloss, & Schloss, 1994; Berger, 1995; Spodek & Saracho, 1994). One of the most common challenges to communication is the parent-teacher conference, which most schools schedule once or twice a year. Because this strategy for communicating with parents is the one most often used by teachers, it is important that it be productive and enlightening for all concerned.

Unfortunately, many parents and teachers look upon the conference with tension, anxiety, or fear. Parents sometimes feel afraid that they will be criticized, blamed for their child's behavior, or made to feel inferior because they do not understand education jargon. Teachers frequently worry that they will be held responsible for their child's lack of progress. They do not want to give negative information or be misunderstood (Candelaria, 1987). Yet, the parent-teacher conference is the one event in the teaching profession for which teachers have received little or no training. It is no wonder that it is often approached with fear and trepidation.

To be productive, parent-teacher conferences must be recognized as one of the necessary ingredients of a successful parent-teacher partnership. Conducted on a regular basis, they provide an ideal forum to facilitate the exchange of information about children (Gee, 1992). This chapter presents suggestions for conducting effective conferences and utilizing the information shared for the benefit of the child.

Parent-teacher communication should be an ongoing process.

PURPOSE OF THE CONFERENCE

Parents are their children's first and most influential teachers. Their influence does not stop once their children are enrolled in an educational setting. The pressures of parenting and teaching have much in common; both parents and teachers play a vital role in children's growth and development. They both create and structure a learning environment in which the child is the major focus. The home and the school need each other, and the child needs both. Parent-teacher communication should be an ongoing process throughout the child's school experience. Parent-teacher conferences can be beneficial for parents, teachers, and children alike as they share bits of information which, when integrated into current knowledge, can then be acted upon (Rich, 1987).

Parent-teacher conferences provide an excellent avenue to encouraging parent involvement in the school. While teachers and parents both benefit from working together, the real beneficiary is the child. Benefits of the conferences for both parents and teachers are shown in the boxes on pages 211 and 212.

PREPARING FOR THE CONFERENCE

The process of preparing for a conference should be as complete and detailed as possible. Positive parent-teacher communication should be established, and

BENEFITS FOR TEACHERS

Teachers will:

- understand parents' impressions and expectations of the school program.
- gain a better understanding of the program's effect on the child.
- obtain additional information about the child.

- encourage parents' understanding and support of the program.
- communicate the child's school progress and supplement ideas and activities that can stimulate development.
- develop a working partnership with the parents.

conference materials prepared in advance (Canter, 1989; Elksnin & Elksnin, 1989). This initial positive communication can be facilitated by inviting and encouraging parents to visit and observe the classroom, by placing "warm" telephone calls, by sending welcoming letters and happy-grams, by setting up a school open house, and by soliciting home profile sheets.

The home profile sheet is a list of nonthreatening questions that the children use to "interview" their parents (custodial, noncustodial, or others who will be coming to the conference). The questions should be developed with input from the children. They might include favorite songs, foods, colors, animals, books, and hobbies; their birthplace; and questions such as "What would you like to know about my school?" When the profile sheets are returned, the children draw pictures of the people they have interviewed. The drawings are mounted on construction paper and posted in the classroom with a sign that reads "Welcome Families" (see Figure 9.1). Parents will enjoy seeing their child's drawings. The process serves to welcome parents and stimulate conversation. After some form of positive communication has occurred, parents are more likely to be receptive to the conference (*Instructor*, 1986).

The teacher should begin collecting samples of the children's work at the start of the school year. Keeping anecdotal records and samples of children's work, noting special interests and abilities, shows parents the time and attention the teacher has given their child. The records should reflect the child's growth in self-esteem, language mastery, social skills, and personal relationships, as well as progress in academic subjects, if applicable. A portfolio is an excellent means of organizing each child's materials. The portfolio offers the teacher a means of individualizing a child's progress over time. It consists of a collection of children's work and gives the parent and teacher an opportunity to share accurate and current information about how the child is functioning in the classroom (Clark, 1986). Allow the children to help decide what goes into their portfolio; this gives them the opportunity to be involved in the conference. Children may even wish to include their own thoughts about their progress.

BENEFITS FOR PARENTS

Parents will:

- gain a better understanding of their child's school program.
- learn strategies that can enhance their child's development.
- understand their child's personal growth.
- get information on the school's philosophy on teaching and learning styles.

- communicate concerns, questions, and suggestions that can lead to a better school experience for their child.
- provide experiences that contribute to their child's physical, emotional, and intellectual growth.

Plan a conference agenda that will prevent or limit conference anxiety. Some elements to consider are the establishment of rapport, a statement of the meeting's purpose, the communication of specific information, an opportunity for parent input and information exchange (strategies for parents, strategies for teachers), recommendations, plans for follow-up contacts, a conference summarization, and the conference termination (Elksnin & Elksnin, 1989; Stephens & Wolf, 1989). An easy rule of thumb to remember as you plan is to make the conference like a sandwich: Start on a positive note, go to points that need improvement, and end on a positive.

Mail a conference invitation to the home. The invitation should ask the parents to select an available conference date and time that is convenient for them. The invitation should indicate the length of the conference, its location, and its agenda. Special consideration should be given to parents who have more than one child enrolled in the school. If possible, back-to-back conferences should be made available to them (Berger, 1995).

The invitation also should encourage the parents to prepare a list of questions (Rich, 1987). Suggest that they prioritize the questions, as there may not be time to answer them all. If this happens, arrange for an additional conference or perhaps a telephone call to bring closure.

Here are some sample questions that parents might want to ask the teacher:

- What are my child's strengths and weaknesses?
- Is my child involved in any special instruction?
- What is your policy on homework?
- How is my child doing with the various subjects?
- How can I better help my child at home? What specific things can I do?
- Are there any special problems relating to discipline or socialization?

- How well does my child communicate?
- Is my child motivated?

If there are more questions than the school's conference time blocks can accommodate, encourage parents to make an additional appointment to address all their concerns.

A few days before the conference, a confirmation letter should be sent to the home reminding the parents of date and time. Be sure to enclose the school telephone number and request that they call immediately and reschedule if they're not able to keep the appointment.

Also prepare for the conference by considering its physical environment. Proper lighting, temperature, and privacy help make the surroundings more comfortable (Riepe, 1990). The environment must help parents feel more relaxed and less intimidated. Having adult-sized furniture and seating arranged so that parents and the teacher can sit side by side will help parents feel welcome. Provide paper and pencils for note taking.

Be considerate of the parents who are waiting for their appointments. Arrange for a waiting area. Prepare the area with information regarding the school and the special services it provides. Include a newsletter and information on the school's volunteer program, curriculum, philosophy, and homework and grading policies; suggestions on how parents can help at home; and invitations to various school events. Make a "Conference in Progress" sign that can be hung on the door to prevent interruptions (*Instructor, 1986).*

A final step of preparation is to look over the objectives of the meeting, the anecdotal notes, records, reports, samples of work, child's name, the parent's name, and any other information pertinent to the conference.

CONDUCTING THE CONFERENCE

It is important to remember that many parents are going to be apprehensive about the conference. The teacher must work at putting parents at ease. One of the most effective ways of doing this is to greet each parent at the door in a friendly way. Know and use the parent's name. Do not assume that the parent has the same name as the child. State your own name clearly and in the next sentence refer to the child in question. After this initial exchange, refer to the agenda and begin the conference.

A successful conference includes the following:

BUILDING RAPPORT

To many parents, the school environment is intimidating. This may be due to negative experiences that might even date back to their childhood. Regardless, the teacher must work at putting parents at ease, encouraging them to feel welcome, and assuring them that they have not wandered into enemy territory. An

FIGURE 9.1
Children's Interview with a Parent

initial bit of small talk related to the weather or another neutral topic might help. The child-parent interview is a perfect ice breaker. Avoid emotionally laden topics such as religion or politics (Stephens & Wolf, 1989). Some parents may only want to engage in small talk, as it provides a way to avoid discussing the present issues at hand. Always begin with a positive remark and make sure that everyone present knows that the purpose of the conference is to share information and work together to help the child.

OBTAINING INFORMATION FROM THE PARENT

Eliciting information from the parent is key to the success of the conference. The teacher must be a sensitive, active listener. Begin with general, open-ended questions such as, "What does Donna say about her school activities?" or "What did she share about our field trip to the orchard?" Avoid negative questions such as, "Does Donna still refuse to do her homework?" Instead try, "How does Donna feel about doing her homework?" Structure questions that will allow the parents to share perceptions about the topic and give the teacher an opportunity to provide suggestions. This process allows the teacher to obtain information before providing suggestions. It also gives the parents an opportunity to share their knowledge about the child.

The teacher also can gain insight into parental expectations, which can have instant benefits during the conference as well as in future work with the child.

PROVIDING INFORMATION

The teacher must express openness to questions and advice about the child. Indicate an understanding of the parents' views by making brief comments and asking clarifying questions. Be truthful about problem areas, but present them in a way that makes your concern for the child evident. This is the opportune time to examine a portfolio of the child's work in order to share both progress and concerns. Be prepared to give the parents specific ideas, activities, and strategies that they can use at home to help their child.

SKILLS THAT MAXIMIZE ACTIVE LISTENING

Effective communication is the most essential ingredient to the success of the parent-teacher conference. If a conference is to be effective, the teacher must employ active-listening skills. Being a good listener requires concentration, effort, and a willingness to give credence to what another is saying (Simpson, 1990); all efforts are fruitless unless the teacher wants to hear what the family has to say. Active listening literally means being active in the listening process. A listener can use four basic skills to make sure that he or she clearly understands what the speaker has stated. These skills are reflecting, paraphrasing, clarifying, and drawing out.

A teacher should organize a portfolio for parent-teacher conferences.

REFLECTING

Reflecting is the ability to restate as exactly as possible what another person has said. Keep in mind the example of a mirror reflecting exactly the image that appears before it.

The importance of reflecting as a basic communication skill is that the ability to say back to a speaker what you heard lets the speaker know that your interpretations, judgments, or meanings have not slanted or loaded what was stated. Reflecting does not imply that you agree with what was said, only that you heard it and know what words the speaker used to convey the message. For example:

SPEAKER: "I don't want to talk with you right now. I'm angry with my son for forgetting to bring his homework home last night."

LISTENER: "You don't want to talk with me now because you are upset with your son for forgetting to bring his homework home last night."

When using reflective listening it is important that the listener reflect the sender's message without adding emotional inflections to the response, which could indicate judgment.

PARAPHRASING

When paraphrasing, the listener attempts to restate the important elements of a speaker's lengthy or complex statement in his or her words because it would be difficult to repeat the statement word for word.

Try to use some of the speaker's words, but more important, focus on the meaning and the points he or she makes that you believe are the most significant to him or her. For example:

SPEAKER: "I can't talk with you now. I'm so angry with my son for forgetting to bring his homework home last night. I've given him reminders each day before he leaves for school, and he always promises, but he never remembers. I'm the kind of parent who can't relax when I know how important it is for my child to do his homework. How can I work effectively with my other children when he makes me so upset?"

LISTENER: "You don't want to talk right now because you have had an argument with your son, and you want to wait to talk with me after you have resolved this issue with him."

The ability to listen, and to demonstrate that you have heard what the speaker has said by reflecting or paraphrasing, is a valuable skill because it promotes the feeling that the speaker and listener are at the same level of understanding in their communication.

CLARIFYING

The clarifying question seeks to elaborate on what the speaker has said. The clarification can be in two areas. One is the problem of definition: What the words mean to the speaker may not be what the same words mean to the listener. The clarifying question can be used to establish a working definition of a word or phrase. The intent is to clarify meanings, not to nitpick on dictionary definitions or shades of meanings. The intent is also to avoid the kind of arguments that occur when the listener tries to convince the speaker that "_____ doesn't mean that." The listener tries to accept the definition offered by the speaker as the operational definition for the discussion they are having. For example:

SPEAKER: "I'll tell you what the problem is—it's violence and crime in the streets. It's getting so a decent citizen isn't safe anymore. We need more law and order to control the lawless element in this society."

LISTENER: "I understand that you think violence and crime is a problem and that we need more law and order in our society. Can you tell me what law and order means to you?"

The other type of clarifying question seeks to find out why the speaker has placed value and importance on certain concepts or words. For example:

SPEAKER: "I think kids in school should be allowed more freedom than they have now. They should be free to inquire into all kinds of things. Instead, they are locked into a system that tells them what to learn and when to learn about it."

LISTENER: "You think kids in school should be free to learn and explore. What specific things do you feel they should be free to explore?"

The key to this skill is that the listener is attempting to understand the importance and the value that the speaker places on the statements made during the conversation. The listener may be in total disagreement with the speaker, but this skill permits him or her to begin with a common agreement about something they are disagreeing about. It helps to prevent the kinds of arguments that sometimes occur when both parties are close to agreement, but the words they use in communicating their position continue to keep them apart.

There are times, however, when thoughts and feelings are not expressed clearly or fully. Even though the listener has heard the speaker accurately, he or she may not understand what the speaker means, or there is a sense that there may be more to the message than what was said. In these instances, it may be necessary to clarify ideas and draw out the speaker.

DRAWING OUT

Drawing out is a skill that is used to allow the speaker the opportunity to expand upon what has been stated. It is used to clarify parts of the message that may not be in the original statement, but still are a part of the total context of the communication interaction.

There are several situations in which a drawing-out question can be useful. If the speaker is focusing the majority of the message in the past, ask about the present. If it seems necessary for the listener's understanding to find out how the speaker came to his or her present position, ask about past events and how they relate to what is being said. For example:

SPEAKER: "This is really a poor place to work. Why, when I worked for Smedly Midlap and Sons, we had coffee breaks, lunch in the buildings, an exercise program, bowling leagues and . . . and . . . and . . ."

LISTENER: "I hear you talking about what it was like at the other place you worked, but can you tell me what makes this a poor place to work?"

Additional examples of drawing-out questions are:

■ Are there other factors that caused you to arrive at that decision?
■ Have you considered other ways of handling that problem?
■ Is this generally how you feel about things like this?

NONVERBAL COMMUNICATION

Communication is generally thought of as being verbal, but nonverbal communication is just as important. We communicate not only with spoken words, but with gestures, postures, eye contact, facial expressions, and different levels of voice volume and intonation to reveal our thoughts, feelings, intentions, and personalities. Close attention to nonverbal communication will enhance the perception of what is being said by all participants as messages are sent and received (Haitt & Lieberman, 1993).

CONCLUDING THE CONFERENCE

Summarize the areas of strength and weakness. Be sure you are in agreement as to how you will work together to reach the goals that have been set. Establish timelines for completing the planned activities. Clear up any misinterpretations. If another conference is needed, schedule it at this time. Close the conference on a positive note by inviting the parents to call, write, or stop in to express any concerns. Stand up and see them to the door.

FOLLOW-UP STRATEGIES

Within a week after the conference, the teacher should send home a note or letter thanking the parents for their participation. This letter should include a conference summary that highlights what was discussed and planned. Include such details as the goals of the conference, information presented, information gained, and agreements made. A telephone call is a helpful follow-up, especially if the family needs another conference or a referral for other services.

SUMMARY

A successful parent-teacher conference should provide parents with new information about their child and practical suggestions on how they can work as partners with the teacher for the benefit of the child. To accomplish this, the teacher must employ active listening skills and be prepared to offer parents realistic approaches for working with their children at home. Both parties will benefit from the conference, but the ultimate beneficiary is the child.

ACTIVITIES FOR DISCUSSION, EXPANSION, AND APPLICATION

1. Why is it necessary to prepare portfolios of children's work prior to the parent-teacher conference?

2. What is the value of involving the child in obtaining family information via the home profile?

3. Interview a preschool teacher and a teacher in grades K-3. Compile a list of each teacher's parent conference strategies and compare. What are the similarities? What are the differences?

4. What can the teacher do to create a comfortable environment for the parent-teacher conference?

5. List some strategies for building rapport with the parents before the conference begins.

6. Compile a checklist of questions that a teacher might ask parents and questions that parents might ask the teacher. Using these questions, role-play a parent-teacher conference.

REFERENCES

Alper, S.K., Schloss, P.J., & Schloss, C.N. (1994). *Families of students with disabilities: Consultation and advocacy.* Boston: Allyn & Bacon.

Anderson, P.A. (1988). Nonverbal communication in the small group. In R.S. Cathart & L.A. Samovar (Eds.), *Small group communication* (5th ed.). Dubuque, IA: William C. Brown Publishers, 333–365.

Berger, E.H. (1995). *Parents as partners in education: Families and schools working together* (4th ed.). Englewood Cliffs, NJ: Prentice Hall.

Candelaria, C., & Knox, L. (1987). Tips for more productive parent teacher conferences. *Learning, 16*(2), 60–61.

Canter L. (1989). How to speak so parents will listen. *Teaching Pre K-8, 19,* 34–36.

Clark, B. (1992). Optimizing learning: The integrative education model in the classroom. In L.R. Williams & D.P. Fromberg (Eds.), *Encyclopedia of early childhood education.* New York: Garland.

Elksnin, L.K., & Elksnin, N. (1989). Collaborative consultation: Improving parent teacher communication. *Academic Therapy, 24*(3), 261–269.

Gee, E.W. (1992). Perspectives on children: Evaluation trends. In L.R. Williams & D.P. Fromberg (Eds.), *Encyclopedia of early childhood education.* New York: Garland.

Haitt, M., & Lieberman, N. (1993). *A guide for implementing home visits.* School Board of Broward Country, FL.

Kroth, R.L., & Simpson, R.L. (1977). *Parent conferencing as a teaching strategy.* Denver: Love.

Rich, D. (1987). *Teachers and parents: An adult to adult approach.* Washington, DC: National Education Association, The Home and School Institute.

Riepe, L.D. (1990). For the benefit of all: Planning and conducting effective parent teacher conferences. *Exchange 74,* 47–49.

Simpson, R.L. (1990). *Conferencing parents of exceptional children* (2nd ed.). Austin, TX: PRO.ED, Inc.

Spodek, B., & Saracho, O.N. (1994). *Right from the start.* Boston: Allyn & Bacon.

Stephens, T.M., & Wolf, J. (1989). Parent-teacher conferences: Finding a common ground. *Educational Leadership 47,* 28–31.

The updated guide to parent conferences. (November/December 1986). *Instructor, 96*(4), 56–58.

PART THREE

Support

Chapter 10

PARENT AND COMMUNITY VOLUNTEERS

READERS WILL BE ABLE TO:

- Support the rationale for the utilization of parent and community volunteers.
- Describe the steps that must be taken to organize and conduct a school volunteer program.
- Identify procedures to be followed in determining needed volunteer services.
- Explain the value of recognizing volunteers for the services they provide.

A valuable strategy for involving parents in the education of their child is to involve them as volunteers. Because every school volunteer program will have unique needs that will require unique solutions, there is no one way to conduct a volunteer program. However, in this chapter we provide some specific steps and procedures that will assist in avoiding some of the problems that might occur when initiating a volunteer program.

THE BEGINNINGS OF VOLUNTEERISM

Volunteerism is not new to the United States, and it is not new to educational programs that serve children from birth through high school. Parents and community members have volunteered services to schools since they began. In the early days of the nation, farmers cut wood and gave it to the schoolmaster to use in heating the schoolhouse. Later, immigrants who had learned English assisted in teaching newly arrived immigrants. Following World War 1, when communities were establishing high schools, volunteers often built the outdoor athletic fields, baseball diamonds, and running tracks. During the Great Depression of the 1930s, many school hot lunch programs depended on volunteer labor.

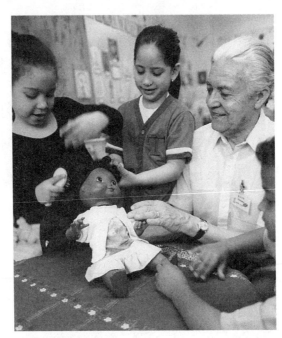

Volunteers build a community partnership in the classroom.

Today, parents, teenagers, college students, carpenters, lawyers, secretaries, teachers, retirees, males and females covering the occupational range from professional to semiskilled all participate in volunteer activities. However, while the roots of volunteer services are deep, the concept of organized, coordinated volunteerism in schools is a fairly recent phenomenon that has rapidly gained in popularity during the decades of the '60s, '70s, and '80s.

Many school volunteer programs have been initiated primarily to solve some of the problems that schools have faced over the past three decades. Some of these problems are overcrowded classrooms, children who need individual attention, the need for individualized tutoring and small group teaching, the need to bring into the classroom a broad base of talent that no one individual teacher can provide, and the need to develop a positive public relations system that in the long run will result in additional public support for the schools.

A great impetus to involve parents and community in the schools has come from the federal government. Our last four U.S. presidents have devoted time to make rather lengthy public service announcements that have stressed the vast number of volunteer efforts that take place daily in this country. In 1968 the federal interagency requirements of the Department of Health, Education, and Welfare stated that all federally funded programs will show some form of parent and community representation in participation and in an advisory capacity. These guidelines have had a great influence on schools using volunteers and in the reception of volunteers once they have agreed to help in the schools or at home. School volunteers are unpaid personnel who usually work on a part-time basis and who perform important tasks that supplement but do not replace the work of employed staff members within the school.

When starting a volunteer program, use caution. It is easy to get carried away with a good idea and attempt to do too much too fast. Many successful programs have started with one teacher or one classroom and gradually expanded. In reviewing the various steps that the authors advocate as essential to a successful program, we hope that those who are using this book will recognize that each step needs to be taken with care.

As with any new program, the concept and procedures for implementing it must be presented to the board of education or board of directors for approval. The question of program cost will certainly arise. Although volunteers do not receive money for their time and effort, there are costs involved. The amount of money needed will depend on the scope and size of the program. Funds will be needed for office supplies, equipment, telephone service, and postage. These initial costs are often underwritten by local citizens, foundation or program grants, and, in some instances, the school boards. The adoption of a volunteer program frequently depends on how detailed the planning is and the projected speed with which the program will progress.

THE NEED FOR A VOLUNTEER PROGRAM

There is a need to bring volunteers into the schools to enrich the learning process and expand the learning environment of the children. For example, a great need exists to assist teachers so they can provide more individualized instruction in their classes; this can be accomplished by relieving them of some of their nonteaching duties and tasks.

There is also a need to provide our schools with resource people who are able to share special talents, skills, and expertise normally not available in schools and early childhood settings. This is especially true at the elementary level, where the teacher is expected to teach a wide range of subject matter. Additionally, there is a need to provide opportunities for concerned members of the community to participate effectively, improving the educational program of the schools. There's also a need for volunteers to help stimulate greater citizen understanding and support of school programs through their participation and work in the program. Finally, there is a need for the school to obtain valuable ideas from the community, as well as relevant information about the problems and needs of the community.

Volunteers working within a school system can obtain insights into and get a more valid view of the problems facing the schools. Volunteers frequently become the most ardent supporters of the public schools. However, volunteers should not be used to save a school district money. Volunteers should never be used in lieu of teaching assistants or other certified personnel. Such uses are an abuse of the volunteer concept and only result in the underrating of the expert services that trained, professionally certified staff can provide. A well-planned and well-organized volunteer program will provide enrichment and expand the learning opportunities for children. The use of volunteers should complement and enhance the role of professional educators, rather than supplant or undermine that role.

Not all volunteer programs have been successful. Some school personnel look upon volunteers as more trouble than they are worth. Others scratch their heads in bewilderment, saying, "I don't know why they volunteered; they don't intend to stay." Volunteers who come in good faith often feel they are not wanted and wouldn't be missed if they were absent. Often they ask, "What is my role?" As well, school volunteer coordinators, teachers, and other school personnel who utilize volunteers also ask, "What is my role?" Once the choice is made to use volunteers, they must be looked upon as a vital part of the total school operation and must be given full-time consideration. To do less will increase the possibility of failure.

What Jobs Will the Volunteers Do?

There are many potential jobs for volunteers, ranging from routine tasks to fairly sophisticated levels of responsibility. Some general categories of service are: members of advisory councils; assistants in classrooms, tutorial and special programs; library and office helpers; and clerical assistants. Volunteers also may help with arts and crafts, skill recreation, group guidance, neighborhood work, public relations, and community education.

Housekeeping jobs are sometimes assigned to volunteers to relieve teachers and other professionals of routine and drudgery. Giving volunteers these kinds of assignments is less threatening to staff members because they are easier to control. However, it is harmful to volunteers who are serious about their work and want to do meaningful, responsible tasks. It is erroneous to assume that volunteers represent a free source of labor that can fill roles that should be held by paid employees. Even though a volunteer may have the proper qualifications, staff jobs must be done by people who can be held accountable.

Frequently, once volunteers arrive at the school, they are assigned jobs that are not thought out, planned, or even needed. Volunteers who have come to the school eager to give their time and talent sometimes find they are given only minimal tasks, and when those tasks are completed, they are left to sit and watch the activities that are going on around them. For that reason, some volunteers will choose not to return. If teachers have not been properly oriented to a volunteer program or have not been given the opportunity to indicate what volunteer services they need in their room or the total school program, it can be predicted that volunteers will not be used effectively. To avoid this possibility, teachers must be given an opportunity to determine the kinds of volunteer assistance they will need. This seven-step process can be used to get input from teachers about their specific needs (Rockwell, 1993).

FIRST-GRADE TEACHER'S VOLUNTEER NEEDS

- Person to read to the children.
- Someone with knowledge of carpentry who can make simple and inexpensive materials for my room.
- A clerical assistant.
- Helper on field trips.
- Resource people for careers.
- Someone to make paint smocks.
- Someone to help create and decorate bulletin boards.
- A gardener (and land).
- Musicians.
- Someone to film special classroom events.

DETERMINING NEEDED SERVICES

1. Examine the total program to determine volunteer needs for specific roles and responsibilities. The entire staff can meet with the volunteer coordinator to make a list of jobs volunteers could do. It is critical that no limits are put on the ideas and services they feel are needed. All ideas should be listed.
2. Review the inventory of needs and identify the services on the list that are currently available from regular staff at the school. In most schools, an existing pool of talent can provide some of the services requested.
3. Determine which services requested are available from existing local agencies by referral. Beware of the long waiting lists that often occur in some agencies.
4. Subtract steps 2 and 3 from step 1 to get the remainder of services that volunteers might provide. If the initial inventory in step 1 was complete, the remainder will include services that no paid source could provide.
5. Determine which of the remaining services could be provided by volunteers.
6. Translate the lists of needed services into a list of volunteers.
7. Write clear and concise job descriptions for each service a volunteer can provide.

At top is a first-grade teacher's list of volunteer needs.

Frequently, teachers and other school personnel think of using volunteers in school activities not directly connected with the academic program. Generally, state regulations and contractual agreements between teachers' organizations and boards of education permit the use of volunteers in supportive services. Here are examples of supportive activities:

1. Attendance clerk: checks and records student attendance.
2. Library aide: shelves books; makes simple repairs on damaged books.
3. Media aide: keeps instructional and media equipment in working order.
4. Lunchroom monitor: helps monitor lunchroom conduct.

5. Playground monitor: helps on playground during free play, and not during PE.
6. Classroom assistant: collects material for, and helps prepare, class displays and bulletin boards.
7. Chaperone: assists teacher on field trips.
8. General aide: catalogs and files instructional materials; helps construct educational games and kits.

Volunteers with extra knowledge, exciting experiences, and specialized skills should be utilized in the classroom. In most states, only the approval of the local school administration is required in order to have special resource people in the classroom. Police officers and firefighters frequently are used in the "Community Helper Unit" in the primary grades, and local government officials are used in high school social studies classes. Some examples of special resource volunteers are:

1. a carpenter (demonstrates the use of his or her tools).
2. an artist (explains a famous masterpiece).
3. a parent who has spent the summer in another country (gives a slide presentation).
4. an attorney who has worked as a public defender (tells of his or her experiences).
5. an automotive factory worker (explains the automated assembly line).
6. a registered nurse (discusses the training, skills, and tasks involved in professional nursing).
7. a farmer (describes how recent flooding has affected crop production).
8. a native of Mexico (models traditional garments and teaches the children a song in Spanish).
9. a local musician (demonstrates various styles of music on the piano).
10. a parent (conducts a storytelling session during the lunch hour).

Occasionally, school volunteers will be needed to provide specialized help on a continuing basis, such as two or three times a week for a semester or more. Also, it may be appropriate to have a volunteer assist during an entire unit of instruction. The volunteer mentioned in number 8 above could be used during the entire unit on Mexico. If this occurs, the teacher should carefully outline the duties of the volunteer, the specific instruction the volunteer is to provide, and the beginning and ending dates of such instruction. Generally, it is a good idea to provide this information in writing to the proper school administrator. Of course, any instruction on either a onetime or a continuing basis should be closely supervised by certified personnel.

One area of school volunteer work frequently overlooked are activities that can be done at home or in the community. For example:

1. a parent who serves as a liaison between neighborhood groups and the school.
2. a group of volunteers trained to conduct a communitywide survey for the school.

SCHOOL VOLUNTEER JOB DESCRIPTION

SCHOOL: Franklin   TEACHER: Ms. Janet Kniepkamp

POSITION: Playhouse Builder   GRADE LEVEL: Kindergarten

JOB DESCRIPTION: Assist a team of volunteers to plan and build a playhouse for the kindergarten classroom.

TIME NEEDED: Day: 3 Saturdays   Time: 9:00 a.m.–12:00 p.m.

                Start: September   Finish: September

SPECIAL REQUIREMENTS: Construction and/or decorating skills preferred, but not required.

---

3. volunteers who help disseminate information to the community regarding the importance of impending bond issues.
4. volunteers who collect recycled materials to be used by the teacher in a classroom activity.
5. a parent who sews and decorates cloth bags to be used by the teacher with a toy or book lending library.
6. a volunteer who prepares and distributes a weekly calendar of school and community activities that take place in school facilities.

LEGAL CONCERNS

Generally, there are few legal concerns related to this kind of volunteer service because such help is not directly related to the academic program or the instructional process.

Legal regulations regarding the use of volunteers will vary from state to state. Some programs require criminal background checks and health papers. Those considering using volunteers for parent and community involvement should seek information from local and state authorities.

JOB DESCRIPTIONS

Accurate job descriptions are needed so that volunteers will know what is expected of them. Job descriptions should identify specific details for each service provided by volunteers, list the skills required, and describe the time commitment needed to provide the service. Above is an example of a job description form.

When teachers write job descriptions, they have an opportunity to thoroughly think through the task for the volunteer. After the job descriptions are written, they should be assembled in a job description catalog for distribution by classroom and grade level to each teacher, secretary, and principal in the district.

WHERE WILL THE VOLUNTEERS COME FROM?

Volunteers will be drawn from all segments of the community. A wide range of occupations and economic and social roles enrich a school volunteer program (Henderson, Marburger, & Ooms, 1993) The most abundant source of volunteers will be parents of the children served by the program (Berger, 1995). Another excellent source will be friends and acquaintances of staff members or of other volunteers. Certain volunteer tasks can be accomplished by upper elementary, junior high, or high school students. College students can provide a variety of useful talents.

Most volunteers are middle-aged. Surveys indicate that 40% to 60% of volunteers are between 30 and 55 years old (Rockwell, 1993). Retirees become excellent volunteers because they usually are devoted and loyal in their service. In addition, a person who has spent 30 or more years on a job or a series of jobs has accumulated a wealth of information and skills that can be extremely helpful to the school. Retirees also can provide a link to an older generation that many children don't have because their grandparents are deceased or live far away. It has been estimated that 100,000 older people are involved as volunteers in programs serving young children (Seefeldt & Warman, 1990).

RECRUITMENT

The recruitment of volunteers can and should cut across the categories of age (from elementary school students to retired adults); sex (both males and females); occupation (professional to semiskilled); economics (all income levels); racial, ethnic, and religious differences; and education.

The method of recruiting will depend on the size of the program and the available volunteer pool in the community. In general, recruitment is not too difficult after the recruitment targets have been identified. Parents, naturally, are the major source of volunteers in a program that emphasizes community involvement. In a program that emphasizes parent involvement, the major source of volunteers is readily identified. When recruiting community volunteers, talks given to local civic groups are effective. Speakers appearing before local groups should stress the need for volunteers and be prepared to answer questions about the goals and purposes of the program. Community understanding and support are vital in providing a quality program.

Other approaches are school tours and brochures or letters mailed to target groups. These brochures should describe the need for volunteer services as well as give examples of jobs that need to be filled by volunteers. Volunteers who already work in the program can potentially be the most effective recruiters.

⬛ THE VOLUNTEER COORDINATOR

The volunteer program will be different in each school depending on the number of children, the size of the community, public transportation facilities, and other community resources. In establishing guidelines for a school volunteer program, it is necessary to plan carefully.

First, designate an individual or individuals who will be responsible for the direction and supervision of volunteer services. A full-time coordinator will be needed for larger programs. Smaller programs might be able to combine this position with another assignment. For example, in some small elementary schools, the building principal is the volunteer coordinator. In an early childhood setting, the position often is assumed by the director. In Head Start programs, the coordinator of parent involvement usually fills the role. In some situations the position might be filled by a qualified volunteer who is willing to serve as the coordinator.

The job of the volunteer coordinator is a multifaceted one. Success or failure of the program depends on a coordinator's ability to manage the many factors involved. The coordinator must be proficient in human relations, communications, and managerial skills. The coordinator also must have the time, interest, and necessary skills to:

1. understand the policies and procedures of the school.
2. make school personnel aware of the benefits of volunteer service.
3. explore and determine the level of support and cooperation the school will provide the volunteer program.
4. provide an important link between the school and the community.
5. orient volunteers to the value and goals of the program.
6. maintain regular communication with all volunteers.
7. stimulate continuing community support and interest in the program.
8. exemplify the kind of model that volunteers can imitate in the performance of their duties.
9. constantly evaluate the efforts of the volunteers and of the entire school volunteer program in an effort to improve it.

Although not all volunteer coordinators will perform these duties, they highlight the range of duties a coordinator might be asked to perform.

It is the job of the volunteer coordinator, working under the direction of the principal, the director, or a designated assistant, and in cooperation with the teachers and staff, to develop clear answers to the following questions.

- What kinds of volunteer services are needed?
- How many volunteers are desired?

*An interview is an important early step in communicating
expectations to a potential volunteer.*

■ When are these volunteer services needed and for how long?
■ What performance objectives are required?
■ For which age or grade levels are volunteer tutors needed?
■ What special problems are involved?
■ What facilities and resources will be available?

After questions such as these are answered, you're ready to get a program
under way. Here are the steps to follow; the order can be changed, depending
on the circumstances. All of the items listed need to be given some attention
during the operation of a program (Rockwell & Comer, 1978).

1. Publicize the volunteer program. News stories in the local paper, public
   service announcements on radio and cable television stations, posters in
   grocery stores and laundromats, and notes and letters sent home from
   school with the children are all effective.
2. Speak to groups such as the PTA, PTO, civic organizations, etc.
3. Recruit volunteers.
4. Interview volunteer prospects.
5. Process teachers' requests for volunteer assistance.
6. Assign volunteers to situations that best match the needs of teachers.
7. Develop and maintain schedules.
8. Keep an information file on regular and substitute volunteers.
9. Orient the volunteers in the following areas:

      a. Goals of the program

      b. Needs of the school staff

      c. School regulations

      d. Physical arrangement of the school

      e. Location of materials and supplies

      f. Existing school programs and services

      g. Neighborhood recreational help and supporting social services

10. Provide preservice training for the volunteers. This training will vary depending on where the volunteers are to be placed and what training the teachers, and the volunteers themselves, think they need. Training also should cover general skills and duties of the volunteers, child development, appropriate developmental practices, and human relations skills, including self-image and effective communication.

11. Introduce volunteers to the school staff.

12. Secure and be responsible for the use of inventory and necessary supplies.

13. Maintain volunteer records and supplies.

14. Notify volunteers in advance if their services are not needed on a particular day.

15. Follow up on absences and their cause. Make adjustments to remove the cause, if possible. For example, if the volunteer is not able to attend because of a lack of transportation, perhaps the coordinator can arrange transportation.

16. Secure substitutes or alternate volunteers if necessary.

17. Observe volunteers and be prepared to make constructive suggestions to help them improve in the volunteer role.

18. Guide and counsel volunteers with individual conferences and group meetings. Inservice training programs should be ongoing, depending on volunteer and teacher needs.

19. Continually investigate and search for school and community resources that might offer services to the volunteer program.

20. Confer regularly with volunteers, school officials, and teachers to maintain morale.

21. Provide continuous formal recognition of volunteers throughout their service. Publicity in the news media and the school newsletter, letters of appreciation, trophies, pins, certificates, and recognition dinners are all widely used methods of recognizing volunteers. A coordinator generally knows of the assistance that the volunteers have provided, but formal recognition provides an opportunity for awareness at the community level.

22. Evaluate the volunteer program and offer recommendations for strengthening it.

It is a big job to find a volunteer coordinator who can effectively carry out all of these duties. The volunteer coordinator may well be the key to the success of the entire program and must be selected with great care.

▣ VOLUNTEER INTERVIEWING AND JOB PLACEMENT

Each volunteer should be interviewed before being accepted. The interview should take place at the school or center and be conducted by the volunteer co-ordinator, the principal, or the center director. The purpose of the interview is to judge the individual's motivation, assess his or her skills, and determine where the volunteer should be placed in order to make the greatest contribution to the program (Shea & Bauer, 1993).

From the interview, the volunteers learn the purpose of the program, why they are needed, and what is expected of them. The interview should be carefully planned so that the prospective volunteer fully understands the satisfactions that can be gained through service, as well as the obligations that must be met. Volunteers should not be seen as free labor and therefore exempt from conforming to expectations (such as preparing adequately for the task, being regular and punctual, writing records, attending training meetings, etc.) that must be met in order to conduct an efficient, high quality program (Cook, Tessier, & Klein, 1992).

When interpreting the program to a prospective volunteer, the interviewer should review the lists of tasks or job descriptions developed from the aforementioned inventory of needs. While the responsibility for the assignment of volunteers rests with the staff, based on an assessment of abilities and competencies, assignments must be mutually agreeable to both staff and volunteer.

The most important qualifications for a volunteer are a dedication to the welfare of children and a willingness to commit time and energy on their behalf. Some volunteers may possess an intellectual and emotional commitment, but still be unable to work directly with children. A well-conducted interview will help determine where volunteers of this nature may serve best. It is important that an alternative be available for these volunteers. An appropriate activity might include soliciting funds, equipment, and materials from community groups. These volunteers also could aid in interpreting the program to the community, serve on a newsletter publication staff, or prepare teaching materials in their homes.

People to be avoided as volunteers are those who cannot discipline themselves to accept the school program. If they can't keep appointments or complete training, they are going to bring more confusion than help to the children and the staff. Desirable traits that the interviewer should look for in prospective volunteers are helpfulness, sincerity, creativity, dependability, reliability, confidentiality, and responsibility (Rasinski, 1995). The interviewer should have knowledge of the volunteer needs of other community agencies, as it might not be possible to use everyone who offers to help but an applicant may possess skills that could be better utilized by another agency. Cross referral by local groups can be beneficial to all involved.

SELECTION OF AN ADVISORY COMMITTEE

An advisory committee for volunteer services is essential to the program. Such a committee should represent a broad spectrum of community agencies and organizations, as well as the teachers and parents of the children who will be the beneficiaries of the services provided. Examples of agencies that might be invited to serve include the local volunteer bureau, Boy Scouts, Girl Scouts, Urban League, YMCA, YWCA, Council of Churches, County Homemakers, Junior League, PTA, PTO, Council of Negro Women, Council of Jewish Women, labor groups, and student organizations. It is also important to contact groups that have traditionally supported child-related programs, such as the American Legion, Shriners, Kiwanis, Lions, local teacher organizations, and the American Association of University Women.

The advisory committee should meet well in advance of the initiation of the program to approve the general plan and to help formulate a presentation to the board of education or other funding agency or both. In some communities the program is funded by one of the service organizations previously mentioned, while formal approval of the program to operate in the schools is granted by the board of education. The advisory committee also should continually monitor and evaluate the program.

ESTABLISHING POLICY

It is important that a guiding philosophy be developed for the program. This philosophy will vary from program to program. If developed with care, the philosophy will serve the school well in the recruitment and orientation stages, as well as throughout the life span of the program.

An example of a philosophy might be:

1. The volunteer program is an integral part of our program.
2. Volunteers are viewed as partners of the staff and are members of the school team.
3. Volunteers should complement rather than replace the existing staff.
4. Volunteers are not paid. They donate their time and talents and therefore have special meaning and value to children.
5. Volunteers bring a richness in the variety of talents, skills, and interests they contribute. They invest time and energy to meet the regular and special needs of children on an individualized and group basis.
6. Volunteers relieve school professionals so that their time and energy may be directed to areas of greatest need and concern.

The statement of philosophy for the program should be general in nature and be tailored to each individual program. However, a clearly stated written philosophy is the key to all successful school volunteer programs. It should touch on matters of crucial importance, such as the intended role and function of the volunteer and the relationship of volunteers to the staff.

SETTING GOALS AND OBJECTIVES

The goal of a program is a broad description of what the program is to accomplish over a period of time, usually one school year. The objective of a program is a specific statement of a step toward the goal and must be measurable in some way.

The writing of a philosophy and the selection of goals for the program should involve the school administration, the advisory committee, and all staff members. Generally, goals are determined first, and then specific, measurable objectives are developed to meet each goal. This step cannot be omitted. At the end of the program, it is essential to be able to measure the degree to which the program did or did not accomplish its goals.

For example, a community might think that home-school relations could be improved by increasing the number of parents working at the school and becoming familiar with the school program. This goal might be stated as follows: The volunteer program will strengthen home-community school relations. An objective for the goal could be that during the school year, 50 parents will participate in a parent volunteer program. Another goal could be that parent volunteers will provide individual instruction for school students. Still another goal could be that parents will provide enrichment activities for the students. An objective for this goal might be that 25% of the students will participate in an enrichment activity presented by a parent. Enrichment activities are defined as experiences that broaden student understanding of the topics the teacher has already introduced.

WORKING WITH VOLUNTEERS

ORIENTATION

At least one formal orientation session should be held for all volunteers before any volunteer work begins. It should cover the most important details that volunteers should know before they begin working (Swick, 1991). Include the goals and purposes of the school, the school's philosophy as it relates to volunteer services, specific duties and responsibilities of volunteers, the relationship of the volunteers to the staff, and an overview of specific do's and don'ts.

One useful method of further conveying the information covered in the orientation is to prepare a volunteer handbook (Henderson, Marburger, & Ooms, 1993; Rockwell & Comer, 1978). This handbook, which can be given to all volunteers, includes the detailed information presented at the orientation and provides a handy reference for volunteers throughout their contact with the program.

Training volunteers is crucial.

TRAINING

Orientation should be followed by training. The training program should be perceived as an ongoing process involving on-the-job training as well as informal small group and individual preplacement sessions. As many staff members as possible should participate in these sessions with the volunteers. This eliminates communication problems between the professional staff and the volunteers. It also will help increase the volunteers' awareness of the professionals' role and provide an opportunity for professionals to become aware of the problems and concerns of the volunteers. Training sessions can contribute to the development of harmony and a cooperative spirit for the volunteer program.

The training program's format should be varied. Informality should prevail. Videos and demonstrations are useful training tools; lengthy formal lectures should be deemphasized. If possible, new volunteers should have an opportunity to hear from experienced volunteers. The training session's content depends on what jobs the staff has decided it needs volunteers to do.

Obviously, the training should fit the job. Classroom volunteers will need to understand their role in the classroom. If possible, the teacher who has requested the help will assist in or conduct the training sessions. If the job is clerical, the volunteer should be trained to use the computer, the laminating machine, and any other "hardware" the school may possess. Nothing is more discouraging to volunteers than to receive training that is not relevant to the job they have volunteered to do (Shea & Bauer, 1993).

SUPERVISION

Supervision, whether group or individual, must be regular. Volunteers need and are entitled to have their performance assessed on a regular basis. They need to share successes and also be supported during periods of frustration and feelings of inadequacy. If supervision and/or opportunities for volunteer feedback are omitted, a high turnover rate can be predicted (Swick, 1991). Volunteers desire guidance in their work and can be distressed by a lack of direction. A good program of supervision and support will help volunteers be accountable for their commitments, show up on time, do their work in a thorough fashion, and be a valuable contributing member of the school or center team.

EVALUATION

A vital component of the volunteer program is evaluation. Evaluation serves as a systematic, constructive form of feedback to help a program be better. If changes are called for as a result of evaluations—be they self, teacher, coordinator, principal, director, or total program—then those changes should be made. Evaluation information should be sought from all who have participated in the program. All volunteers should engage in a self-evaluation of their contributions. Staff members who utilize volunteer services also should evaluate the volunteers.

Obviously, evaluation helps those in charge of a volunteer program to see whether volunteers have been doing what they were expected to do. Matching the evaluation results with the overall objectives of the program will provide the volunteer coordinator and the advisory committee with information about the goals of the program. If the objectives have been met, then the program has done what it set out to do. If some of the objectives have not been met, then either the program needs to be adjusted so those objectives can be met in the future, or perhaps the objectives need to be modified. It is possible that a thorough evaluation process will discover that totally new objectives need to be formulated and considered by the advisory board. If the volunteer program is to be viable and ongoing, then evaluations, whether constructive or critical, must be heeded.

RECOGNITION

Every volunteer, regardless of the time devoted to the program, should receive frequent praise and encouragement for their services. Much satisfaction is gained when the volunteers feel they have been accepted as colleagues by their co-workers. Another form of satisfaction results from their contribution to the progress and growth of an individual child or group of children.

Staff members must make a continual effort to express their acceptance of the volunteer and the skills the volunteer is contributing. In addition to this effort, a dinner, reception, or some type of recognition ceremony should be held near the end of the school year to publicly recognize the volunteers for their services.

SUMMARY

Volunteers are some of the most important members of the education team. They are the extra hands, eyes, and legs that teachers frequently need for a successful day. It is a wonderful feeling to know that there are people who are willing to give freely of their time and talent to serve in this capacity. Volunteers have many responsibilities. They should be dependable and show maturity, cooperation, and the ability to accept suggestions and instructions willingly. They must be eager to learn and to do assigned duties; and they must feel free to consult with staff members when they have questions about the program. They also need to genuinely care for children. A good program, well conceived, can help volunteers achieve all of these qualities.

ACTIVITIES FOR DISCUSSION, EXPANSION, AND APPLICATION

1. Identify barriers that might be present when a school volunteer program is attempted.
2. What are the volunteer resources in your community?
3. What major topics should be addressed in a volunteer orientation session?
4. What volunteer services do you think are needed for your program?
5. What are some ways that volunteers can be recognized for their services?
6. Do a survey of the volunteer training programs that are conducted in the early childhood centers of your community. Do a similar survey for training programs conducted in the elementary schools.
7. Contact and interview two parents, two teachers, and two administrators and ask their opinion on the use of volunteers in school settings. Share the interviews in class.

REFERENCES

Berger, E.H. (1995). *Parents as partners in education: Families and schools working together* (4th ed.). Englewood Cliffs, NJ: Prentice Hall.

Boyer, E.L. (1992). *Ready to learn: A mandate for the nation.* Lawrenceville, NJ: Princeton University Press.

Cook, R.E., Tessier, A., & Klein, M. (1992). *Adapting early childhood curricula for children with special needs* (3rd ed.). Columbus, OH: Merrill.

Henderson, A.T., Marburger, C.L., & Ooms, T. (1993). Beyond the bake sale: An educator's guide to working with parents. Washington, DC: National Committee for Citizens in Education.

Rasinski, T.U. (1995). *Parents and teachers helping children learn to read and write.* Fort Worth, TX: Harcourt Brace College Publishers.

Rockwell, R.E. (1993). Parent involvement. In B.J. Howery (Ed.), *Early childhood handbook.* Springfield, IL: Illinois State Board of Education.

Rockwell, R.E., & Comer, J.C. (1978). *School volunteer programs: A manual for coordinators.* Athens, OH: Midwestern Teacher Corps Network, Ohio University.

Seefeldt, C., & Warman, B. (1990). Young and old together In L.R. Williams & D.P. Fromberg (Eds.), *Early childhood education*. New York: Garland.

Shea, T.M., & Bauer, A.M. (1993). *Parents and teachers of exceptional students—a handbook for involvement*. Boston: Allyn & Bacon.

Swick, K.J. (1991). *Teacher-parent partnerships to enhance school success in early childhood education*. Washington, DC: National Education Association.

Chapter 11

Parents as Decision Makers: Empowerment in Process

READERS WILL BE ABLE TO:

- Analyze the historical and legislative evolution of parent involvement as decision makers in regular and special education movements.
- Outline parental rights and responsibilities for involvement.
- Discuss levels of parent empowerment in school relationships and how they apply to programs for young children.
- Identify current trends for parental decision making in programs for young children.
- Explain how teachers and parents can promote meaningful parent involvement in leadership roles within early childhood systems.

If educators believe that one goal of parent involvement is to empower parents to be more effective as their child's first teacher and partners in their child's education, the acceptance of parents as decision makers is a test of that conviction. Parents already possess the right and power to make decisions concerning their child and to choose their degree of parental participation. Since the role of participant inherently includes choice making, parents exert their right as decision maker when they choose to have their child attend a particular program or school, when they participate in parent meetings and conferences, or are available when the teacher visits.

Yet, the parental role as program and policy decision maker has broadened. More early childhood and elementary centers than ever before recognize that the power of parents to assist programs and enhance outcomes for children is generated by the program philosophy of partnership and from the opportunities provided parents to undertake real responsibilities, not token tasks.

Parent Involvement: A Historical Evolution

In the United States, the parents' role in education has been an evolving one. During the 18th and 19th centuries, parents and schools had a cooperative partnership: The schools taught some reading, writing, and arithmetic; parents taught (or arranged for) the craft skills needed to earn a living, as well as the social, religious, and moral foundations they valued. Parents did more than just select the local schoolmaster. Because the teacher often lived on a rotating basis with local families who had children in the school, the parents strictly monitored the teacher's behavior and activities. Parents paid for their child's schooling and often decided the curriculum; to them, the school and teacher were in their employ.

The industrial revolution and the change from a rural, agricultural lifestyle meant that families could no longer prepare their children for the varied jobs available to them. The influx of immigrant families was in need of education in the language and learning traditions of their new country. Schools quickly took over the preparation of children for adult work, as well as some of the family responsibilities for child health and well-being. Children were required to be vaccinated before entering school, and school lunches and physical education became part of many school programs. During the late 19th and early 20th centuries, teacher training requirements increased and, instead of being any literate, studious individual willing to teach children, teachers now belonged to a distinct profession. To direct parent participation in their children's school lives, local and national Parent-Teacher Associations were soon visible in schools across the country. At that time, however, their activities were restricted to hosting social events, supervising field trips, and fundraising (Elkind, 1991).

LEGISLATION IMPACTS POLICIES

Depending on the state, children are required by law to begin school between ages 5 and 7 and to attend until ages 16 to 18. Parents have established the right to choose where this education will take place: public, parochial, private schools, or even at home. Over time, other legal protection has been won for parental rights. For example, parents worked to secure the Family Educational Rights and Privacy Act, passed in 1974, which assured parents the right to review their child's school records, correct incorrect or misleading information, and maintain privacy regarding the information held in school files.

Important changes in parent involvement can be traced to the legislation, policy-making, and research generated during the 1960s. The passage of the Civil Rights Act of 1964 increased the awareness of the rights of all individuals. Throughout the country, students in high schools and colleges demanded a voice in decisions that affected their lives. Programs were initiated during the "War on Poverty" that assured the involvement of program participants—the poor—in the planning and delivery of services.

Head Start, the national model preschool program for low-income children and families, was developed during this time. It was the first program to really involve parents in the education of their children. It has maintained the expectation that parents should be active participants in their children's classroom and "owner" of the program through active involvement on advisory boards and policy councils, and as paid classroom assistants. These involvement strategies provided researchers with documentation from which to substantiate the value of parent involvement in early childhood programs and the longitudinal value of early childhood education as well (O'Brien, 1990).

The PTA, which recently has become more policy-oriented, has been joined by the Head Start Parent Association and Parent Action. Parents in these groups have organized to ensure that they will have a voice in public policies that affect them and their children. However, the full strength of public advocacy on the part of parents has yet to be fully seen (Weissbourd, 1994).

SPECIAL EDUCATION LAWS SECURE PARENT/FAMILY RIGHTS

The quest for appropriate educational opportunities for all children has led program policymakers and parents to a shared decision-making process. During the late 1950s and 1960s, parents of children with disabilities took a hand in developing services for their children. At a time when public schools did not welcome children with disabilities, parents often developed their own special education programs outside of the public system. Active as fundraisers, teachers, administrators, and advocates, parents undertook the legal challenges to acquire rights and opportunities for their children. Parents developed into an organized group of political advocates who contributed to a series of successful litigations, ultimately leading to the congressional passage of Public Law 94-142 (Education for All Handicapped Children Act of 1975) and Public Law 99-457 of 1986.

As public schools assumed the responsibility for educating all children, many parents were given a passive role. They were often expected to accept the professional's decisions for placement and programming and remain outside the school, unless needed as room mother or fundraiser. As the full impact of PL 94-142 began to be felt, some parents began to assume the empowered role as a partner in the educational decision making for their children and themselves via the Individualized Educational Program (IEP) for children aged 3 to 21 and with PL 99-457, the Individualized Family Service Plan (IFSP) for younger children and their families.

Although this role as a decision-making partner has been outlined and protected by law, parents do not always exercise it for a variety of reasons. Many organizations (often with broad-based parental support and membership) offer special legal rights awareness classes to educate parents with children in special education. Parents also may form support groups to share advocacy and other information.

When parental partnership expectations are not met and communication at the local level breaks down, parents with children in special education may initiate legal action called due process against the special services provider. This is sometimes averted through mediation; however, parents do have this power protected by federal legislation. In 1991, the Individuals with Disabilities Education Act took effect and updated terminology and expanded and affirmed services for all individuals with disabilities (Turnbull & Turnbull, 1990). The gains made by these parents have been influential in developing increased opportunities for all parents. (See Chapter 4 for additional information on families of children with special needs.)

PARENT RIGHTS AND RESPONSIBILITIES FOR INVOLVEMENT

A popular focus of education has been the right of all children to a successful learning experience. Parents frequently have taken action to defend this right, battling such issues as segregation, gender equity, and restrictions on home schooling.

Although the emphasis in education often appears as children's rights, parental rights exist as well. According to Henniger (1987), these parental rights and responsibilities in the educational process include:

- **The right** to personal feelings about education.
- **The responsibility** to be knowledgeable about educational goals, techniques, and principles.

- **The right** to personal feelings about a child's place in the educational system.
- **The responsibility** to listen carefully and openly to professionals.

- **The right** to meaningful communication with the child's teacher.
- **The responsibility** to ensure that communication flows two ways.

- **The right** to plan and maintain parent groups.
- **The responsibility** to support and develop leadership capabilities in themselves and in others.

- **The right** to know the school's policies and program plans.
- **The responsibility** to be supportive of the plan or to take an active role in changing the policies.

- **The right** to be represented in policy-making decisions.
- **The responsibility** to get involved and participate when possible.

It is because of the need to be represented in policy decisions that affect their children that parents develop into decision makers. Through the developmental process of building a supportive parent involvement policy and practice, energy and momentum emerge. The momentum grows within parents and professionals as they realize that their efforts can equal results. For example, positive parent conferences with relaxed communication may result in a new classroom volunteer with many good ideas, or a major contributor to the advisory committee. The resulting positive feelings can build a progression of enhanced self-esteem, satisfaction, the desire for additional interaction, and the willingness to assume new responsibilities and face new challenges. For many parents this will be a gradual process; for others, an exciting invitation.

LEVELS OF PARENT EMPOWERMENT

Of course, not all parents begin their involvement with their child's program as empowered child advocates. Rasinski and Fredericks (1989) recognize four levels of home-school relationships that correspond to a degree of empowerment for parents. These tiers of involvement are: parent as monitor, parent as an information source, parent as participant, and the empowered parent.

The most simple and basic level open to nearly all parents is that of **monitor.** Parents can take an interest in what is going on in the program through the child ("What did you do today?"), or by reading newsletters and other one-way communications sent home by the teacher. In the next tier, the parent is an **information source.** Parents maintain the lines of communication via two-way communication strategies such as phone calls, notes, passbooks, and parent-teacher conferences. Parents move to the next level of involvement—**participant**—by participating in such activities as meetings and special events, and by being a program volunteer.

The highest level of involvement is that of **empowerment.** Empowerment involves parents and teachers working together for the good of many children and families. This may involve developing program plans, advising staff and administration, and taking leadership in coordinating program efforts such as supervising the parent space, organizing the parent library, or coordinating the program volunteer effort. This level of collaboration emerges from a strong personal commitment to the success of the program goals and requires mutual trust and cooperation between parents and program staff. Unlike the lower levels of involvement, many aspects of empowered decision making may not actively involve all parents, since there typically are a limited number of positions available and limited participation potential for parents.

Empowerment is not an "add it on later" idea, but an important element in planning parent involvement opportunities, especially for families that may be considered "at risk," are poor, belong to a minority racial group, or have non-mainstream culture and language. According to Family Matters at Cornell University, empowerment is one of the keys to overcoming social class and cultural barriers as they relate to involvement in schools. Low-income parents who feel excluded and powerless have responded well to decision-making opportunities in Head Start and other school programs promoting parent participation (Davies, 1989).

PARENTS CHOOSE INVOLVEMENT LEVEL

Not only must opportunities for parent involvement exist at all levels, but parents and professionals alike must be sensitive to the ability of parents to respond. A family system viewpoint takes into consideration the variables of unique family characteristics, interactions, and life stages. Consequently, the level of parent involvement is reflective of the particular values, strengths, and

Empowerment means that parents take an active role in partnership with the school.

needs of each family. For some parents, the role of decision maker, active team member, or child advocate will be realistic and achievable. For others, many aspects of this role will be beyond their capacity to respond.

Parent involvement upholds the belief that parents should share the rights and responsibilities of decision making and be a part of the educational process. These assumptions, however, may conflict with parental needs or preferences. Not all parents may be interested in or be able to make a commitment to higher levels of involvement. Although a parent may be a capable decision maker or an excellent leader, the parent's personal need to set limits on "extra" activities and preserve a sense of balance within the family must be respected. Professionals must recognize that parent involvement is a dynamic activity that will develop (or fluctuate) with the rest of life's experiences.

CURRENT TRENDS IN PARENT DECISION MAKING

It is evident that parent involvement in decision making can take many forms. Some programmatic options for young children may be determined by parents, such as enrollment in a particular preschool program or the choice of a graded or ungraded classroom. Parents can assist with "teacher tasks" of decision making, such as collecting informal assessment data to document their child's progress. Evaluative reviews for many center and school programs often include self-study evaluations as a significant component of that process. Parents typically are asked to participate in this type of program review. Federal grant initiatives since the 1970s also have responded to the need for parental input into the program by supporting programs that emphasize parent empowerment components. Partners in Policymaking, a model empowerment and self-advocacy training program from Minnesota, originated this way (Zirpoli, Hancox, Wieck, & Skarnulis, 1989).

PARENT ADVISERS

As programs for young children continue to seek more effective and "family friendly" strategies, parents often are asked to serve as advisers, both formally or informally, to ensure that the parental perspective is represented and parental expertise is utilized. The parent adviser may actually assist in developing policy through an advisory committee, parent/faculty board, or focus group. Many community and federal preschool programs, such as Head Start and Title I, utilize parents in this way (Rich, 1987).

Parents who have been consulted have a heightened sense of ownership. When their agenda is the same as the professionals' agenda, true partnerships emerge. Planning parent meeting topics, agendas, and formats, for example, *without* consulting parents about their interests and *without* exploring options with them is likely to result in low or fluctuating attendance (Liontos, 1992).

A parent advisory committee may be developed for a particular short-term purpose or be ongoing. A classroom advisory committee might select materials for the parent space, for example. A committee on after-school child care could serve the larger school and community. Parent advisory committee activities may include such objectives as: organizing parent volunteer projects; selecting criteria for the selection of personnel; initiating suggestions for program improvements; assisting in selecting and organizing parent activities; providing input from other parents and encouraging their participation; representing and linking other private and public organizations, clubs, and agencies in the area; and monitoring and evaluating the program (Honig, 1979). Utilizing parents as advisers establishes a vital trust with them and respect for their concerns, which will bring lasting benefits to programs.

PARENTS IN ORGANIZATIONS

PTAs and similar organizations frequently provide another opportunity for parents to support programs and to speak on behalf of children and youth in the schools, in the community, and before governmental agencies and other organizations that make decisions affecting children and families. PTAs have broadened the expectations of parent involvement in schools and programs beyond fundraising. Parents have banded together to form building or program organizations, such as the Preschool PTA, when these are not established for the entire school. It is important to realize that parents may need leadership

GUIDELINES FOR SUCCESSFUL PARENT ADVISORY PARTICIPATION

1. Parents are involved in significant school-related areas, such as curriculum, allocation of funds, personnel, or parent activities.

2. Advisory groups meet regularly to discuss issues and make recommendations. This also builds a sense of purpose, trust, and partnership.

3. Parent involvement has real, not token, impact. Recommendations are listened to and have a real effect on decision making.

4. All advisory group members should receive some training on the group's function, policies, specific focus areas (district budget or curriculum), effective group process, and related skills, as needed.

5. Parents may benefit from leadership training in parliamentary procedure, communication and group management skills, or problem-solving techniques.

6. All advisory group members should have an opportunity to exchange information with veteran advisory members in groups with similar functions. Technical assistance from consultants or workshops offer these opportunities.

7. The needs of all members should be considered. Child-care arrangements for those needing this service during meetings may be welcomed. Assistance with transportation or reimbursement for mileage may be critical for parent participation in advisory activities. Clerical services and office supplies should be available to all advisory members.

8. Written materials (guidelines and regulations, program summaries, handbooks, etc.) should be available to all members.

9. Meetings should be arranged with consideration for all members and run efficiently and purposefully with respect to time and responsibilities.

10. Advisory group members should be recognized for their contribution to the group in a tangible way: an annual dinner, an award, coverage by the local media, etc.

SOURCE: Adapted from information in Lyons, Robbins, & Smith. (1982). *Involving Parents: A Handbook for Participation in Schools*. High/Scope Press.

training to feel ready to be involved in this way. This type of assistance is available from the state or local PTA or through parent resource books. Parent groups could invite professionals from time to time as guest speakers to describe their work and answer any questions. Parent organizations, through their publications, should inform their members of activities that exemplify family-school partnerships and make suggestions about actions they might take locally, illustrating ways in which difficulties could be overcome (McConkey, 1985).

Parent involvement at this level can have unexpected positive outcomes for program and staff. In some communities, parents have developed a resource team of parents willing to share their interests and talents as they relate to

Parent advisory councils can play a major role.

school activities. Parent advisory councils also have played a major role in restoring funding for class activities such as field trips. Parent advocacy can help schools by improving the working conditions of teachers, supporting decreased class sizes, improving parent-teacher relationships, increasing school attendance, improving facilities, and acquiring learning materials and resources (Swick, 1991).

PARENTS ON COUNCILS AND TASK FORCES

Opportunities for genuine parent involvement are increasing in many communities. In order to better solve local problems and address concerns (from playground planning to neighborhood violence and gangs), strategies such as problem-solving teams or task forces are being adopted in the educational sector. These methods not only provide social support for the school system, they also empower the parents who serve on them.

These task forces or councils may be composed of a community coalition of school, organizations, government, and business interests focusing on a particular issue. The National Association of State School Boards of Education, in its report "Caring Communities: Supporting Young Children and Families," recommended that community initiatives focus on early childhood issues (National Association of State School Boards, 1991). Parents are frequently asked to serve with these groups to represent the family perspective (Hester, 1989). This type of involvement is an important requirement of federal special education, compensatory education, and early childhood programs, and a key component in many school restructuring efforts (Council of Chief State School Officers, 1989).

In the effort to guide state implementation of legislation affecting the development of program policy for children from birth through 2 years of age and their families (PL 99-457), many states included parents and professionals on interagency coordinating councils and created local councils with similar membership. Although this effort continues in state-level planning councils, the local interagency coordinating council provides an opportunity for grassroots parental input and offers support for many parents to participate in council activities. These same local councils provide the professional with coordinated information on related family services available within the council area/community that may help other families make more appropriate decisions (Early Integration Training Project Center for Special Needs Populations, 1991).

PARENTS AS ADVOCATES

Parents also can participate in this empowerment stage of involvement as advocates, individually or in groups. Parents may assume decision-making roles regarding school issues, problems, and programs. Not all parental advocacy efforts, however, are connected directly to the school or program. Parents often take the initiative to meet a need with a grassroots effort and provide leadership for continuation of the group as long as the need exists. Parents have assumed responsibility for action through support groups founded across the nation in response to a need—from being the parent of a premature infant to Mothers Against Drunk Driving (Galinsky, 1990). Mother's Centers, part of a national movement begun at the grassroots level, are designed for the support, training, and nurturing of adults and children in the local community (Shirk, 1993).

In Denver, an organization called Family Star has been working with neighborhood residents to strengthen and revitalize the community. Family Star grew out of a 1988 meeting of 60 neighborhood residents concerned about a crack house located across the street from an elementary school. Families built the collaboration, now an incorporated nonprofit organization, and have been successful in attracting financial support from a variety of sources to develop many initiatives that strengthen families and provide a better start for the neighborhood children. An Infant-Parent Education Center, which employs formally trained neighborhood residents, also includes parent participation in the center's management (Children's Defense Fund, 1992).

Parents have effected change by assuming leadership roles on school boards, by lobbying Congress members at town meetings, by organizing letter-writing campaigns, by speaking on forums, and by giving testimony at public hearings. Although there may be limited opportunities for parents to participate in some of the above activities (school boards, for example), many parents could help with mailings or jot a note on a postcard to let their position be known on such topics as budget cuts and preschool programs, both of which are advocacy activities.

PARENTS ON THE TEAM: SHARED POWER

Nationally, parent empowerment has grown through multilevel, progressive changes. Yet those changes have not been uniform, and the challenge of includ-

INFORMATION AND SKILLS FOR DECISION MAKING

In order to be effective contributors to any decision-making effort, parents need to possess appropriate and equivalent background information common to others in the group. This may include:

- Knowledge about the program, school, district, community, local leadership, and past and current priorities that will will affect their actions.
- Information about past activities that impact the current situation and/or information about other groups with a similar focus.
- Knowledge of laws, rules, regulations, policies, and the like that pertain to the situation.
- Information on model programs, curricula, or best practices that would give valuable perspective.

- Information about organizational finances that would influence suggestions or impact the potential outcomes.

Appropriate skills are necessary to function as part of a decision-making group. Parents and other team members may need to have or acquire:

- Listening and communication skills.
- Team building skills.
- Documentation skills (notetaking, letter writing).
- Research skills (locating information).
- Telephone skills.
- Interpersonal or political networking skills.
- Assertiveness and advocacy skills.

ing parents as active team members remains. Oliver Moles (1987) pointed to documented surveys that affirm parental interest in the roles of advocate and decision maker, and that state education agencies support parents as such. At the local level, however, teachers, principals, superintendents, and school board presidents did not necessarily value parents as decision makers. "The elements of confrontation and power sharing are likely to make local educators and school officials uneasy with these forms of parent involvement" (Moles, 1987).

Any change in the traditional school structure or organizational pattern is threatening. The controversy over giving parents any true power challenges the paradigm of school as we have known it. Yet the burgeoning school reform movement in the United States involves new collaborations, including those with businesses and parents. Davies (1989) suggests that external forces such as mandates, laws, citizen protests, and citizen organizations demanding change may be necessary to change traditional school systems. "Without public dissatisfaction," Davies emphasizes, "politicians are unlikely to make substantial shifts in the allocation of public resources. This points to the need for . . . work outside the schools by grassroots parent and community organizations to press for school reform and improved results."

Parents in some countries have the opportunity to instigate services using private and/or governmental monies and to employ professionals directly for

TIPS FOR WRITING LEGISLATORS

■ **Avoid impersonal form letters.**
Share your own personal examples or stories. Handwriting is fine; it does not need to be typed or on fancy paper. Your meaningful illustrations may just end up in a speech to illustrate why others should vote for the measure!

■ **Keep your letter short and to the point.**   Focus on only one issue per letter, told simply. Avoid professional jargon, since the legislator may not understand unfamiliar terms.

■ **Learn the facts.**   Contact the League of Women Voters or other groups to learn the details of the legislation. Be sure your information is correct and that it supports your ideas.

■ **Write more than once to support your ideas.**   Input is critical when you want to gain support for a new bill or want your legislator to sponsor a new measure; you want your legislator to use influence to pass the proposed measure out of committee; and, finally, before the bill you support comes to a vote.

■ **Ask your legislator to respond to your letter.**   Include your name and address on the letter (envelopes are usually thrown away).

■ **Thank your legislator if his/her vote matches your recommendations.**
Be sure to add that you will share the information with others.

SOURCE: Adapted from Goffin & Lombardi (1988). *Speaking Out: Early Childhood Advocacy.* Washington, DC: NAEYC.

their children's services. In the United States, magnet, charter, and alternative schools are already appearing, approximating this concept. In some areas, it already is possible for parents to choose early intervention services for their child from a variety of providers. Instead of monies going to a particular program, funding and services would follow the child. If parents are not satisfied, they could change providers. In education, this is not yet a familiar practice, nor necessarily a comfortable one (McConkey, 1985).

Kagan and Weissbourd (1994) have outlined many facets of these positions concerning parental choice and point out that some minority interest groups also favor control of the schools and their tax dollars to more effectively bring culturally and linguistically relevant curricula and methods into the schools. This type of parental decision-making controversy is marked with flash points in the power struggles that surround this issue.

In many communities, these concerns significantly affect the actualization of parent involvement at the decision-maker level. They can be legitimate concerns or generalizations about all parents based on a negative philosophy or negative interactions with a few parents in the past. These concerns may relate to a threat to power or control, or a fear of the untried. When some parents have a new opportunity to work with professionals, some tension on both sides is not unusual. Professionals sometimes have caused grievances for parents which were not addressed or reconciled. Parents may have caused similar

SALUTATIONS FOR WRITING PUBLIC OFFICIALS

Federal Officials:

The President
The President of the United States
The White House
Washington, DC 20500

Dear Mr. President,

U.S. Senator
The Honorable (full name)
U.S. Senate
Washington, DC 20510

Dear Senator (last name),

U.S. Representative
The Honorable (full name)
U.S. House of Representatives
Washington, DC 20515

Dear Congressman/Congresswoman (last name),

State Officials:

Governor
The Honorable (full name)
Governor, State of _____
State Capitol
City, State ZIP Code

Dear Governor (last name),

State Senator
Senator (full name)
State Capitol
City, State ZIP Code

Dear Senator (last name),

State Representative
Representative (full name)
State Capitol
City, State ZIP Code

Dear Representative (last name),

Local Officials:

Mayor
The Honorable (full name),
City or Town Hall
City, State ZIP Code

Dear Mayor (last name),

Members of local councils and boards
Councilman or Supervisor (full name)
City, Town, or County Seat
City, State ZIP Code

Dear Councilman or Supervisor (last name),

Adapted from Goffin & Lombardi (1988). *Speaking Out: Early Childhood Advocacy.* Washington, DC: NAEYC.

discomfort for professionals. These feelings and issues may be "brought to the table" during the forum. Anger and frustration with the system or with parents should be openly recognized. Respecting the individuals involved may require giving time to an open discussion between parents and professionals in order to share perspectives and experiences, which can build empathy and understanding (Zipper, Hinton, Weil, & Rounds, 1993). Parents and other team members also may need to acquire information or develop team-building skills related to working on a committee.

CHALLENGES FOR TODAY AND TOMORROW

Despite the difficulties or discomfort for many schools and programs, it is time to seriously consider working together with parents. Today, as factors threaten the existence of many human services and school supports, there is an increased need for parent-school partnership. Programs for families and children are frequently underfunded or abolished in difficult times, thwarting the goals to create the best community program possible.

Elkind (1991) points out that, "The humanitarian needs of young children are today in conflict with other economic demands upon public budgets and the profitability of private companies. There are no simple answers to these questions. Both sides have solid arguments. Unlike retired persons, however, who have effectively organized to have their financial and medical needs recognized, young children cannot organize, and parents and early childhood educators must advocate for them." School conditions, large class sizes, reduced opportunities for extracurricular opportunities (such as field trips), and inadequate materials for activities frustrate parents and professionals alike. Schools are stymied by educational accountability issues that are impacted by societal factors outside the school. As change agents, taxpayers, and voters, parents have proven themselves to be a formidable force.

Teachers must remember that parents aren't "just parents." They may be connected to local businesses, religious organizations, and civic groups. In these capacities, parents can be helpful in a variety of ways. Parents can use their influence with businesses to encourage them to donate services, such as taxicab rides to parent meetings, furniture and equipment, or space for meetings; or to hire parents from the program. Parents who are active in local clubs and organizations can encourage those groups to sponsor fundraising events to benefit the family education program, collect used clothing, or sponsor a parent education course in partnership with the school (Allen, Brown, & Finlay, 1992). (See Chapter 12 for more information on community networks and collaborations.)

A CALL TO ACTION

Education professionals and early childhood programs provide a logical, nurturing connection for parents to recognize their power to promote change. By providing opportunities for parents to develop authentic decision-making skills at the local level, and by assisting parents to network with local support groups and national associations, schools and programs can help parents empower themselves. Educators can share critical legislative and educational information acquired through their professional organizations with parents, and model advocacy activities on behalf of their programs and parents. Many professional organizations have parent membership divisions and can assist parents through educational materials and programs to become involved with their schools and governmental agencies.

Teachers can facilitate other empowering opportunities for parents through their class or program involvement strategies. Classroom parent advisers can select toys for the school-home lending library and select activities for home visiting that parents would respond to most favorably. When parent involvement strategies are successful, teachers can share these experiences with others via local newspapers, professional newsletters, journals, or magazines, or at meetings and conferences. The impact of these newspaper articles and meeting presentations can be strengthened dramatically by doing them in collaboration with parents.

Providing parents with opportunities and skills at the local level can empower them to work for appropriate change and improvement in education and in their communities. Professionals can provide general guidelines for writing legislators so that parents can feel more comfortable with this type of advocacy, or parents can host a meeting with the school principal to expand the preschool parent lending library into a parent resource center for the whole school. Legislators and other leaders in government, business, and civic organizations can be invited to visit the school to learn firsthand the importance of these efforts. Teachers can create valuable opportunities for parents to actualize the goals of their advocacy efforts.

SUMMARY

Parents and programs are dynamic and ever-changing. Empowerment is recognized as a purposeful developmental process that aims to help families gain mastery over their lives and environments; parental decision making is a function of the empowerment evolution that takes place within each parent (Turnbull, 1992). It also can be a function of the program's parent involvement philosophy. The process of parent involvement utilizes the natural resources at hand—in people, environments, and organizations—and builds on internal skills for communication, coordination, and leadership. The process nurtures motivation through encouragement, guidance, and an opportunity to promote positive changes in the lives of the children, the family, the professionals, and within the program itself.

Involving parents in decision making is part of the natural progression of parent involvement strategies. Educators do not give parents anything they do not already possess when they are involved in decision-making activities. It is important to remember that involvement at this level of empowerment is dependent on personal variables (personality, values, and opportunity, for example), on external supports, or on disincentives. Because of this, program administration and professional support is critical. Parent involvement at the empowerment level can be challenging for some programs to achieve. It is therefore important for educators to realize that parent decision making has had an erratic historical evolution and that history is still being made. It is up to each teacher and each program to decide what their contribution will be.

ACTIVITIES FOR DISCUSSION, EXPANSION, AND APPLICATION

1. What evidence of the current trends toward increased parent decision making are found in early childhood programs in your community or area? Interview personnel from several programs to learn what leadership roles are available to parents and what strategies are being employed to include parents in decision making. What factors contribute to the levels of quality involvement? What would cause positive changes? Negative changes?

2. Identify five strategies one could suggest to the programs above to promote more meaningful parent involvement in decision making. If things were changed in this manner, what would be the positive and negative perceptions from the staff perspective? From the parent perspective?

3. What aspects of the historical evolution in parental decision making described in this chapter, for regular and special education, are recognizable in the communities and programs you studied? Is this a linear evolution? Why or why not?

4. Interview a parent with a young child in a school or center program. What types of opportunities and what levels of involvement are available to the parent within or as an extension of the program? What is available outside the program?

5. Discuss current concerns and issues facing educational programs and families in your community. Which do you feel strongest about? Identify the most appropriate individual(s) to contact regarding your concerns. This could be a federal or state legislator; a school board president; a state, regional, or local superintendent of education; or a mayor, alderman, or ombudsman. Write a letter describing your views on the issues and what actions you would like to see taken to produce the desired outcomes. Share your response from this individual with your group.

ADDITIONAL RESOURCES

Beach Center on Families and Disability Publications, The University of Kansas Institute for Life Span Studies, 3111 Haworth Hall, Lawrence KS 66045.

Children's Defense Fund publications, 122 C ST. N.W., Washington, DC 20001. It's time to stand up for your children. CDF's nonpartisan voting record of 19__ (updated each year). State child-care fact book.

Child Welfare League of America. (updated biennially) SWLA Washington workbook for child advocates ( )th Congress. Washington, DC: Child Welfare League.

Markel, G., & Greenbaum, J. (1985). Parents are to be seen AND heard: Assertiveness in educational planning for handicapped children. Ann Arbor, MI: Greenbaum & Markel Associates.

National Parent-Teacher Association. A leader's guide to parent and family involvement. Chicago: National PTA.

National Resource Center for Family Support Programs. Starting and operating support groups, A guide for parents. Chicago: Family Resource Coalition.

Pizzo, P. (1983). Parent to parent. Boston: Beacon Press.

Shur, J., & Smith, P. (1980). Where do you look? Whom do you ask? How do you know? Washington, DC: Children's Defense Fund.

REFERENCES

Allen, M., Brown, P., & Finlay, B. (1992). *Helping children by strengthening families.* Washington, DC: Children's Defense Fund.

Bowman, B. (1994). Home and school. In S. Kagan & Weissbourd (Eds.), *Putting families first.* San Francisco: Jossey-Bass.

Children's Defense Fund. (1992). *The state of America's children yearbook.* Washington, DC: Children's Defense Fund.

Council of Chief State School Officers. (1989). *Family support education and involvement: A guide for state action.* Washington, DC: Council of Chief State School Officers.

Davies, D. (March 1989). *Poor parents, teachers, and the schools: Comments about practice, policy, and research.* Paper presented at the annual meeting of the American Educational Research Association, San Francisco.

Dunst, C., Trivette, C., & LaPointe, N. (1994). Meaning and key characteristics of empowerment. In C. Dunst, C. Trivette, & A. Deal (Eds.), *Supporting & strengthening families.* Cambridge, MA: Brookline Books.

Early Integration Training Project Center for Special Needs Populations. (1991). *Go ask Alice: A guidebook for parents serving on state and local interagency councils.* Columbus, OH: Ohio State University Research Foundation.

Elkind, D. (1991). *Perspectives on early childhood education.* Washington, DC: National Education Association.

Galinsky, E. (1990). Raising children in the 1990s: The challenges for parents, educators, and business. *Young Children, 45*(2), 2–3, 67–68.

Henniger, M. (1987). Parental rights and responsibilities in the educational process. The Clearinghouse, 60, 226–229.

Hester, H. (1989). Start at home to improve home-school relations. *NASSP Bulletin, 73*(513), 23–27.

Honig, A. (1979). *Parent involvement in early childhood education.* Washington, DC: NAEYC.

Liontos, L. (1992). *At-risk families and schools: Becoming partners.* Eugene, OR: ERIC Clearinghouse.

Lyons, P., Robbins, A., & Smith, A. (1982). *Involving parents: A handbook for participation in schools.* Ypsilanti, MI: High/Scope Press.

McConkey, R. (1985). *Working with parents: A practical guide for teachers and therapists.* Cambridge, MA: Brookline Books.

Moles, O. (1987). Who wants parent involvement? Interest, skills, and opportunities among parents and educators. *Education and Urban Society, 19*(2), 137–145.

National Association of State Boards of Education. (1991). *Caring communities: Supporting young children and families.* Alexandria, VA: National Association of State Boards of Education.

O'Brien, S. (1990). Parents and schools together. *Childhood Education,* Winter, 106–109.

Rasinski, T., & Fredericks, A. (1989). Dimensions of parent involvement. *The Reading Teacher,* November, 180–182.

Rich, D. (1987). *Teachers and parents: An adult-to-adult approach.* Washington, DC: National Education Association.

Shirk, M. (1993). A nurturing support system for moms. *St. Louis Post Dispatch,* Oct. 20, p. 4F.

Swick, K. (1991). *Teacher-parent partnerships to enhance school success in early childhood education.* Washington, DC: National Education Association.

Turnbull, A., & Turnbull, H. (1990). *Families, professionals, and exceptionality: A special partnership.* Columbus, OH: Merrill.

Turnbull, R. (1992). Family empowerment. *Families and Disability newsletter, 4*(2–3), Lawrence, KS: Beach Center on Families and Disability.

Weissbourd, B. (1994). The evolution of the family resource movement. In S. Kagan & B. Weissbourd (Eds.), *Putting families first.* San Francisco: Jossey-Bass.

Zipper, I., Hinton, C., Weil, M., & Rounds, K. (1993). *Service coordination for early intervention: Parents and professionals.* Cambridge, MA: Brookline Books.

Zirpoli, T., Hancox, C., Wieck, C., & Skarnulis, E. (1989). Partners in policymaking: Empowering people. *Journal of the Association for Persons with Severe Handicaps, 14*(2), 163–167.

Chapter 12
UTILIZING COMMUNITY NETWORKS AND COLLABORATIONS: LINKING EDUCATION AND HUMAN SERVICES FOR FAMILY SUPPORT

READERS WILL BE ABLE TO:

- Recognize concerns with existing family service delivery systems.
- Develop a rationale for education and human service collaboration in support of young children and families.
- Identify common resources and components of community infrastructure for family support.
- Explain ways to enhance the collaborative process of service delivery through educational linkages.
- Indicate ways teachers can empower families with young children to seek information for family supports.
- Describe opportunities educators have to advocate for families and services and to provide leadership for collaborative networking.

The rapid and complex changes in American social structure have created undeniable stress for families. The stressors arising from the economic and social revolution of the past 50 years threaten to overwhelm families and create a high risk for dysfunction, evidenced by the increase in child abuse, violence, teen parenthood, alcohol and other drug abuse, and family dissolution. These symptoms are more than typical family responses to the normal change process, as they reflect major structural changes in society. Families increasingly face not one, but several difficult issues.

Undeniably, economics plays a central role in family stress. Demands for highly educated workers, employment uncertainty, a decline in wages, the impact of technology upon the work force, and the increased cost of living (particularly the increased cost of raising children) all have combined to create a powder keg. For example, within the family system, the initial difficulty may be that of a parent who loses his or her job when the factory lays off workers. For the parent, the impact of joblessness and the accompanying frustrations may result in depression and maladaptive coping, such as alcohol abuse or violent behaviors toward family members. There may be discomfort in the need to access unfamiliar family supports, such as food stamps, medical clinics, or thrift shops. It may be necessary to develop new skills, such as job hunting, preparing inexpensive but healthful meals, or coping with the changes thrust upon the family. These family stressors and responses may become part of a child's or family's eligibility for particular programs or services. They also become risk factors in the development of young children (Swick & Graves, 1993).

NEW COMMUNITY PARTNERSHIPS

There is a need for those educating young children who recognize the interconnectedness of family problems and child development to become proactive in the emerging movement toward community collaborations. As funding for social service programs dwindles, and family needs for intervention escalate, it is not only logical but essential for those with a vested concern for children and families to work together in a new kind of partnership. Parents, educators, social service workers, and health-care providers are creating a unique, interagency paradigm in an effort to provide multidimensional interventions for the complex problems that place families in jeopardy.

This approach to an integrated service system for children and families is built upon the individual community supports provided by schools, hospitals, agency services, government, organizations, volunteers, and businesses. The call to develop community networks and coordinate services for children and families is being heard in all corners of existing systems. Schools and educational programs frequently are the hubs for these initiatives. Therefore, it is crucial for educators to recognize these opportunities, develop skills that contribute to successful collaborations, and network resources for enhanced educational, social/emotional, economic, and medical outcomes for families.

Educators in early childhood traditionally have sought out resources and services to support "their" children and families. Working with families to utilize and broaden their network of support is a primary strategy for empowering parents. The new age of collaboration also offers leadership opportunities for educators to develop community networks that broaden the service base of individual programs and brighten the future for young children.

SERVICE SYSTEM PARADOX POSES PROBLEMS FOR FAMILIES

The increasing number of economic and social stressors has contributed to changes in family dynamics. Adequate supports for coping with these changes, however, have not been available for families. The system of social supports that does exist is outmoded, duplicating some services and inadequately providing others. These often fragmented, inflexible, and underfunded services may create eligibility policy barriers that become sources of additional stress for families (Kunish, 1993).

The 1992 report by the Center for the Future of Children described concern at the lack of a holistic approach to meeting family needs and the administrative obstacles within programs that make it difficult to deliver services effectively. Families as clients seldom have input into program development, and professionals often are frustrated by rigid rules and restrictions. Programs may make it difficult to access their services due to variations in eligibility requirements (individual, family, or household) and inaccessible hours or locations. This creates enormous difficulties for families with multiple problems and limited means. A mother with no dependable transportation who must walk with her young children through violent neighborhoods may choose not to keep an appointment for special services, even if it is located nearby. Just as the problems that families experience are interrelated, logical solutions should be integrated, multidimensional, and coordinated in order to address more than one problem at a time.

Educators must realize that many community social service systems are not as holistic or responsive as they could be, nor are they necessarily sensitive to the situational needs of the family. Teachers may find it easy to fault parents for not providing all the basic needs for their children, or for not securing all the services available to help families in distress. Yet these teachers may not fully comprehend the difficulties posed by the social service system.

SYSTEMS ARE FAILING FAMILIES

The current assortment of education, health, and human services for young children and their families is essentially a collection, owned by a variety of programs, not a unified "system." By dividing the problems of children and their families into rigid and distinct categories, irrespective of interrelated causes and solutions, agencies and programs fail those they intend to serve. Historically, the educational system has been one of the major sources of assistance in dealing with the dynamics of social change. Schools, the "bastions of society," traditionally have been expected to preserve the essence of a collective culture and transmit it to the children, in addition to educating them. Yet the educational system is disabled in its ability to respond to the structural changes in society and to the family systems and communities it is supposed to serve. Frequently outmoded school designs for space, time, curriculum content, and family policy prohibit responsiveness to the educational support needs of today (Swick & Graves, 1993).

Those paying the greatest price for the social revolution are children under 6 and their families. Teachers of young children working with both children and their families on the "front lines" are acutely aware of this. Educators are frustrated by the number of children coming to their programs with recognizable problems related to housing, nutrition, medical care, and other environmental concerns that interfere with the readiness to learn. Educators also are confounded by the difficulties in accessing the systems that are supposed to assist the families.

▲ A Call for Community Action

The first national education goal of the 1989 report on America 2000 was that, "By the Year 2000, all children in America will start school ready to learn." The U.S. Department of Education challenged states and communities to clarify what contributions for readiness were already in place and determine what could be done to enhance readiness and support to families to achieve this goal (U.S. Department of Education, 1989). Since then, many state agencies and community task forces have assessed resources and defined action plans to increase collaborative efforts toward this goal.

The National School Readiness Task Force, chaired by then-Governor Bill Clinton, asserted that the system of family services must support the development of caring communities. These communities provide comprehensive support for young children aged birth through 4 years and their families by filling in gaps in health, family support, and child care. They must work to link services that bring more continuous and convenient help to families. Community-based family support programs are growing. Able to reach young families and deliver the services needed to route them on a path of self-sufficiency, these local programs for parent support and education are succeeding where systems have failed.

It isn't surprising, then, to see progressive schools involved with these programs. Schools not only implement developmentally appropriate teaching and assessment practices and increase parent involvement and professional development for staff, they also work in greater numbers with community agencies to provide appropriate and effective services to children and families (Kunish, 1993; Epstein, 1994).

Communities Look to Schools

Society is again looking to schools, the central structures in each community, to provide more than education. Programs for young children throughout the nation are forging new projects that offer education, health care, and family and child-care support services. The addition of both the parent involvement and family empowerment components make these education service coalitions unique. Getting parents involved in their child's program is a beginning step in these programs, followed by active involvement in goal-setting and other decision making about their child (Kunish, 1993). These programs are sometimes described as being "profamily." According to Melaville, Blank, and Asayesh (1993), profamily systems are:

- **Comprehensive:** a variety of opportunities and services are available, from prevention to crisis intervention.
- **Preventive:** prevention initiatives receive the most emphasis.
- **Family-centered and family-driven:** families are seen and served holistically, with sensitivity to their needs and respect for their abilities.

- **Integrated:** separate services share information so that families face less repetition and confusion.
- **Developmental:** family plans are revised as needs change.
- **Flexible:** policies that govern responsivity to family needs are adaptable.
- **Sensitive to cultural, gender, and racial concerns:** the system is sensitive to diversity in policy and practice
- **Outcomes oriented:** performance is measured by improved outcomes for children and families, not just numbers served.

In the present system, at-risk families frequently receive a patchwork of services from a variety of sources: for example, a state-funded preschool for a younger child, violence prevention services for an adolescent, and job assistance for parents. Often the service providers are not aware of each other. This is clearly a call to collaborate. Bruner (1992) asserts that, "Reducing the number of separate interventions and individuals working with the family, and providing more support for those that remain, would be a better use of resources."

Not all families and children with risk indicators are receiving a variety of services, however. For example, parents of preschoolers may benefit from parenting guidance, joint problem solving, or encouragement, but may not need other social services. These families simply need a collaboration with a caring adult, like a teacher or community service worker. Even if the child is doing well in his neighborhood or school, the community may pose a health and safety threat to the well-being of *all* children and families. Violence and societal health issues like AIDS are examples of this rationale for collaboration. Interventions to these and other complex societal problems should be community-wide, and all groups should have ownership in the solution.

OWNERSHIP ISSUES

The notion of ownership when it comes to the troubles in our country's social service system is an interesting one. There appears to be a great deal of "finger pointing" whenever difficulties affecting child welfare surface. Education has been a source of much attention in this regard. The variable consequence of "ownership" is the issue of paying for the solution. Society has been hesitant to commit financial or personnel resources to assist families, programs, or schools until children are seriously harmed or the situation has become a crisis.

Although prevention is generally cheaper and more effective than crisis intervention and remediation, it only recently has become more evident in comprehensive program planning. By sharing the ownership of societal problems, collaborative funding mechanisms enhance the responsiveness of the system to communities (Education and Human Services Consortium, 1991). Collaborative models frequently interest policymakers because the good (and funding) is diffused throughout the collaboration. Much of the awareness of collaboration and its benefits comes from the business arena. As economic conditions fluctuated and became more complex in the 1970s and early 1980s, businesses (such as the automotive and computer technology industries) studied the potential courses of action, joined together, and documented their collaborative management strategies. In the 1980s, as financial resources became more scarce, collaborations such as partnerships with designated vendors became accepted as cost-effective in the restructuring of service strategies (Kagan & Rivera, 1991).

INCENTIVES FOR EDUCATIONAL SYSTEM INVOLVEMENT

The educational reform movement, through state and local school improvement efforts, also has provided some incentive for schools to more seriously view relationships with parents and to seek out community resource networks. Schools are useful for facilitating collaborations for many reasons. They offer a common access to the majority of children and families whose diverse needs may cross multiple service systems, thus ensuring a more equitable distribution of services. The community or neighborhood school provides a central location where some services may be provided, thus minimizing expenses and service duplications and maximizing staff time. School linkages increase the opportunity to reach families and children with information and services, thus enhancing services and building public support and advocacy for early care and education (Kagan & Rivera, 1991). Schools also open the doors to creative, integrated service options. Most families are familiar with the elementary or secondary schools in their community and many have a network of families they know through school. Successful initiatives also involve school staff in planning, operating, and governing the program or system (Melaville et al., 1993).

By the nature of their business, educational systems are concerned with the quality of services for children and families. A common collaborative initiative that demonstrates these concepts is a community literacy initiative. Adult education agencies, community colleges, community libraries, government agencies, private industry, local volunteers, and preschool programs join forces to provide classes in adult literacy, English as a Second Language, or GED preparation.

A GUIDE TO SOCIAL SERVICES

Teachers of young children are typically aware of or involved in parent education and prevention activities designed to strengthen family functioning and parenting skills. Communication flows both to and from families in the continued sharing of information. The flyer sent home concerning an upcoming public health vaccination clinic is a small step toward programmatic collaboration. Community program and resource information often is shared by social workers within the schools and incorporated within parent involvement strategies like program newsletters, home visits, or parent meetings. Educators learn firsthand from the families of the children they teach about the social, economic, physical, and educational issues that are of greatest concern. Teachers may recognize a need for prevention services or be the first persons outside the family to be aware of a potential crisis situation. Trusting partnerships with educators allows families to sometimes confide troubling circumstances affecting them that require specialized services.

It is crucial that teachers recognize the need for and assist the family in locating services; however, these situations occasionally tax the educator's awareness of available community resources. Although preservice education for some early childhood educators includes information on social service networking, many teachers scramble for information to share with families when the need arises. This is sometimes complicated by the lack of familiarity with available services if the teachers do not live in the community or have not needed to learn about such services. Some professionals are hesitant to engage in some parent involvement activities because of the fear of not knowing how to assist families if a particular situation comes up that they don't know how to handle.

FAMILY SUPPORT PROGRAM MODELS

Families that have developed trust with an early childhood educator may hesitate to go outside their "comfort zone" of professionals for assistance with personal difficulties. Many early childhood programs, like Head Start, may have a small team of professionals who work closely with families. This team may include teachers, social workers, or parent/family coordinators, whose role is to assist families in accessing parent involvement activities sponsored by the program or in locating resources in the community. When it is not possible to delegate the family concerns to another team member, the teacher may assume a family liaison role to facilitate service access and to empower the family to seek assistance.

An increasing number of programs serving young children and their families are developing collaboration projects and "one-stop" shopping approaches to providing comprehensive services. These programs may be sponsored by health-care facilities, mental health clinics, schools, and social service agencies. Head Start has been successful in using federal funds to assist with community initiatives to provide early childhood programming, health services, job training, GED and parenting classes, and child care for younger children at one site (Families and Work Institute, 1993).

Government grants, charitable foundations, and organization initiatives have all funded sources for family support programs. Programs frequently target a particular client group for services, such as urban or rural families, migrant families, a particular cultural or ethnic group, teenage parents, young military families, parents of children with disabilities, or families at risk for abuse or neglect. Epstein (1994) has been involved with two parent-support models, the Parent-to-Parent Dissemination Project and the Child Survival/Fair Start project. In *A Guide to Developing Community-Based Family Support Programs* (1994), Epstein, Larner, and Halpern offer a design for program development that includes these steps:

1. *Identify a client population.*
   Decide how narrow or broad the definition for eligibility will be. How many families, with what type of needs, can be helped?

2. *Set program goals.*

Identify realistic objectives based on the resources of the program and the needs of the families. Family support program goals address concerns for parents, for children, and for communities.

3. *Select a program format.*

Typically, programs offer one or more of these types of service delivery: home-based programs, stand-alone, group-based programs, and family support centers.

4. *Determine how services will be scheduled.*

The onset, frequency, and duration of services must be considered and weighed against the desired outcomes for the program.

5. *Select a curriculum.*

Programs may adopt a packaged curriculum, modify an existing curriculum, or create an individual curriculum from scratch.

6. *Establish a staffing structure.*

Staff roles and responsibilities must be defined. Programs typically have a supervisor and family workers. Issues regarding staff recruitment, staff development, and the establishment of a working relationship with families must be resolved.

7. *Determine the evaluation design and conduct the evaluation.*

Both formative (what was done, how was it done, numbers served, frequency and content, etc.) and summative (outcomes related to gains, improvements, etc.) evaluations should be included.

INFORMAL MODELS

Under the current system, social service assistance may be a confusing web of eligibility requirements, paperwork, access, waiting lists, and information from within the same agency. Educators have, depending on the ability of the family to help itself and the educator's relationship with the family, assisted families with initial telephone contacts to find out requirements, locations, office hours, and such. When the family has no other person to assist it, educators sometimes help with application paperwork. Some visionary social service providers have developed strategies through collaborations, minimizing the bureaucratic efforts a family must initiate in order to receive or access supports.

LOCATING SERVICES FOR FAMILIES

Throughout the United States there is great diversity in the services available to families and children. Federal, state, business, foundation, local, and private sponsorships make a wide variety of programs available. These variations make it difficult to develop a comprehensive list of programs for the nation. Some federal programs are unilateral and can be located in every state; some federal initiatives may be model, pilot, or grant-sponsored and available only to a

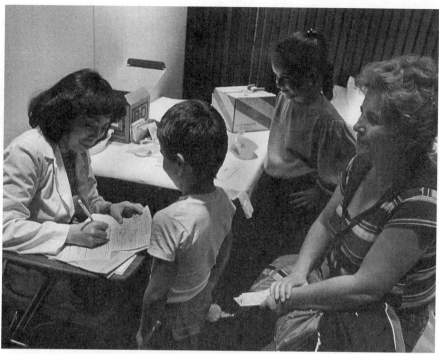

Schools are frequently community centers for comprehensive services for young children.

selected geographical area or community population until the money runs out. These variations in support services are evidence that local communities and regions benefit from uniquely designed program responses. They also reflect the inequality of funding that provides concentrated services in selected areas of a state. This can be confusing for families that relocate and search unsuccessfully for particular supports, and for educators who learn that colleagues in another area have resource programs they cannot access.

Each state, region, or community must therefore develop a directory of services available to families within the designated boundaries. With the heightened awareness of the benefits of community networking, many initiatives have developed a social service directory or list as one of their initial activities. Some communities have produced collaborative directories; others have lists focused to specific needs. That way, information on existing programs or social services is readily available. School district social workers, Head Start programs, and local interagency councils are highly recommended sources of information on community services. Hospitals and clinics, along with mental health, public health, and child and family service programs, also have access to resource information that can be shared. If a program wants to develop its own directory, a format similar to the one in the box titled Community Resource Information may be used.

COMMUNITY RESOURCE INFORMATION

Name of organization/agency:

Sponsoring organization/agency:

Address:

Telephone: Fax:

Director: Contact person:

Months of operation: Days of operation:

Hours of operation: Service area boundaries:

Description of your organization/agency:

Population served: Ages:

                                              Definition:

                                              Income:

                                              Geographic area:

                                              Other:

Description of eligibility criteria/referral criteria:

Length of service availability:

Fee description:

How do consumers gain access to your services?

Coordination/collaborative linkages with:

FEDERALLY FUNDED PROGRAMS

Funding for services for young children and their families is used to support a vast number of initiatives. As of this writing, funds for child care or related services have been available to families through 31 programs in 11 federal agencies. The Social Services Block Grant (Title XX of the Social Security Act) also had subsidized care. Medicaid and the Maternal and Child Health Program financed health-care services. Nutritional needs were addressed through the Child Care Food Program authorized under the National School Lunch and Child Nutrition Act and through the Women's, Infant's and Children's (WIC) Feeding Program. Parents could receive assistance for child care and job training or continuing education through the Family Support Act and the

Aid to Families With Dependent Children (AFDC) program. The Title IV-A At-Risk Child Care Program provided child-care assistance for low-income families that need child care in order to work and are at risk of becoming dependent on AFDC. Before- and after-school care and early childhood development services were available through state initiatives receiving funding from the Child Care and Development Block Grants.

Head Start programs have provided comprehensive models for community and parental involvement. Under the Reauthorization Act (May 1994), new options to the traditional part-day, center-based program include year-round, full-day services; a Transition Project of demonstration grants for Head Start agencies collaborating with local schools; and Parent and Child Centers, which provide prenatal and postnatal services to Head Start-eligible parents and children to age 3.

Even Start is a federal family literacy program that combines early childhood education for children ages 1 to 7 with adult education for parents with poor literacy skills. These programs are typically found in communities with a concentration of low-income families. The Comprehensive Child Development Program is a federal demonstration program designed to provide intensive, integrated support services to children from low-income families from birth to elementary school age. It also provides such support services as early intervention; nutrition and parenting education; vocational training and adult education; substance abuse education and treatment; and assistance in obtaining necessary income support and housing for parents and other household members. Federal budget issues may transform the source and scope of many early childhood services in the years to come. Opportunities exist to renew or reform social service policies in Congress and state legislatures. Citizens and the political system at large have crucial decisions to make that will affect services to children and families.

STATE-FUNDED PROGRAMS

All states commit some general revenues to programs that serve or benefit young children. There is great variation in the size, scope, and focus of these initiatives. These efforts include dependent care tax credits, child care, preschool education, expansion or enhancement of Head Start, and parent education. More than 30 states provide funding for preschool initiatives (many of which target at-risk preschoolers) and/or additions to Head Start (Levy, Kagan, & Copple, 1992).

Despite such diversity of programs and initiatives, detective work still may be necessary to locate specific services. The state lead agency for early intervention services may put out a state services directory. The state department of public health or education also may have a comprehensive guide to services for young children and their families. Some states offer a computerized information service on resources and family supports. Directories such as the Directory of Federally Funded Resource Centers, sponsored by the National Center for Service Integration, list not only national resource centers for child and family welfare and child and family health, but regional educational laboratories, research and development centers, and other federal services. Numerous publications for families have listings in their reference section of available resources and contacts. Do not overlook the community library, community hospitals, local police, and even the telephone book as sources of assistance. An analysis of local services may look like Table 12.1.

Reviewing Educational Systems: A Vital Link

The systemswide trend toward collaboration challenges the traditional education system to broaden its policies and programming to include the needs of families and communities. Early childhood educators are in a unique position to model this process for the entire educational system. Profamily practices in quality early childhood programs also can become the starting point for developing family-sensitive practices in the entire school and community. All of the previously detailed elements of parent involvement come together to prepare for successful collaborations: early partnerships with families, educator skills in communicating sensitively with families, and meaningful parent involvement in order to encourage positive parenting skills. Schools can identify and put into practice educational experiences that communicate a commitment to parent partnerships, support families in developing healthy ways of living and interacting, and integrate parents into the instructional process at all levels.

All this involves looking at the role of school and education in new ways. In order for this to expand beyond a token, trial initiative, schools must examine their philosophical understanding of profamily parent involvement and view their role as an extended family support in much the same way that early educators did (Swick, 1991). In order for educators and schools to achieve their goals for children, partnerships with families must be developed and maintained. Through community partnerships and collaborative resourcing, all families can receive assistance in meeting needs and successfully nurturing upcoming generations.

Reciprocal Benefits

The African proverb, "It takes a whole village to raise a child," has become a slogan of community collaborations. The interconnectedness of resources, the ability to respond, and the corresponding need become evident in many community linkages, but especially so in education. This chart outlines possible lines of collaboration with the school or other educational system.

Educators and Educational Systems Can Provide:

- **Awareness** to communities of the value of parent involvement.
- **Information, resources, support, and training** to communities and businesses on family-centered practices.

TABLE 12.1
Analysis of Local Services

SERVICES	AGENCIES/ORGANIZATIONS
Family assessment	School district
Developmental screening	Special education
Hearing screening	Easter Seals
Vision screening	ARC
Psychological evaluation	Head Start
Audiological evaluation	Mental Health
Medical evaluation	Community/county hospital
Service coordination	WIC
Special education class	Medicaid
Home-based program	Local support groups
Speech/language therapy	Specialized services
Transportation services	Local clubs and organizations
Parent education/training	
Parent counseling/therapy	
Parent support group	
Parent library loan	
Parent-to-Parent	
Medical services	
Dental services	
Child care	
Respite care	
Nursing services	
Prevention services	
Infant program	
Financial counseling	
Substance counseling	
Housing	
Nutrition counseling	
Crisis services	
Supplemental Security Income	
Aid to Families With Dependent Children	
Legal Aid	
Recreation	
Other	

- **A model to communities of respectful practices** and valuing families.
- **Guidance** to communities on the changing roles of parents, families, and communities.
- **Recognition programs** for parents, community organizations, and businesses that are sensitive to families.
- **Partnership opportunities** for parents, organizations, businesses, and communities.
- **Parent-to-parent network information** to parents, organizations, and communities.
- **Special education and educational support services** to children and parents.
- **Locations** for community meetings, health-care services, counseling, employment training for parents, and community organizations.
- **On-site parent education programs** at the workplace to businesses and organizations.
- **Educational programs** like English as a Second Language, GED studies, and literacy for all in the community.
- **Sites and services** for before- and after-school child care, latchkey child programs, and summer programs for children and parents.

EDUCATORS/EDUCATIONAL SYSTEMS CAN RECEIVE:

- **Information, resources, support, and training** from organizations for family-centered involvement.
- **Support** from everyone for early education and family programs.
- **Transportation services** from businesses for family events.
- **Volunteer support** from everyone for school and family programs.
- **Technical assistance** from businesses for marketing school events, public awareness campaigns, grant writing, etc.
- **Job training** from businesses for families.
- **Support for the dissemination of information** and a location for parenting resources from the community.
  (Sources: Children's Defense Fund, 1992; Committee for Economic Development, 1985; Luethy, 1991; National Task Force on School Readiness, 1991; National PTA, 1992; Pooley & Littell, 1986; Rich, 1987; Swan & Morgan, 1993.)

INDIVIDUAL PROFESSIONAL CONTRIBUTIONS TO COLLABORATIONS

Educators can develop their own skills in their new role as collaborator, liaison, or family resource person. Frequently the teacher will be called upon to "sell" the program and concept of parent involvement to parents, agencies, other teachers, administrators, and the community, much like a public relations specialist. As a collaborator, your style of communication and interpersonal interactions should promote openness and respect for the expertise of others as new relationships are formed outside the education system. Projecting a positive attitude and a willingness to share will help in communicating, planning, and problem solving with others in the networks built with each agency and organization. Be patient with people and with the process of collaboration. Collaboration pushes all parties into the unfamiliar when a first contact is made. Time and a commitment to making meaningful linkages are valuable assets (Hazel, Barber, Roberts, Behr, Helmstetter, & Guess, 1988; Jackson, 1992).

INTERPERSONAL DYNAMICS OF COLLABORATION WITH FAMILIES

Parent-teacher collaborations, like all parent involvement, is based on mutual respect; an understanding of the other's perspective and role; and the sharing of knowledge, information, and skills. Each individual in any partnership brings unique values, ideas, perspectives, and skills to the relationship; therefore, each parent partnership will be different. Family-centered practice emphasizes the family's central role in planning and making decisions about services for their child and other family members. The teacher can assist parents in assessing their child's strengths and needs, family resources, priorities, and concerns, and can help identify goals and services with the family. As a family resource provider as well as an educator, the teacher can assist with locating services the family is interested in, and in facilitating parent involvement with other professionals and agencies (Zipper, Hinton, Weil, & Rounds, 1993).

Empowering parents and families to actualize a plan to meet their needs or to problem solve requires positive attitudes and expectations toward them. Professional understanding of the families educators work with requires a true partnership in order to plan a nurturing, healthy environment. Enabling parents to make their own decisions and empowering them to become resourceful in their own lives requires professionals to respect the family autonomy and assist families in responding to their perceived needs.

Families don't want the professional to view their needs and risk attributes as personal or family deficits. They frequently may experience community rejection as a "problem" family. Throughout their lives, other forces have shaped their perception of themselves as somewhat powerless and unable to make better choices for their lives. These perceptions are critical to the parents' ability to guide themselves and their children in proactive directions. Through childhood experiences, education, interpersonal dynamics, and cultural and subcultural parameters, parents have developed a belief system about themselves and their abilities. If this system has negative messages that are not confronted by positive, proactive ones, the parent's ability to function as a self-empowered individual may be diminished. These feelings of powerlessness and low self-esteem affect the parent's relations with others and how events and life circumstances are viewed. Parental behavior patterns and interpersonal relationships are indicators of their locus of control. Do I control my life (internal locus) or do life events or other people control me (external locus)?

The role of the educator may be to help parents see the possibility of choices in their environment and in their lives. As the concept of potential develops, parents will increase their participation in life decisions. The feelings of frustration, along with the lack of self-determination, create a potential for destructiveness and dysfunctional responses. Problems, both real and imagined, appear unsolvable and promote pessimistic responses to life. Stress and anxiety arise from these interpretations of reality (Swick & Graves, 1993).

These parents may feel overwhelmed that they do not have the resources or ideas to cope with their problems; however, the parents often do not realize the risk factors confronting the family. Poverty, intergenerational abuse, and poor family and school experiences may reinforce a negative, limiting perception of life. ("I wasn't good in school, neither is my child. He'll have to find another way.") Parents also can become dependent upon their problems for structure or social identity. Even if it may improve their life, change is threatening to them and to their social status. Some at-risk families are isolated from other views of society, and some of their rigid attitudes may come from inexperience or a lack of exposure to other ways of thinking (Swick & Graves, 1993).

Professionals can best assist these disempowered parents by being empathetic, warm, and responsive to the family's needs and concerns without being judgmental. They should model a positive and proactive attitude to help the family acquire a realistic understanding of the strengths and needs of their children and family system. Attention should be focused on developing autonomy and healthy self-concepts within the family relationships. Educators should emphasize collaborative strategies to facilitate the development of plans the family feels are beneficial to it.

Collaboration itself builds a sense of power for the family within the helping relationship. Here are strategies that teachers can use to become an effective collaborator with the family (Children's Defense Fund, 1992; Swick & Graves, 1993; Steele, 1989).

- Recognize your motivation in assuming the helping role. This is critical.
- Emphasize the family system whenever possible, instead of focusing on an individual child or other family member.
- Treat families with respect, and honor cultural differences.
- Offer flexible, responsive services instead of single-purpose, "quick-fix" provider solutions.
- Focus on the people, not the problem. Build on family strengths instead of emphasizing deficits.
- Offer preventive services to avert crisis.
- Balance your efforts as helper with opportunities for other members of the family's system to help.
- Recognize your strengths and limitations. You can't be all things in the relationship.

- Rely on your network of resources and your supports and mentors. The family itself should be encouraged to take responsibility for its progress.
- Provide the family with the resource contacts through printed information, telephone links, resource fairs, etc.
- Assist the family, if necessary, to access the resources.

ADVOCACY FOR SERVICE SYSTEMS: WHAT TEACHERS CAN DO

Advocacy is defined as speaking or writing in support of something. In early childhood, we advocate for children and families when we share our profession with families, colleagues, administration, community leadership, politicians, and policymakers. Although many issues are important in the field of educating young children, this chapter has centered on service availability and collaborations to meet the needs of young children and their families. The current system has weaknesses that allow children to fall through the cracks in society.

True system collaborations that are effective and sensitive to needs in today's world will evolve when the "turf issues" of service delivery are addressed. Fiscal accountability will no longer ignore duplication of services and programs, and wise decisions for creating systems changes cannot be made from behind a desk in Washington, DC, alone. Policymakers must hear the stories from the field: your stories, your family's stories.

Advocacy takes many forms and has many voices. Early childhood educators should feel empowered with the role of advocate for the types of program and services *they* believe are best practices for children and families. Support programs in your community and in your state that are family-focused. Participate in family system support organizations like the Family Resource Coalition and in professional organizations like the National Association for the Education of Young Children. Encourage businesses in your community to adopt family-friendly policies for parent employees. Educate your school administration about profamily policy and current trends toward school-service linkages. Communicate knowledgeably, sincerely, and effectively. Practice what you believe to be the highest quality of service for families as a model to others. Add your voice of commitment to the cause for quality education for all children. Be an active learner about your school, your children, and the programs that serve their families. Enlist the assistance of your community and family service providers. Expect best practices in early childhood programming and work to achieve levels of excellence. Participate in the democratic process of communicating your beliefs to government, and support genuine leaders in education. Attend town meetings, talk with candidates, and educate them about the issues you see as a professional and what you believe to be an acceptable course of action for change (Children's Defense Fund, 1990; Nall, 1992; National PTA, 1992; Swick & Graves, 1993). Advocacy is a job we all share.

Parents are powerful advocates for early childhood services.

SUMMARY

Providing services to young children and their families can become an overwhelming job until teachers begin to identify and link with a comprehensive network of colleagues in community human services. The "community village" will need to summon all its nurturing resources to ensure the well-being of families and children. Linkages and collaborations can be made on any partnership scale imaginable: person to person, corporation to community, national to neighborhood. Present service delivery systems are not keeping pace with the families needing assistance. The difficulties of systems policies, with their layers of administration and politics, have a human cost in children's lives.

There is a call to communities to become their own problem solvers, and all players are asked to help. For many schools this presents a break from the traditional mold of education; for others it is a natural outreach into the community. Teachers working with those most at risk, namely young children and their families, must be open to utilizing service network systems at many levels and be aware of national, state, and local programs that can help meet needs. Skills are needed to successfully communicate, motivate, and empower families to utilize these systems themselves and the role of the educator is broadening. As leaders in the community, educators have a new opportunity to advocate as caring professionals for services that will best serve the needs of the community, its families, and especially the children.

ACTIVITIES FOR DISCUSSION, EXPANSION, AND APPLICATION

1. The existing family service delivery system has come under fire. Outline the concerns from the following perspectives: the family, the social service worker, the educator, the citizen, and the community.

2. As an early childhood professional, you are requesting release time to meet with community agency program personnel. How would you justify this activity to your reluctant administrator?

3. Using suggestions from this chapter, design a chart of support services available to families with young children from birth through 5 years of age in your community. Indicate type of service/program, source of the service, eligibility requirements, length of service eligibility, and additional benefits available to the family through its participation in the program.

4. Identify typical brokers of social service network information at the national, state, and community levels. Who accesses information on their service? How is this done?

5. Within an early childhood program, identify and detail at least five strategies to empower parents to connect with community resources.

6. As an early childhood professional, discuss what family support services you would advocate for and how you would do it.

7. Insight challenge: Elect one member of your discussion group to assume the role of a parent in search of social service assistance within your community. Have that person make telephone contact to learn what needs to be done in order to receive services. How was he or she treated? Did he or she find out all necessary information? What was positive about the contact? What difficulties, if any, were there? How would a parent without a telephone, child care, or transportation manage to access the service? How great a challenge would the lack of good communication skills be for the parent? How easy to access (office hours, location, etc.) is the service agent? Would this create any problems for working parents, non-English-speaking, or other culturally diverse families?

ADDITIONAL RESOURCES

Boyer, E. (1992). *Ready to learn. A mandate for the nation.* Princeton, NJ: The Carnegie Foundation for the Advancement of Teaching.

Mendoza, J. (1992). *Exploring support systems. A family education program.* Tucson, AZ: Communication Skill Builders.

National Center for Service Integration. (1993). *Directory of federally funded resource centers–1993.* Washington, DC: National Center for Service Integration.

Otterbourg, S. (1991). *Bring business and community resources into your classroom. A handbook for educators.* Washington, DC: National Educational Association.

REFERENCES

Bruner, C. (1992). *Thinking collaboratively: Ten questions and answers to help policymakers improve children's services.* Washington, DC: Education and Human Services Consortium.

Center for the Future of Children. (1992). *The Future of Children, 2*(1).

Children's Defense Fund. (1992). *The state of America's children.* Washington, DC: Children's Defense Fund.

Committee for Economic Development. (1985). *Investing in our children: Business and the public schools.* Research and Policy Committee statement. New York: Committee for Economic Development.

Education and Human Services Consortium. (1991). *What it takes: Structuring interagency partnerships to connect children and families with comprehensive services.* Washington, DC: Education and Human Services Consortium.

Epstein, A. (1994). Supporting today's families. *High/Scope Resource*, Fall. Ypsilanti, MI: High/Scope Press.

Epstein, A., Larner, M., & Halpern, R. (1994). *A guide to developing community-based family support programs.* Ypsilanti, MI: High/Scope Press.

Families and Work Institute. (1993). *Community planning initiatives. National forum on state and community planning in early education and care.* Washington, DC: Families and Work Institute.

Hazel, R., Barber, P., Roberts, S., Behr, S., Helmstetter, E., & Guess, D. (1988). *A community approach to an integrated service system for children with special needs.* Baltimore: Paul H. Brookes.

Jackson, M. (1992). *Resourcing: Handbook for special education resource teachers.* Reston, VA: Council for Exceptional Children.

Kagan, S., & Rivera, A. (1991). Collaboration in early care and education: What can and should we do? *Young Children, 47,*(1), 51–56.

Kunish, L. (1993). Integrating community services for young children and their families. North Central Regional Educational Laboratory Policy Briefs. Report 3, 1–7.

Levy, J., Kagan, S., & Copple, C. (1992). *Are we ready? Collaboration to support young children and their families.* Paper developed through support from the Foundation for Child Development.

Luethy, G. (1991). An example of parent education at the work site. *Young Children, 46*(4), 62–64.

McCarthy, J., Lund, K., & Bos, C. (1986). *Parent involvement and home teaching.* Denver: Love.

Melaville, A., Blank, M., & Asayesh, G. (1993). *Together we can: A guide for crafting a profamily system of education and human services.* Washington, DC: U.S. Department of Education and U.S. Department of Health and Human Services.

Nall, S. (1992). A fresh look at advocacy. *National All Day Kindergarten Network, 2*(1), 1, 3, 6.

National PTA Parent/Family Involvement Committee. (1992). *For our children: Parents and families in education.* National PTA Parent/Family Involvement Summit Report. Chicago: National PTA.

National Task Force on School Readiness. (1991). *Caring communities: Supporting young children and families.* Alexandria, VA: National Association of State Boards of Education.

Pooley, L., & Littell, J. (1986). *Family resource program builder: Blueprints for designing and operating programs for parents.* Chicago: Family Resource Coalition.

Rich, D. (1987). *Schools and families: Issues and actions.* Washington, DC: National Education Association.

Steele, B. (1989). *Developing community networks: A guide to resources and strategies.* Washington, DC: Association for the Care of Children's Health.

Swan, W., & Morgan, J. (1993). *Collaborating for comprehensive services for young children and their families.* Baltimore: Paul H. Brookes.

Swick, K. (1991). *Teacher-parent partnerships to enhance school success in early childhood education.* Washington, DC: National Education Association/Southern Association on Children Under Six.

Swick, K., & Graves, S. (1993). *Empowering at-risk families during the early childhood years.* Washington, DC: National Education Association.

U.S. Department of Education. (1989). *America 2000: What other communities are doing. . . . National educational goal #1.* Washington, DC: U.S. Department of Education.

Zipper, I., Hinton, C., Weil, M., & Rounds, K. (1993). *Service coordination for early intervention: Parents and professionals.* Cambridge, MA: Brookline Books.

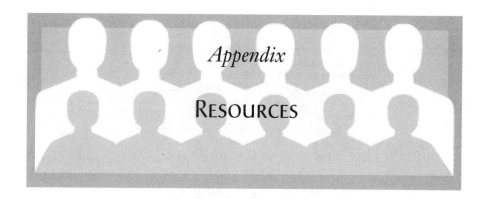

Appendix

RESOURCES

The resource information in this appendix is intended to serve as a starting point. A wide variety of content areas related to parenting and family involvement issues are included in order to assist early childhood professionals and the families they serve. We have purposely deleted compilations of books and videos due to the rapidly expanding market of materials published each year. Most organizations maintain bibliographies of current information in their field and will be able to direct parents, teachers, and administrators to appropriate resources.

GENERAL RESOURCE GUIDES FOR SCHOOLS AND PROGRAMS SERVING FAMILIES

The following books offer expansive listings of organizations that provide helpful resources for schools and programs serving families.

Cutright, M. (1992). *Growing up confident: How to make your child's early years learning years.* New York: Doubleday.

DeFrancis, B. (1994). *The parents' resource almanac: Where to write, who to call, what to buy, and how to find out everything you need to know.* Holbrook, MA: Bob Adams.

Lyons, P., Robbins, A., & Smith, A. (1992). *Involving parents: A handbook for participation in schools.* Ypsilanti, MI: High/Scope Press.

Moore, C. (1990). *A reader's guide: For parents of children with mental, physical, or emotional disabilities* (3rd ed.). Rockville, MD: Woodbine House.

Starer, D. (1992). *Who to call: The parent's source book.* New York: William Morrow. An invaluable resource guide to every 800 number, hotline, and organization that can help you raise a happier, healthier child.

GENERAL EDUCATION RESOURCES

American Reading Council (ARC). 45 John St., Suite 908, New York, NY 10038. Phone: (212)619-6044. ARC provides information on successful literacy programs and helps groups that wish to found or improve a literacy program.

Barbara Bush Foundation for Family Literacy. 1002 Wisconsin Ave. NW, Washington, DC 20007. Phone: (202)338-2006. The foundation sponsors programs that bring parents and children together, encouraging a positive home attitude toward learning. Provides grants and seed money, and trains volunteers and teachers.

Center for the Study of Children's Literature. Simmons College, 300 the Fenway, Boston, MA 02115. Phone: (617)738-2258. The center offers a community education program in the field of children's literature, answers questions, and offers advice to researchers in children's books.

Educational Press Association of America (EDPRESS) and the International Reading Association. Glassboro State College, Glassboro, NJ 08028. These groups publish a list of children's magazines. Write for a price list.

Educational Resources Information Center (ERIC). Office of Educational Research and Improvement, 555 New Jersey Ave. NW, Washington, DC 20208. Phone: (202)219-2289 or (800)LET-ERIC. ERIC is a national information system responsible for developing, maintaining, and providing access to the world's largest single source of information on education research and educational practices. The ERIC system includes a network of clearinghouses, each of which specializes in an area of education. Within their subject areas, the ERIC clearinghouses acquire significant literature for the database, publish research summaries and other products, and provide free reference and referral services. There are several ways to access ERIC documents (these are described in several free guides: *A Pocket Guide to ERIC*, *All About ERIC*, and *For Education Information . . . Call ACCESS ERIC*. Call or write for copies). ACCESS ERIC is a toll-free service offering information on the ERIC network and other education resources. ACCESS ERIC staff members will answer questions, refer callers to education sources, and provide information about the ERIC network.

Friends for Education. 600 Girard Blvd. NE, Albuquerque, NM 87106. Phone: (505)260-1745. This group works to establish and improve public school accountability systems.

National Center for Fair and Open Testing. 342 Broadway, Cambridge, MA 02139. Phone: (617)864-4810. This center explores the problems and inequities in standardized testing.

New Horizons for Learning. P.O. Box 15329, Seattle, WA 98115-0329. Phone: (206)547-7936. This international clearinghouse for information about new strategies in learning publishes a newsletter, *On the Beam*, which describes the latest research in learning and thinking skills.

Reading Is Fundamental (RIF). 600 Maryland Ave. SW, Suite 500, Washington, DC 20560. Phone: (202)287-3220. This organization of volunteer groups works to interest children in reading. It runs reading motivation programs, encourages parents to have children read to at home, and sponsors a book distribution program.

U.S. Department of Education. Office of Educational Research and Improvement, 555 New Jersey Ave. NW, Washington, DC 20208. Phone: (800)424-1616. This office supports and conducts research on education, collects and analyzes education statistics, and disseminates information.

🔲 PARENT EDUCATION

HOME PROGRAMS

Family Infant and Preschool Program (FIPP). Western Carolina Center, 300 Enola Road, Morganton, NC 28655. Phone: (704)433-2661.

Hawaii Healthy Start Program. Department of Health, 741-A Sunset Ave., Honolulu, HI 98816. Phone: (808)733-9022.

The High/Scope Perry Preschool Program. High/Scope Educational Research Foundation, 600 N. River St., Ypsilanti, MI 48198-2898. Phone: (313)485-2000.

Home and School Institute. MegaSkills Education Center, 1201 16th St. NW, Washington, DC 20036. Phone: (202)466-3633. The institute offers programs and materials to help parents stimulate their children's learning in the home. Researches and designs home learning activities that parents can use with their children; offers a series of workshops for parents sponsored by school systems in states across the country; and develops educational strategies that emphasize cooperation between families and schools, schools and the community, and families and businesses. Offers a variety of books on family learning and parent/community involvement in schools.

Home Instruction Program for Preschool Youngsters (HIPPY). Housed in Teacher's Institute, 525 W. 120th St., P.O. Box 113, New York, NY 10027. Phone: (212)678-3500. HIPPY is an international program that offers parents information through home visits, literature, and recommended parent-child activities. Support and training for parents are given by para professionals who are themselves parents of young children from the communities served by the program.

Mother-Child Program. Center for Mother-Child Home Program, 3268 Island Road, Wantagh, NY 11793. Phone: (516)785-7077.

Parents as Teachers (PAT). Parents as Teachers National Center Inc., 9374 Olive Blvd., St. Louis, MO 63132. Phone: (314)432-4330. PAT believes that parents are a child's most influential teachers and that the parent-school partnership should begin at birth. Stresses that children learn more during the first three years of life than ever again, and bases its programs on this belief.

Portage Project. CESA 5, 626 E. Slifer St., Portage, WI 53901. Phone: (608)742-8811.

Resource Mothers Program. National Commission to Prevent Infant Mortality, 330 C St. SW, Switzer Building, Room 2014, Washington, DC 20201. Phone: (202)205-8364.

PARENTING CLASSES

Active Parenting. This is a nationwide parenting education program. Check with local schools, churches, synagogues, or social service organizations to find out whether classes are offered in your community. Alternatively, you can call the Family Resource Coalition for tips on locating parent education classes in your area.

Parent Effectiveness Training (PET). Phone: (800)628-1197. PET teaches parents how to eliminate the power struggles that prevent effective communication. Call for a directory of certified instructors in your state.

Systematic Training for Effective Parenting (STEP). More than 2 million parents have participated in STEP classes, which help moms and dads discover new ways to handle problems, build their child's self-confidence, set limits, and increase cooperation. The classes are offered through many adult education centers, preschools, and elementary schools. For information on groups near you, or on starting a STEP group, contact American Guidance Service, Publishers Building, Circle Pines, MN 55014-1796. Phone: (800)328-2560. (Note: A videotape and print parenting course designed to teach groups the basics of STEP is available.)

GENERAL PARENTAL INVOLVEMENT

Alliance for Parental Involvement in Education. P.O. Box 59, East Chatham, NY 12060. Phone: (518)392-6900.

American Academy of Pediatrics. 141 Northwest Point Blvd., P.O. Box 927, Elk Grove Village, IL 60009-0927. Phone: (708)228-5005 or (800)433-9016.

American Association of School Administrators. 1801 N. Moore St., Arlington, VA 22209.

American Federation of Teachers. 555 New Jersey Ave. NW, Washington, DC 20001.

Appalachia Educational Laboratory. Rural Excel Program, P.O. Box 1348, Charleston, WV 25325. Phone: (304)347-0400.

Association for Library Service to Children. American Library Association, 50 E. Huron Road, Chicago, IL 60611. Phone: (312)944-6780.

Association for Supervision and Curriculum Development. 1250 N. Pitt St., Alexandria, VA 22314.

Center for Early Adolescence. University of North Carolina at Chapel Hill, Suite 233, Carr Mill Mall, Carrboro, NC 27510. Phone: (919)966-1148.

Center on Families, Communities, Schools, and Children's Learning. Johns Hopkins University, 3505 N. Charles St., Baltimore, MD 21218. Phone: (410)516-0370. Through research, evaluation, and policy analysis, this center works to produce new and useful knowledge about how families, schools, and communities influence students' motivation, learning, and development.

Center for the Study of Parent Involvement (CSPI). 303 Van Buren Ave., Oakland, CA 94610. Phone: (415)465-3507. CSPI helps increase and improve the involvement of parents in the education of children. Advises and consults parents, community workers, and educators.

Center on Parent Involvement. Johns Hopkins University, c/o Joyce Epstein, 3505 N. Charles St., Baltimore, MD 21218. Phone: (301)338-7570.

Cornell University Family Matters Project. 7 Research Park, Cornell University, Ithaca, NY 14580. Phone: (607)255-2080/2531.

Council of the Great City Schools. 1413 K St. NW, 4th Floor, Washington, DC 20005. Phone: (202)635-5431.

Designs for Change. 220 S. State St., Suite 1900, Chicago, IL 60604. Phone: (312)922-0317. This group assists parent groups, teachers, students, and others working to improve public schools.

Elementary School Center. 2 E. 103rd St., New York, NY 10029. Phone: (212)289-5929. Center works to improve quality of elementary and middle school education.

Family Resource Coalition. 200 S. Michigan Ave., 16th Floor, Chicago, IL 60604. Phone: (312)341-0900. Fax: (312)341-9361.

Home and School Institute. Special Projects Office, 1201 16th St. NW, Washington, DC 20036. Phone: (202)466-3633.

Institute for Responsive Education. 605 Commonwealth Ave., Boston, MA 02215. Phone: (617)353-3309. The institute fosters greater parental involvement in the schools, especially among poor and minority parents in urban areas. Offers assistance to those seeking school support within their community.

International Reading Association. 800 Barksdale Road, P.O. Box 8139, Newark, DE 19714-8139. Phone: (302)731-1600 or (800)336-READ. Fax: (302)731-1057.

La Leche League International. 9616 Minneapolis Ave., P.O. Box 1209, Franklin Park, IL 60131-8209. Phone: (708)455-7730. Hotline: (800)LA-LECHE.

National Association for the Education of Young Children. 1834 Connecticut Ave. NW, Washington, DC 20009-5786.

National Association of Elementary School Principals. 1615 Duke St., Alexandria, VA 22314.

National Association of Partners in Education. 209 Madison St., Suite 401, Alexandria, VA 22314. Phone: (703)836-4880. This association promotes the value of school volunteer and partnership services and the involvement of citizens and businesses in schools.

National Black Child Development Institute. 1023 15th NW, Suite 600, Washington, DC 20005.

National Coalition of Alternative Community Schools. 58 Schoolhouse Road, Summertown, TN 38483. Phone: (615)964-3670. The coalition consists of regional and local alternative school associations.

National Coalition for Parent Involvement in Education. P.O. Box 39, 1201 16th St. NW, Washington, DC 20036. This coalition is dedicated to the development of strong family-school partnerships. Works to build broad community support for local schools.

National Coalition for Parents Involvement in Education. 119 N. Payne St., Alexandria, VA 22314. Phone: (703)683-6232.

National Coalition of Title I/Chapter I Parents. Edmonds School Building, Ninth and D Streets NW, Room 201, Washington, DC 20002. Phone: (202)547-9286. This is a coalition of parents, educators, administrators, and others who encourage and support community participation in the development of educational programs for disadvantaged children.

National Committee for Citizens in Education. 10840 Little Patuxent Parkway, Suite #310, Columbia, MD 21044-3199. Phone: (301)977-9300 or (800)NETWORK (633-9675).

National Committee for Prevention of Child Abuse (NCPCA). P.O. Box 2866, Chicago, IL 60690. NCPCA has brochures on child sexual abuse as well as other material for parents. Write for a publication list.

National Conference on Parent Involvement. 579 W. Iroquois, Pontiac, MI 48341. Phone: (313)334-5887. The objective of this group is to hold an annual conference to bring together people who are advocates of parent involvement in the schools.

National Education Association Professional Library. P.O. Box 509, West Haven, CT 06516.

National Mental Health Association (NMHA). 1021 Prince St., Alexandria, VA 22314-2971. Phone: (703)684-7722. NMHA provides information, offers emotional support and guidance for families, and helps school systems develop programs for children with mental illnesses. Lobbies for federal mental health legislation and stimulates funding for research. Publications catalog lists, pamphlets, and booklets on all aspects of mental health and mental illnesses. *Focus*, its newsletter, comes out quarterly.

National PTA. 700 N. Rush St., Chicago, IL 60611-2571. Phone: (312)787-0977. Fax: (312)787-8342. National PTA serves as the headquarters for the more than 28,000 local PTA chapters across the country. Seeks to unite home, school, and community in promoting the education, health, and safety of children, youth, and families. Contact the national office for state office information.

National School Board Association. 1680 Duke St., Alexandria, VA 22314. Phone: (703)838-6722.

National School Volunteer Program. 701 N. Fairfax St., Suite 320, Alexandria, VA 22314. Phone: (703)836-4880.

Northwest Regional Educational Laboratory. 101 SW Main, Suite 500, Portland, OR 97204.

Parent Cooperative Elementary Program. Cedar Valley Elementary School, Edmonds School District 15, 20525 52nd Ave. W., Lynnwood, WA 98036. Program offers guidelines and suggestions for starting a parent cooperative at your elementary school.

Parent Cooperative Pre-Schools International. c/o Kathy Mensel, P.O. Box 90410, Indianapolis, IN 46290. Phone: (317)849-0992. This group provides information and research services to members, including individuals and groups interested in nonprofit preschools operated cooperatively by parents.

Parent Involvement Center. Chapter I Technical Assistance Center, RMC Research Corporation, 400 Lafayette Road, Hampton, NH 03842. Phone: (603)926-8888.

Parent Involvement in Education Program. San Diego County Office of Education, c/o Janet Chrispeels, 6401 Linda Vista Road, Room 407, San Diego, CA 92111-7399.

Parents for Public Schools. P.O. Box 12807, Jackson, MS 39263-2807. Phone: (601)982-1222 or (800)880-1222. Fax: (601)982-0002. This nonprofit, grassroots organization is made up of parents who believe their children receive the best available education in public schools and who actively recruit other parents to enroll their children in public schools.

President's Committee on Mental Retardation. 330 Independence Ave., SW, Washington, DC 20201. Phone: (202)619-0634. This office responds to inquiries and serves as an advocate for mentally retarded persons.

Southwest Educational Development Laboratory. 211 E. Seventh St., Austin, TX 78701.

United Parents-Teachers Association of Jewish Schools. 426 W. 58th St., New York, NY 10019. Phone: (212)245-8200. The association works to build a healthy partnership between the Jewish home and Jewish schools. Encourages parental involvement in Jewish education.

University of California Department of Education. Joint Task Force on Parent Involvement, c/o Susan Brand, University of California at Berkeley, Berkeley, CA 95064. Phone: (415)526-3864.

Work and Family Research Council. The Conference Board Inc., 845 Third Ave., New York, NY 10022. Phone: (212)759-0900.

🔲 DIVERSITY, BILINGUAL EDUCATION, AND MULTICULTURAL ISSUES

A Better Chance (ABC). 419 Boylston St., Boston, MA 02116. Phone: (617)421-0950. ABC oversees placement of talented, motivated minority students in excellent public and private schools, counsels students on higher education, encourages leadership roles, and conducts research. Financial aid is available from schools within the organization.

ERIC Clearinghouse on Rural Education and Small Schools. Appalachia Educational Laboratory, 1031 Quarrier St., P.O. Box 1348, Charleston, WV 25325-1348. Phone: (800)624-9120 or (in West Virginia) (800)344-6646. The laboratory serves as a clearinghouse for information on the social, cultural, and economic impact on educational programs for migrants, Native Americans, and Hispanic Americans, with particular emphasis on small schools.

Intercultural Development Research Association (IDRA). 5835 Callaghan Road, Suite 350, San Antonio, TX 78228. Phone: (512)684-8180. The association is involved in research and in training those interested in bilingual education.

National Association for Bilingual Education (NABE). Union Center Plaza, 810 First St., NE, 3rd Floor, Washington, DC 20002. Phone: (202)898-1829. NABE supports bilingual education and equal opportunity.

National Institute for Multicultural Education (NIME). 844 Grecian, NW, Albuquerque, NM 87107. Phone: (505)344-6898. The institute is dedicated to equal opportunity in education for bilingual school-age children.

Quality Education for Minorities. 1818 N St. NW, Suite 350, Washington, DC 20036. Phone: (202)659-1818. This organization works to ensure that minorities in the United States have equal access to educational opportunities. Assists local schools in carrying out educational programs to benefit minority children (African Americans, Hispanic Americans, Native Americans, Puerto Ricans, and others), particularly in the areas of math and science. Helps coordinate educational activities among organizations and institutions.

🔲 EARLY CHILDHOOD ORGANIZATIONS/ INFORMATIONAL RESOURCES

GESELL

Gesell Institute of Human Development. 310 Prospect St., New Haven, CT 06511. Phone: (203)777-3481. The Gesell School Readiness Evaluation, which is performed by a trained professional, provides information related to a child's general level of maturity, separate from academic and intellectual abilities. Used with parents' and teachers' observations, this evaluation is helpful in planning for a child's placement in school. Offers a parents' guide to starting school, as well as a variety of books on school readiness and developmental education, including *School Readiness* (a full explanation of developmental placement), *Is Your Child in the Wrong Grade?* (a handbook for determining whether a child is overplaced), and *Don't Push Your Preschooler.*

HOMESCHOOLING

Holt Associates. 2269 Massachusetts Ave., Cambridge, MA 02140. Phone: (617)864-3100. This organization promotes homeschooling, publishes a newsletter called *Growing Without Schooling*, and runs a mail-order service.

The National Center for Home Education. P.O. Box 125, Paeonian Springs, VA 22129. Phone: (703)882-4770. The center is a division of the Home School Legal Defense Association, which provides legal counsel to families that educate their children at home.

National Homeschool Association (NHA). P.O. Box 290, Hartland, MI 48353-0290. Phone: (313)632-5208. NHA promotes public awareness of home education and encourages the exchange of information and experience among families whose children are homeschooled.

MONTESSORI

American Montessori Society. 150 Fifth Ave., Suite 203, New York, NY 10011. Phone: (212)924-3209. This professional association was formed in response to the growing interest in the Montessori approach to early learning.

Association Montessori International-USA. P.O. Box 421390, San Francisco, CA 94102-1390. Phone: (415)861-7113. A professional association, it trains and certifies teachers in the traditional Montessori method.

North American Montessori Teacher's Association. 2859 Scarborough Road, Cleveland Heights, OH 44118. Phone: (216)371-1566. This association publishes a directory of Montessori schools across the country.

NATIONAL ASSOCIATIONS AND OTHER SUPPORTS

Alliance for Parental Involvement in Education. P.O. Box 59, East Chatham, NY 12060. Phone: (518)392-6900.

American Academy of Pediatrics. 141 Northwest Point Blvd., P.O. Box 927, Elk Grove Village, IL 60009-0927. Phone: (708)228-5005 or (800)433-9016.

Association for Childhood Education International (ACEI). 11501 Georgia Ave., Suite 315, Wheaton, MD 20902. Phone: (301)942-2443 or (800)423-3563. ACEI is a professional organization for those involved in the education of children from infancy through early adolescence. Advocates developmentally appropriate curricular materials. Works to promote the quality and availability of educational programs for children. Promotes cooperation among individuals and groups concerned with children. Encourages professional growth of teachers. Informs the public about the needs of children.

Association for Library Service to Children. American Library Association, 50 E. Huron Road, Chicago, IL 60611. Phone: (312)944-6780.

Bank Street College of Education. 610 West 112th St., New York, NY 10025. Phone: (212)875-4400. The college, founded in 1916, conducts programs of research, consultation, and curriculum development to benefit children. Offers graduate programs for educators and early childhood specialists; operates a demonstration school for children aged 3 to 13, which serves as a working model of the college's approach to learning and teaching; and operates a nonprofit child-care center, which offers a training site for the college's graduate students studying infant/parent development, early childhood education, or special education. Bank Street College's approach to learning places emphasis on child development and individual learning styles; the importance of experiential learning; and the understanding that the emotional life of children is inseparable from their learning, interests, and motivation. Educators, psychologists, and child development experts are on staff. In additional to videotapes, software, and curriculum guides, Bank Street College has produced a variety of books for children, as well as for parents. Books for children include the Bank Street Ready-to-Read Series (published by Bantam); Bank Street Mind Builders (summer learning activity kits and books for children and parents, published by Cowles Educational Corporation); Bank Street Museum Books (including *Dinosaurium*, *Oceanarium*, and *Planetarium*, published by Bantam). Parent guides include *Kids and Play* and *Love and Discipline* (both published by Ballantine), as well as *Raising a*

Confident Child, The Preschool Handbook, The Elementary School Handbook, and *Buy Me! Buy Me! The Bank Street Guide to Choosing Toys* (all published by Pantheon). In addition, the Child Study Children's Book Committee at Bank Street produces lists of recommended titles for children. [Note: For those within easy traveling distance, Bank Street College offers Saturday workshops for parents and children (science projects, cooking activities, tie-dye workshops, musical instrument making, etc.); workshops for parents only (positive discipline that works, choosing a school for your child, etc.); and performing arts programs for families (magic shows, storytelling, dance, and music).]

Family Resource Coalition. 200 S. Michigan Ave., Suite 1520, Chicago, IL 60604. Phone: (312)341-0900. Fax: (312)341-9361.

Head Start. Department of Health and Human Services, Administration for Children and Families, 370 L'Enfant Promenade SW, Washington, DC 20447. Phone: (202)401-9215. Since its establishment in 1965, this national program has served more than 13.1 million children and their families. Offers "comprehensive developmental services" for America's low-income preschool children aged 3 to 5 years and social services for their families.

International Reading Association. 800 Barksdale Road, P.O. Box 8139, Newark, DE 19714. Phone: (302)731-1600 or (800)336-READ. Fax: (302)731-1057.

La Leche League International. 9616 Minneapolis Ave., P.O. Box 1209, Franklin Park, IL 60131-8209. Phone: (708)455-7730. Hotline: (800)LA-LECHE.

National Association for the Education of Young Children (NAEYC). 1509 16th St. NW, Washington, DC 20036-1426. Phone: (202)232-8777 or (800)424-2460. Fax: (202)328-1846. NAEYC is a nonprofit professional organization of more than 80,000 members, dedicated to improving the quality of services provided to young children and their families. Provides educational opportunities and resources to promote the professional development of those working for and with young children. Works to increase public knowledge and support for high-quality early childhood programs (including those of preschools, primary schools, kindergartens, child-care centers, cooperatives, church schools, and others). Advocates developmentally appropriate educational methods for young children. Operates a voluntary, national accreditation system for quality early childhood programs. Write for a list of accredited schools within your state. Publishes *Young Children*, a bimonthly journal. Also publishes brochures, books, videos, posters, and information kits.

National Clearinghouse on Family Support and Children's Mental Health. Portland State University, P.O. Box 751, Portland, OR 97207-0751. Phone: (800)628-1696. The clearinghouse assists families of children with serious emotional disorders and also aids professionals in mental health care.

National Committee for Prevention of Child Abuse (NCPCA). P.O. Box 2866, Chicago, IL 60690. NCPCA has brochures on child sexual abuse as well as other materials for parents. Write for a publications list.

National Education Association (NEA). 1201 16th St. NW, Washington, DC 20036. Phone: (202)833-4000. This association's 2.1 million members include elementary and secondary school teachers, administrators, principals, college professors, students, and others concerned with education.

National Mental Health Association (NMHA). 1021 Prince St., Alexandria, VA 22314-2971. Phone: (703)684-7722. NMHA provides information, offers emotional support and guidance for families, and helps school systems develop programs for children with mental illnesses. Lobbies for federal mental health legislation and stimulates funding for research. Its catalog lists pamphlets and booklets on all aspects of mental health and mental illnesses. *Focus*, its newsletter, comes out quarterly.

National PTA. 700 North Rush St., Chicago, IL 60611-2571. Phone: (312)787-0977. Fax: (312)787-8342.

President's Committee on Mental Retardation. 330 Independence Ave. SW, Washington, D.C. 20201. Phone: (202)619-0634. Committee responds to inquiries and serves as an advocate for mentally retarded persons.

▓ PARENT SUPPORT

CHILD SUPPORT HELPLINES

American Child Support Collection Association. Children's Services, P.O. Box 691067, San Antonio, TX 78269. Phone: (800)729-2445. A national network of professional agencies that specialize in child support collection.

Association for Children for Enforcement of Support. 723 Phillips Ave., Suite 216, Toledo, OH 43612. Phone: (800)537-7072. A nonprofit agency that offers advice on obtaining child support.

National Child Support Advocacy Coalition. P. O. Box 4629, Alexandria, VA 22303. Phone: (908)828-2901. Affiliates of this organization conduct workshops on starting the collection process, obtaining a support order (a legal document ordering a parent to provide support), and shopping for legal assistance.

Office of Child Support Enforcement. Administration for Children and Families, U.S. Department of Health and Human Services, 370 L'Enfant Promenade SW, Fourth Floor, Washington, DC 20447. The goal of this federal program, carried out by state and local Child Support Enforcement (CSE) offices, is to ensure that children are financially supported by both parents. Helps parents locate an absent parent for child support enforcement, establish paternity if necessary, determine child support obligations, and enforce child support orders (legal documents ordering a parent to provide support). Here is the telephone number for the office in your state.

Alabama (205)242-9300

Alaska (907)276-3441

Arizona (602)252-0236

Arkansas (501)682-8398

California (916)654-1556

Colorado (303)866-5998

Connecticut (203)566-3053

Delaware (302)421-8300

District of Columbia (202)724-5610

Florida (904)488-9900

Georgia (404)894-4119

Hawaii (808)587-3712

Idaho (208)334-5710

Illinois (217)782-1366

Indiana (317)232-4894

Iowa (515)281-5580

Kansas (913)296-3237

Kentucky (502)564-2285

Louisiana (504)342-4780

Maine (207)289-2886

Maryland (410)333-3979

Massachusetts (617)621-4200

Michigan (517)373-7570

Minnesota (612)296-2499

Mississippi (601)354-0341

Missouri (314)751-4301

Montana (406)444-4614

Nebraska (402)471-9125

Nevada (702)885-4744

New Hampshire (603)271-4426

New Jersey (609)588-2361

New Mexico (505)827-7200

New York (518)474-9081

North Carolina (919)571-4120

North Dakota (701)224-3582

Ohio (614)752-6561

Oklahoma (405)424-5871

Oregon (503)378-5439

Pennsylvania (717)787-3672

Rhode Island (401)277-2409

South Carolina (803)773-5870

South Dakota (605)773-3641

Tennessee (615)741-1820

Texas (512)463-2181

Utah (801)538-4400

Vermont (802)241-2319

Virginia (804)662-9629

Washington (206)586-3162

West Virginia (304)348-3780

Wisconsin (608)266-1175

Wyoming (307)777-7892

Parenting Hotline. Phone: (900)535-MOMS (the cost is $1.95 for the first minute and 95c for each additional minute). The hotline is a service of *Parenting* magazine and the National Parenting Center. Callers select an age group (pregnancy, newborns, infants, toddlers, preschool, preteen, or adolescence), then choose a topic from the ever-changing menu.

Parents Stressline. Phone: (800)421-0353 (Monday through Friday, 8:30 a.m. to 5:00 p.m., Pacific Standard Time). The hotline is a service of Parents Anonymous, a nonprofit program for parents who fear they will abuse their children. Trained staff members help diffuse feelings of anger and hostility and refer callers to mental health professionals and community resources, when appropriate.

ADOPTION

Adoptee/Natural Parent Locators-International. P.O. Box 1283, Canyon Country, CA 91351. Phone: (805)251-4477. This organization helps adoptees, natural parents, and adoptive parents locate each other through a computer-based registry of adoptees and parents.

Adoptive Families of America. 3333 N. Highway 100, Minneapolis, MN 55422. Phone: (612)535-4829. This nonprofit organization provides problem-solving assistance and information about the challenges of adoption to members of adoptive and prospective adoptive families.

Adoptive Parents Committee Inc. (APC). 210 5th Ave., New York, NY 10010. Phone: (212)683-9221. APC is dedicated to the improvement of adoption and foster care laws. Educates the public and adoptive parents about all matters involving adoption and foster care.

Aid to Adoption of Special Kids (AASK). 450 Sansome St., San Francisco, CA 94111. Phone: (415)434-2275. AASK, a nonprofit, California-licensed adoption agency with branch offices nationwide, helps place older children, sibling groups, minority children, and emotionally, mentally, and physically disabled children in permanent homes.

American Academy of Adoption. P.O. Box 33053, Washington, DC 20033-0053. This group offers a state-by-state directory of adoption attorneys.

American Adoption Congress. 1000 Connecticut Ave. NW, Suite 9, Washington, DC 20036. Phone: (202)483-3399. This organization serves as a public information center on adoption and related issues. Conducts research, develops educational programs, and sponsors conferences.

Committee for Single Adoptive Parents. P.O. Box 15084, Chevy Chase, MD 20815. The committee acts as an information service to current and prospective single adoptive parents of both sexes. It supports the rights of children to an adoptive family regardless of any handicap or any difference in race, creed, color, religion, or national origin.

Concerned United Birthparents Inc. (CUB). 2000 Walker St., Des Moines, IA 50317. Phone: (515)263-9558 or (800)822-2777.

Edna Gladney Center. 2300 Hemphill, Fort Worth, TX 76110. Phone: (800)GLADNEY (452-3639) or (in Texas) (800)772-2740. The Gladney Center provides supportive and caring services for those involved in adoption.

Families Adopting Children Everywhere (FACE). P.O. Box 28058. Northwood Station, Baltimore, MD 21239. Phone: (410)488-2656. FACE offers support services to adoptive parents and their families. Disseminates information concerning adoption.

International Concerns Committee for Children. 911 Cypress Drive, Boulder, CO 80303. Phone: (303)494-8333. Committee helps those interested in adopting children from foreign countries.

International Families. P.O. Box 1352, St. Charles, MO 63302. Phone: (314)423-6788. An organization and support service for families interested in foreign adoption, this group publishes a newsletter, provides information, and makes referrals.

Latin America Parents Association (LAPA). P.O. Box 339, Brooklyn, NY 11234. Phone: (718)236-8689. This nonprofit volunteer association of adoptive parents helps people who want to adopt children from Latin America.

National Adoption Center. 1500 Walnut St., Suite 701, Philadelphia, PA 19102. Phone: (215)735-9988 or (800)862-3678 (800 TO-ADOPT). The center promotes adoption opportunities for children with special needs, including minority, handicapped, and older children, as well as sibling groups.

National Adoption Exchange. 1218 Chestnut St., Suite 204, Philadelphia, PA 19107. Phone: (215)925-0200. The exchange is a national network that brings children waiting for adoption together with parents who want to adopt them.

National Adoption Information Clearinghouse. 11426 Rockville Pike, Suite 410, Rockville, MD 20852. Phone: (301)231-6512. Fax: (301)984-8527. This clearinghouse answers questions about adoption and provides referrals to adoption experts. Issues fact sheets, brochures, and reports covering a wide range of adoption topics.

National Committee for Adoption. 1930 17th St. NW, Washington, DC 20009-6207. Phone: (202)328-1200. The committee focuses on children needing to be adopted by supporting local adoption agencies and running the National Adoption Hotline.

National Foster Parents Association. Information and Services Office, 226 Kitts Drive, Houston, TX 77024. Phone: (713)467-1850. This association seeks to identify and help meet the needs of children in foster care and those who care for them. Works to improve the foster parenting image.

National Organization for Birthfathers and Adoption Reform (NOBAR). P.O. Box 1993, Baltimore, MD 21203. Phone: (301)243-3986. NOBAR is an advocacy and support group for fathers who have given their children up for adoption or risk losing them through adoption.

North American Council on Adoptable Children (NACAC). 970 Raymond Ave., Suite 106, St. Paul, MN 55104. Phone: (612)644-3036. NACAC works on behalf of special-needs children, those with physical or mental handicaps, older children, sibling groups, and minority children.

Operation Identity. 13101 Black Stone Road NE, Albuquerque, NM 87111. Phone: (505)293-3144. Through its newsletter and referrals, Operation Identity provides emotional support for everyone involved in the adoption process.

Orphan Voyage. 2141 Road 2300, Cedaredge, CO 81413. Phone: (303)856-3937. This organization provides information, education, and networking for adults separated from their natural families by adoption.

Resolve Inc. National Office, 1310 Broadway, Somerville, MA 02144-1731. Phone: (617)623-0744. This group offers support, counseling, and referrals to those experiencing problems of infertility and others striving to build a family.

Yesterday's Children. P.O. Box 1554, Evanston, IL 60204. Phone: (312)545-6900. The group provides counseling and assistance for adoptees in search of their biological families.

FATHERS AND MOTHERS

Committee for Mother and Child Rights Inc. Route 1, Box 256A, Clearbrook, VA 22624. Phone: (703)722-3652.

Fathers Are Forever. P.O. Box 4804, Panorama City, CA 91412. Phone: (818)846-2219 or (800)248-DADS (3237).

Fatherhood Project. c/o Bank Street College of Education, 610 W. 12th St., New York, NY 10025. Phone: (212)222-6700. This national clearinghouse provides information on father-participation programs. It works to increase the role of fathers as nurturers involved in rearing children.

Formerly Employed Mothers at Loose Ends (FEMALE). P.O. Box 31, Elmhurst, IL 60126. Phone: (312)279-8862. FEMALE's newsletter and group meetings help women move from the paid work force to at-home mothering.

Minnesota Early Learning Design (MELD). 123 N. Third St., Suite 804, Minneapolis, MN 55401. Phone: (612)332-7563. An association of more than 60 discussion groups nationwide for parents of children through age 2, MELD also offers programs for Hispanic families, teenage mothers, handicapped parents, and parents of older children.

Mothers at Home. P.O. Box 2208, Merrifield, VA 22116. Phone: (703)352-2292. This organization helps mothers who prefer to stay at home to raise their children.

Mother's Connection. 468 Rosedale Ave., White Plains, NY 10605. Phone: (914)946-5757. This network for at-home mothers of young children provides mothers' groups, play groups, and babysitting exchanges to lessen the sense of isolation.

Mothers Matter. 171 Wood St., Rutherford, NJ 07070. Phone: (201)933-8191. This small group offers educational materials that help with parenting skills and increase the enjoyment of parenting.

National Center for Family Studies. Catholic University of America, 620 Michigan Ave. NE, Washington, DC 20064. Phone: (202)635-5996 or (202)635-5431. The center conducts research projects on all aspects of the family. Offers information, referral, and advisory services.

One and Only. P.O. Box 35351, Station E, Vancouver, BC V6M 462, Canada. Phone: (604)222-2931. One and Only will refer you to local groups that provide emotional support, information, and networking for parents of an only child or of children more than 5 years apart.

Parental Stress Services. 600 S. Federal, Suite 205, Chicago, IL 60605. Phone: (312)427-1161. In this organization for both parents and children in stressful family situations, participants meet separately in groups run by volunteers in an effort to understand themselves and family matters.

Parents' Resources Inc. P.O. Box 107, Planetarium Station, New York, NY 10024. Phone: (212)873-0609. This organization supports groups for parents to help each other. Offers referrals if you are looking for a group and technical assistance if you wish to start one.

GAY AND LESBIAN PARENTS

Custody Action for Lesbian Mothers Inc. (CALM). P.O. Box 281, Narberth, PA 19072. Phone: (215)667-7508.

Federation of Parents and Friends of Lesbians and Gays (FLAG). P.O. Box 20308, Denver, CO 80220. Phone: (303)321-2270. This national organization comprises 200 chapters for families with gay members. It is dedicated to increasing understanding within families and educating the public as a whole.

Gay and Lesbian Advocates and Defenders (GLAD). P.O. Box 218, Boston, MA 02112. Phone: (617)426-1350. GLAD, which focuses on the New England states, is active in the legal defense of lesbians and gay males who are denied their rights because of their sexual preferences. The rights of child custody and visitation are among the many areas this group covers.

Gay and Lesbian Parents Coalition International. P.O. Box 50360, Washington, DC 20091. A coalition of lesbian and gay parenting groups across the country, this group provides information, education, and support services.

GRANDPARENTS

Foster Grandparent Program. ACTION, 806 Connecticut Ave. NW, Room M-1006, Washington, DC 20525. Phone: (202)634-9349. The program enrolls low-income volunteers aged 60 or older to assist children who have special needs in health and education. Offers advisory and information services and distributes brochures.

The Foundation for Grandparents. Box 326, Cohassett, MA 02025. This nonprofit organization works to enhance intergenerational relations. Organizes Grandparents Conferences, which bring together grandparents and grandchildren from around the country, along with experts in the field of intergenerational relations. Publishes a quarterly newsletter called *Vital Connections.*

Grandparents'-Children's Rights Inc. 5728 Bayonne Ave., Haslett, MI 48840. Phone: (517)339-8663. This group provides information and advocacy for grandparents denied the right to see their grandchildren. Encourages grandparents to form groups to discuss issues, work for legal change, and swap information.

Grandparents Raising Grandchildren. 3851 Centraloma Drive, San Diego, CA 92107. Phone: (619)223-0344. This organization is for grandparents or other relatives who are bringing up a child, or who are worried about a possibly abusive situation that a child may be in.

Grandtravel. Chevy Chase, MD. Phone: (800)247-7651. This travel agency specializes in trips for grandparents and grandchildren. Washington, DC, Colonial Williamsburg, and the coast of Maine are among their domestic destinations.

Vistatours. Phone: (800)248-4782. Offers trips for grandparents and grandchildren. Destinations include Nevada, New England, and South Dakota.

SINGLE PARENTS

America's Society of Separated and Divorced Men (ASDM). 575 Keep Street, Elgin, IL 60120. Phone: (312)695-2200. ASDM supports fathers' rights to their children. Fights unreasonable child support, alimony, and custody rulings. Offers counseling and makes referrals.

Divorce Anonymous. P.O. Box 5313, Chicago, IL 60680. This group assists divorced persons in dealing with emotional conflicts.

Joint Custody Association. 10606 Wilkins Ave., Los Angeles, CA 90024. Phone: (310)475-5352.

Mothers Without Custody. P.O. Box 27418, Houston, TX 77227-7418. Phone: (713)840-1622. An association of women living apart from one or more of their minor children. Helps establish local self-help groups.

National Organization of Single Mothers. P.O. Box 68, Midland, NC 28107-0068. Phone: (704)888-KIDS. The organization helps new members form or join local support groups.

Parents Sharing Custody. 420 S. Beverly Drive, Suite 100, Beverly Hills, CA 90212-4410. Phone: (310)286-9171. An association of parents sharing custody of children after divorce. Educates parents on maintaining their parental roles and works to protect the rights of children.

Parents Without Partners. 401 N. Michigan Ave., Chicago, IL 60611-4267. Phone: (312)644-6610. With over 800 chapters, this is by far the largest parenting organization in the United States. Offers education and referral services. Provides information and support services to anyone raising children alone.

Single Mothers by Choice. P.O. Box 1642, Gracie Square Station, New York, NY 10028. Phone: (212)988-0993. This is an organization of single professional women who either have or are considering having children outside of marriage.

Single Parent Resource Center. 141 W. 28th St., New York, NY 10001. Phone: (212)947-0227. The center offers a manual for single parents who would like to organize a support group.

Single Parents Society. 527 Cinnaminson Ave., Palmyra, NJ 08065. Phone: (609)424-8872. The society's discussion groups, newsletter, events, and instructional programs work to improve the circumstances and support the interests of once-married parents.

United Fathers of America. 595 City Drive, Suite 202, Orange, CA 92668. Phone: (714)385-1002. This group offers information, counseling, and support services to individuals whose families are disrupted due to divorce.

Unwed Parents Anonymous. P.O. Box 44556, Phoenix, AZ 85064. Phone: (602)952-1463. This organization offers support to unwed parents. Provides information and advice on child rearing, child care, relationships, finances, and other issues affecting parent and child.

Women on Their Own. P.O. Box 1026, Willingboro, NJ 08046. Phone: (609)871-1499. This group offers information, referral services, and support to single, divorced, separated, or widowed women raising children on their own.

SPECIAL INTERESTS

Resource Guide, *Exceptional Parent*, P.O. Box 3000, Dept. EP, Denville, NJ 07834. Phone: (800)247-8080. Published yearly. Although several reference books offer directories of organizations, one of the most current is the annual Resource Guide issue of *Exceptional Parent: The*

Magazine for Families and Professionals. It lists state and national resources for information and advocacy on specific disabilities and conditions, parent training/information centers, technology centers, disability-related electronic bulletin boards, professional organizations, and a directory of products and services.

Al-Anon Family Group Headquarters. P.O. Box 182, Madison Square Station, New York, NY 10010. This organization assists spouses, parents, and other relatives of alcoholics to understand and cope with common problems.

American Association of University Affiliated Programs for Persons With Developmental Disabilities (AAUAP). 8630 Fenton St., Suite 410, Silver Spring, MD 20910. AAUAP is a national organization representing university-affiliated programs throughout the United States that provide technical assistance, training, and information.

The Association for the Care of Children's Health (ACCH). 7910 Woodmont Ave., Suite 300, Bethesda, MD 20814. ACCH is an organization of family members and professionals; it offers information and support for children needing specialized health and developmental services.

Beach Center on Families and Disability. The University of Kansas, Bureau of Child Research, 3111 Haworth Hall, Lawrence, KS 66045. Beach Center is the first federally funded national rehabilitation research and training center on families and disabilities. Offers information, resources, and research on Parent-to-Parent programs.

Children-In-Hospitals Inc. 31 Wilshire Park, Needham, MA 02192. This group assists parents with chronically or terminally ill children.

Compassionate Friends. P.O. 1345, Oak Brook, IL 60521. The group assists parents whose children have died.

Council for Exceptional Children (CEC). 1920 Association Drive, Reston, VA 22091-1589. CEC is a professional organization dedicated to advancing the quality of education for all exceptional children and improving the conditions under which special educators work. Focuses on particular areas (such as early childhood) and offers publications for professionals.

Families Anonymous. P.O. Box 344, Torrance, CA 90401. This organization assists parents, relatives, and friends of youth with alcohol, drug, or other behavioral problems.

Family Resource Coalition. 230 N. Michigan Ave., Suite 1625, Chicago, IL 60601. The coalition is a national grassroots federation of individuals and organizations. Promotes the development of prevention-oriented, community-based programs to strengthen families.

Gam-Anon. P.O. Box 4549, Downey, CA 90241. This group assists spouses, relatives, and friends of the compulsive gambler.

Nar-Anon Family Group. P.O. Box 2562, Palos Verdes Peninsula, CA 90274. The organization assists spouses and relatives of drug addicts in understanding and coping with common problems.

National Center on Parent-Directed Family Resource Centers. Parents Helping Parents, 535 Race St., Suite 140, San Jose, CA 95126.

National Coalition Against Domestic Violence. 1728 N Street NW, Washington, DC 20036. This coalition assists battered women and their children with support, legal, and welfare advocacy and educational materials.

National Easter Seal Society. 230 W. Monroe, Chicago, IL 60606. Easter Seals sponsors activities involving advocacy, research, public education, government relations, and resource development. Conducts local programs that serve people with disabilities.

National Fathers Network. The Merrywood School, 16120 NE Eighth St., Bellevue, WA 98008. Phone: (206)747-4004 or (206)282-1334. This organization puts fathers of children with special needs in contact with support groups located around the country.

National Information Center for Children and Youth with Disabilities (NICHCY). P.O. Box 1492, Washington, DC 20013. Phone (800)695-0285. NICHCY provides fact sheets, article reprints, resource information, specialized packets, and bibliographies on topics of interest to parents, as well as contacts for parent organizations and disability-related groups.

National Lekotek Center. 2100 Ridge Ave., Evanston, IL 60201. Phone: (800)366-PLAY. Lekotek offers play-centered programs and toy-lending library services for children with special needs.

National Organization for Rare Disorders (NORD). P.O. Box 8923, New Fairfield, CT 06812. NORD acts as both a clearinghouse for information and a family network system for disorders affecting fewer than 200,000 people.

National Organization on Disability (NOD). 910 16th St. NW, Suite 600, Washington, DC 20006. NOD promotes public awareness and supports legislation to improve the lives of people with disabilities.

National Parent Network on Disabilities (NPND). 1600 Prince St., Suite 115, Alexandria, VA 22314. NPND provides information and resources to promote advocacy efforts for people with disabilities and their families.

Parents Anonymous Inc. 9030 W. Imperial Highway, Suite 332, Inglewood, CA 90303. This group assists parents who feel they are abusing or neglecting their children (physically, sexually, or emotionally).

Parents Helping Parents. 535 Race Street, Suite 140, San Jose, CA 95126. Phone: (408)288-5010. This is an organization of parents, professionals, and others working to help families with special needs children, including those with physical, mental, emotional, or learning disabilities.

Parent-to-Parent. March of Dimes, 1275 Mamaroneck Avenue, White Plains, NY 10605. This organization assists parents of children with birth defects or special needs.

Parents Without Partners. 7910 Woodmond Ave., Washington, DC 20014. Group assists single parents.

Prison Families Anonymous Inc. 131 Jackson St., Hempstead, NY 11550. The group assists spouses and relatives of prisoners.

RESNA Technical Assistance Project. 1700 N. Moore St., Suite 1540, Arlington, VA 22209-1903. RESNA provides information on state assistive technology programs.

SEFAM Family Support Program. c/o James May, Merrywood School, 16120 NE Eighth St., Bellevue, WA 98008.

Self-Help for Interracial Couples. Wright Institute Graduate School of Psychology and Y House (Campus Branch), 2728 Durant, Berkeley, CA 94704. This group assists women in racially mixed relationships help one another deal with issues and problems experienced in relationships with partners or children of different or mixed races.

Sibling Information Network. 62 Washington St., Middletown, CT 06457. This program offers a clearinghouse of information on siblings of children with disabilities and issues related to families of individuals with disabilities.

Sibling Support Project. P.O. Box 5371, CL-09, Seattle, WA 98105-0371. This project offers training and technical assistance for organizing peer-support and education programs for siblings of people with disabilities.

Specialized Training of Military Parents. c/o Washington PAVE, 12208 Pacific Highway SW, Tacoma, WA 98499. This organization provides information about testing and assessment, parental rights and responsibilities, and networking with military resources.

Widow-to-Widow. Widowed Resources Center, 25 Huntington Avenue, Boston, MA 02115. This group assists widowed persons with help and information.

SPECIAL NEEDS

National Alliance for the Mentally Ill. 200 North Glebe Road, Suite 1015, Arlington, VA 22203-3754. Phone: (703)524-7600. This national network of nearly 1,000 self-help groups is for families of those suffering from severe mental illness. It provides information and parental support.

Parents Involved Network. 311 S. Juniper St., Room 902, Philadelphia, PA 19107. Phone: (215)735-2465. Groups within this network help parents of children with severe emotional problems.

Reassurance to Each (REACH). 328 E. Hennepin Ave., Minneapolis, MN 55414. Phone: (612)331-6840 or (in Minnesota) (800)862-1799. REACH self-help groups, for friends and families of the mentally ill, supply information and emotional support. Provide guidelines for starting new groups.

Technical Assistance for Parent Programs. Federation for Children with Special Needs, 95 Berkeley St., Suite 104, Boston, MA 02116.

STEPFAMILIES AND FOSTER FAMILIES

National Foster Parent Association. Information and Services Office, 226 Kilts Drive, Houston, TX 77024. Phone: (713)467-1850. This is the nation's largest group promoting the care of children in foster homes. Offers foster parents information on their legal rights. Publishes *National Advocate* Newsletter.

Remarried Parents Inc. 175 Fifth Ave., New York, NY 10010. This organization assists remarried people discuss difficulties surrounding remarriage and parenting.

Stepfamily Association of America Inc. (SAA). 602 E. Joppa Road, Baltimore, MD 21204. Phone: (301)823-7570.

The Stepfamily Foundation. 333 West End Ave., New York, NY 10023. Phone: (212)877-3244 or (800)SKY-STEP. This organization gathers and disseminates information on stepfamilies and stepfamily relationships. Offers over-the-phone counseling and makes referrals. Publishes *Step News*, a quarterly newsletter. Offers books, pamphlets, audiocassettes, and videotapes on common stepfamily concerns.

STATE INFORMATION OFFICES

If you need to identify which office in your state government can answer a particular question, the referral services below can help.

Alabama (205)261-2500	Louisiana (504)342-6600
Alaska (907)465-2111	Maine (207)289-1110
Arizona (602)542-4900	Maryland (301)974-2000
Arkansas (501)371-3000	Massachusetts (617)727-2121
California (916)322-9900	Michigan (517)373-1837
Colorado (303)866-5000	Minnesota (612)296-6013
Connecticut (203)566-2211	Mississippi (601)354-7011
Delaware (302)736-4000	Missouri (314)751-2000
District of Columbia (202)727-1000	Montana (406)444-2511
Florida (904)488-1234	Nebraska (402)471-2311
Georgia (404)656-2000	Nevada (702)885-5000
Hawaii (808)548-2211	New Hampshire (603)271-1110
Idaho (208)334-2411	New Jersey (609)292-2121
Illinois (217)782-2000	New Mexico (505)827-4011
Indiana (317)232-3140	New York (518)474-2121
Iowa (515)281-5011	North Carolina (919)733-1110
Kansas (913)296-0111	North Dakota (701)224-2000
Kentucky (502)564-2500	Ohio (614)466-2000

Oklahoma (405)521-2011
Oregon (503)378-3131
Pennsylvania (717)787-2121
Rhode Island (401)277-2000
South Carolina (803)734-1000
South Dakota (605)773-3011
Tennessee (615)741-3011
Texas (512)463-4630

Utah (801)538-3000
Vermont (802)828-1110
Virginia (804)786-0000
Washington (206)753-5000
West Virginia (304)348-3456
Wisconsin (608)266-2211
Wyoming (307)777-7220

Illustration Credits

Figure 5.1 Reprinted/excerpted from *Families and Education: An Educator's Resource for Family Involvement* by Marie App with permission from the Wisconsin Department of Public Instruction, 125 South Webster Street, Madison, WI 53702.

Figure 5.5 Reprinted with permission of Beth Jennings, kindergarten teacher, Edwardsville, IL, Community Schools.

Figure 5.7 Mary Anne Posnanski, parent educator, Edwardsville, IL, Community School.

Figure 5.11 Reprinted with permission of Diana Baker, first-grade teacher, Bradley, IL.

Figure 5.13 Reprinted by permission of Linda Pokorny, kindergarten teacher, Edwardsville, IL, Community Schools.

Figure 5.15 Used by permission of Susan Lucco, Edwardsville Public Library.

Figure 5.16 Reprinted with permission of *Growing Together*.

Figure 5.17 Reprinted by permission of Dawn Robin, The Family Tree.

Figures 5.14, 5.18 Reprinted with permission of Lynda C. Andre, Edwardsville Parent Education Project—Family Matters.

Figures 6.1, 6.2 Reprinted by permission of Teresa Harris.

Figure 8.1 From *Discovery Science, Explorations for the Early Years, Pre-Kindergarten*, by D. Winnett, R. Rockwell, E. Sherwood, and R. Williams. Copyright ©1996 by Addison-Wesley Publishing Company. Reprinted by permission.

Photographic Credits

Index